Beginning Scala 3

A Functional and Object-Oriented Java Language

Third Edition

David Pollak
Vishal Layka
Andres Sacco

Apress®

Beginning Scala 3: A Functional and Object-Oriented Java Language

David Pollak
San Francisco, CA, USA

Vishal Layka
Bruxelles, Belgium

Andres Sacco
Ciudad Autonoma de Buenos Aires, Argentina

ISBN-13 (pbk): 978-1-4842-7421-7
https://doi.org/10.1007/978-1-4842-7422-4

ISBN-13 (electronic): 978-1-4842-7422-4

Managing Director, Apress Media LLC: Welmoed Spahr
Acquisitions Editor: Steve Anglin
Development Editor: James Markham
Coordinating Editors: Mark Powers
Copyeditor: Mary Behr

Cover designed by eStudioCalamar

Cover image by Zack Tullos on Unsplash (www.unsplash.com)

Distributed to the book trade worldwide by Apress Media, LLC, 1 New York Plaza, New York, NY 10004, U.S.A. Phone 1-800-SPRINGER, fax (201) 348-4505, e-mail orders-ny@springer-sbm.com, or visit www. springeronline.com. Apress Media, LLC is a California LLC and the sole member (owner) is Springer Science + Business Media Finance Inc (SSBM Finance Inc). SSBM Finance Inc is a **Delaware** corporation.

For information on translations, please e-mail booktranslations@springernature.com; for reprint, paperback, or audio rights, please e-mail bookpermissions@springernature.com.

Apress titles may be purchased in bulk for academic, corporate, or promotional use. eBook versions and licenses are also available for most titles. For more information, reference our Print and eBook Bulk Sales web page at www.apress.com/bulk-sales.

Any source code or other supplementary material referenced by the author in this book is available to readers on GitHub (https://github.com/Apress). For more detailed information, please visit www.apress.com/source-code.

Printed on acid-free paper

To my grandparents, who taught me the importance of learning new things all the time.

To my wife and daughter for supporting me during the process of writing this book.

—Andres Sacco

Table of Contents

About the Authors

 **David Pollak** has been writing commercial software since 1977. He wrote the award-winning Mesa spreadsheet, which in 1992 was the first real-time spreadsheet. Wall Street companies traded billions of dollars a day through Mesa. In 1996, David sold his company to CMP Media and became CTO of CMP Media's NetGuide Live and was one of the first large-scale users of Java and WebLogic to power an Internet site. In 1998, David released Integer, the world's first browser-accessible, multiuser spreadsheet. Since 2000, David has been consulting for companies such as Hewlett-Packard, Pretzel Logic/WebGain, BankServ, Twitter, and SAP. David has been using Scala since 2006 and is the lead developer of the Lift web framework. David blogs at `https://blog.goodstuff.im.` `http://groups.google.com/group/liftweb/.`

 **Vishal Layka** is the Chief Technology Officer of Star Protocol and has over a decade of experience in JVM languages. Vishal is actively involved in machine learning, inferential statistics, and pattern recognition using R, Python, Mahout, and Spark. When he needs a break from technology, Vishal reads eclectically from calculus to star formation.

ABOUT THE AUTHORS

 **Andres Sacco** has been a professional developer since 2007, working with a variety of languages, including Java, Scala, PHP, NodeJs, and Kotlin. Most of his background is in Java and the libraries or frameworks associated with it, but since 2016, he has utilized Scala as well, depending on the situation. He is focused on researching new technologies to improve the performance, stability, and quality of the applications he develops.

In 2017, he started to find new ways to optimize the transference of data between applications to reduce the cost of infrastructure. He suggested some actions, some applicable in all microservices and others in just a few of them; the result of these actions was a cost reduction of 55%.

About the Technical Reviewer

Orlando Méndez is a software professional who started to code professionally in 2000. He has worked with different languages and technologies for (public) finance, retail, and embedded systems. His interest in Scala started with a talk Martin Odersky gave in 2010 in the Netherlands.

When not tinkering with code or (micro) computers, Orlando enjoys spending time with his family, running outdoors, or simply looking at the cosmos in his backyard in rural Chile. You can find him online in the Twitter-verse at the @0rkk0 account.

Acknowledgments

I would like to thank my family members and friends for their encouragement and support during the process of this book:

- My wife, Gisela, was always patient when I spent long hours at my computer desk working on this book.

- My little daughter, Francesca, helped me relax when I was writing each chapter.

- My friends, German Canale and Julian Delley, always trusted me to write a book and supported me when I felt bad.

I would especially like to thank Orlando Méndez for his guidance, which helped improve the quality of this book.

My sincere thanks to the wonderful team at Apress for their support during the development of this book. Thanks to Mark Powers for providing excellent support and Jim Markham for his valuable editorial feedback. And, last but not least, thanks to Steve Anglin for giving me the opportunity to work on the latest edition of this book.

—Andres Sacco

Introduction

When you learn common programming languages like C++, Java, Python, or C#, you notice that they all have basically the same structure for defining variables, control (`for`/`while`), and objects. The semantics change because you cannot define a class or variable using the same word in all languages, but the concept does not change, so for any developer, it's easy to learn another language. It's almost like having a mind map that enables you to use your existing knowledge to do something differently. Scala is not an exception to this mind map and these common structures. The main difference with this language is that it supports both functional and object-oriented programming paradigms. Understanding that both can exist in the same language is the most difficult part for some developers. See Figure 1.

Difference in the syntax between languages			
Java	**C#**	**Python**	**Scala**
Variables int number = 1;	int number = 1;	number = 1	val number = 1
Classes public class Example { // Add code }	class Example { // Add code }	class Example: // Add code	class Example { // Add code }
Iteration for (int i = 0; i < 5; i++) { System.out.print(i); }	for (int i = 0; i < 5; i++) { Console.WriteLine(i); }	for x in range(5): print(x)	for (i <- 1 to 5) println(i)

Figure 1. *Differences in syntax*

Scala is not just another language that tries to do the same things differently. The spirit or philosophy of this language is to maintain code cleanly and simply. Don't feel bad if you don't understand at the beginning. Most developers coming from other languages take time to assimilate because it's not the same as popular languages like Java, Python, or C#. Scala is not for a specific situation. In particular, you can use it to create different things like libraries or applications (web or microservices) and data streaming using Akka. A friendly approach when you don't have a lot of experience in Scala but do have experience developing applications in other languages is to create something small to interact with other components. In this way, you can grow your skills with Scala. See Figure 2.

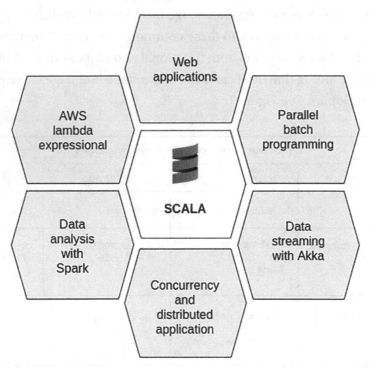

Figure 2. *Applications*

There are some external tools for solving specific problems with your system which are developed with Scala, but you can use them in some Java applications. The following are some of these tools:

- Gatling is an open-source tool to do load tests. This tool is used as an alternative to JMeter but one of the benefits is that you create tests that can run in the test step of your pipeline.

- Akka is a toolkit runtime that simplifies the construction of concurrent and distributed applications.

Who This Book Is For

This book is for folks with some programming background in any language who want to know more about the benefits of functional programming and Scala in particular. Take into consideration that if you have experience in another language, the differences between that language and Scala are not trivial; you can't just translate the syntaxes from one language to another. You need to understand some concepts that are not the same in languages like Java, C#, or C++.

Also, this book updates the knowledge that some Scala developers have from previous versions because Scala 3 introduces a lot of extra features and changes from Scala 2.

Prerequisites

You should have the Java JDK 11 or higher installed on your machine and Scala 3.0.0 or higher. Scala 3.0.0 works with Java JDK 8 but future versions may not be supported (however, there is no specific timeline). Martin Odersky said at the Scala Days of 2020 conference that he recommended using the latest LTS Java version, which is 11.

How This Book Is Structured

This book is structured in four blocks:

- The first block of chapters (1-3) gives you a basic understanding of the Scala syntax.

- The second block of chapters (4-8) offers a basic tour of some of the key features like functions, pattern matching, collections, and traits.

- The third block of chapters (9-10) gives a brief overview of the interoperability between Java and Scala.

- The fourth block of chapters (11-14) demonstrates how to use a build tool like SBT to create an application (web or REST), best practices, and how to test your code.

Source Code

You can download all the source code used in this book from `github.com/apress/beginning-scala-3`.

CHAPTER 1

Getting Started with Scala

Scala is not one of those popular languages that you learn at university, so most people don't even know that it exists. However, there are many benefits or reasons for using it. Scala was born as a language with a relatively small number of features but with the idea of doing things simply and clearly. For that reason, most of the developers who know something about Scala use it for different projects, and some of them collaborated to create the recent version of Scala.

Why Use Scala?

Scala is a language that any developer can use for a variety of purposes, from simple to complex applications, because it offers a mixed paradigm, a simple and elegant syntax to declare variables or to use the different features which not appears in other languages. Let's see some of the reasons to use Scala:

- Scala is a simple, clear, and expressive language with the idea of reducing the complexity of some operations, such as creating variables.

    Variables in Java

    ```
    private int number = 4;
    private int otherNumber = 2;
    ```

    Variables in Scala

    ```
    val number = 4 //One alternative to declare a variable
    val otherNumber:Int = 2 //Another alternative to do the same
    ```

    When it comes to declaring classes, the differences between these two languages grow:

© David Pollak, Vishal Layka, and Andres Sacco 2022
D. Pollak et al., *Beginning Scala 3*, https://doi.org/10.1007/978-1-4842-7422-4_1

Class in Java

```java
public class Person {
  private String name;
  private String passport;

  public Person(String name, String passport) {
      this.name = name;
      this.passport = passport;
  }
}
```

Class in Scala

```scala
class Person(name:String, passport:String)
```

In Java, there is a library[1] called Lombok that helps reduce the number of lines of code in the POJO objects that automatically generate set, get, toString, or equals methods. You need to add this library in your code to obtain these benefits. In Scala, these benefits exist without adding any library.

- Connected with the last point, Scala has a lightweight syntax. For that reason, most of the keywords that exist in other languages (such as continue or break in Java) do not exist in Scala. Also, in Scala it's optional to use a keyword like new to instantiate an object, so you can use it or not.

- Scala has some of the best practices that other languages have, like immutability in the variables, anonymous functions, pattern matching, and more.

- Scala is a multi-paradigm language because it combines an object-oriented language with a functional language so you can create objects that receive functions. This characteristic has existed for a long time and is a key difference from other languages. For example, Scala has a lot of methods to iterate and filter collections before Java 8.

---

[1] https://projectlombok.org/

- Scala uses the JVM (Java Virtual Machine) to exploit all the benefits of the improvements in the performance of each new version. Also, you can interact with libraries of other languages that use JVM, such as Java.

- Recently, Scala started offering the possibility of using GraalVM[2] or Scala Native[3], which improves performance in compilation, the use of memory, and the time to start Scala applications. In the case that you want to use Scala Native, you need to use version 2.11.x or up which includes Scala 3. You can see a complete benchmark about the difference between each alternative in an article on Medium[4].

- Scala has a great number of libraries to reduce the time to do certain operations like iterate using a `for` loop. Also, the Scala community has grown a lot since the first version and now offers many conferences and talks (`https://scala-lang.org/events/` lists some of them) about complex problems that you can solve using Scala.

Migrating to Scala 3

Developers who have experience using the previous version of Scala (2.x.x), which has several books and tutorials that explain all the features, may feel uncomfortable migrating to a new version because it introduces a lot of features and deprecates others. So why migrate to Scala 3? To answer this question, consider the following benefits of this new version:

- One of the most important features of this new version is the compilation time. As said by Martin Odersky at ScalaCon, "The compilation time is 3000 lines/second." (It might be longer the first time you compile your code; these things depend on how many libraries you have in your project.)

- Several new features simplify the life of the developer. Here are some of them:

---

[2] www.graalvm.org/
[3] https://scala-native.readthedocs.io/en/latest/
[4] https://medium.com/viruslab/revisiting-scala-native-performance-67029089f241

- **Optional braces/parentheses**: This one of the most requested features for the new version. The idea is simply to reduce the complexity of the code by removing the braces or parentheses in all declarations, but you need to help the compiler by using the correct indentation (similar to Python).

  In the following example, you can see an if/else in both versions:

  Scala 2

  ```
  val number = 1
  val isZero = if (number == 1) { true } else { false }
  ```

  Scala 3

  ```
  val number = 1
  val isZero = if number == 1 then true else false
  ```

  Another example of this feature is the case of the for loop:

  Scala 2

  ```
  val a = 0

  for( a <- 1 to 10) {
      println( "Value of a: " + a )
  }
  ```

  Scala 3

  ```
  val a = 0
  for a <- 1 to 10 do println( "Value of a: " + a )
  ```

- **Enumerations:** Most developers who use Java know the concept of enumeration because it helps to have an object that contains all possible values for one particular object.

  ```
  enum Color:
    case RED, YELLOW, GREEN;
  ```

  This enum not only lets you define possible values, but you also have different methods to simplify the use of this type of object, such as obtaining the correct value of the enum from a String.

  ```
  val color = Color.valueOf("BLUE")
  ```

- **Implicits:** This feature went through a redesign in Scala 3 to simplify the use. For this reason, there are new keywords, `given` and `using`, to replace the old version.

- **Intersection and union types:** The intersection type lets you combine different types in one. The order of the types is not important because they always produce the same result. You can see something similar in Java when you have a class that implements multiple interfaces. In the case of the union type, it accepts two different types without any problem, such as a method that has a param, a String, or an Int (String | Int). You can send any of these types, and your method needs to have the logic to do something different in both cases.

- Retro compatibility with the latest version of Scala, 2.x.x. The idea of Scala 3.x.x is to include the binaries of Scala 2 so that the transition from one version to another becomes a complex task so you can have parts of the code with an old version and parts with the new version. The official page offers a complete guide[5] to do this migration and shares some common problems that you may run into during the migration from one version to another. Also, there is a video[6] that covers most of the migration guide in a way that could be better.

History

Although you may not have heard much, or indeed anything, about Scala, this language has existed for a long time. The design of the language started in 2001 at École Polytechnique Fédérale de Lausanne[7] (EPFL) by Martin Odersky, but the first version was launched in 2003. Since that year it has grown in the number of developers that use it for different things.

Martin Odersky offered several courses on different platforms and took part in some conferences with the idea of letting more people know all the benefits of Scala.

---

[5] https://docs.scala-lang.org/scala3/guides/migration/tutorial-intro.html
[6] www.youtube.com/watch?v=RDY3NMZYWwY&ab_channel=47Degrees
[7] www.epfl.ch/en/

In 2006, a new version of Scala (2.0) was released. It included features like rewriting the compiler, supporting generics from Java, and others. Over the next 15 years, updates only included extra features or bug fixing but nothing big enough to merit an increase to version 3.0. Regardless, Scala continued to grow in popularity, and some companies started to use it, like Twitter, which moved some parts of its back end from Ruby to Scala. The New York Times uses it in parts of its system with Akka and Play Framework, and certain teams at Apple, Google, and Walmart use Scala as part of their backend platform.

In 2012, a new version was launched, with the idea to include many features, simplify the syntax (some which appears in version 2.x.x), and improve the performance of the compiler. Scala 3.0.0 was launched on May 14, 2021, and 100 contributors collaborated on the new features.

Some considerations about this new version:

- Some considerations related with the compilation.

  - The current speed is more or less 3000 lines/second, but the first time you compile, it could take longer. After that, the velocity of compilation increases because Scala 3.0 has a very aggressive mechanism of caching.

  - The velocity of compilation will decrease if you have several external libraries, which generate a lot of code behind the scenes.

- You can consider Scala 3.0 as a new language because it introduces a lot of changes related to new features and some features from version 2.0 have been removed or will be deprecated in the following versions.

- You don't need to migrate everything from Scala 2.x.x to Scala 3.x.x because the latest version uses the binaries of Scala 2.13.

- Most of the features provided by different contributors generated a lot of discussions about the best approach.

- In 2020, Martin Odersky, with the rest of the contributors, decided to launch a survey to find out which features are the most exciting for developers. The results showed that enums, unions/intersections, and opaque types are the most relevant for developers.

Figure 1-1 shows a brief summary of the timeline of Scala's evolution, with an emphasis on the steps towards the latest version (Scala 3.0).

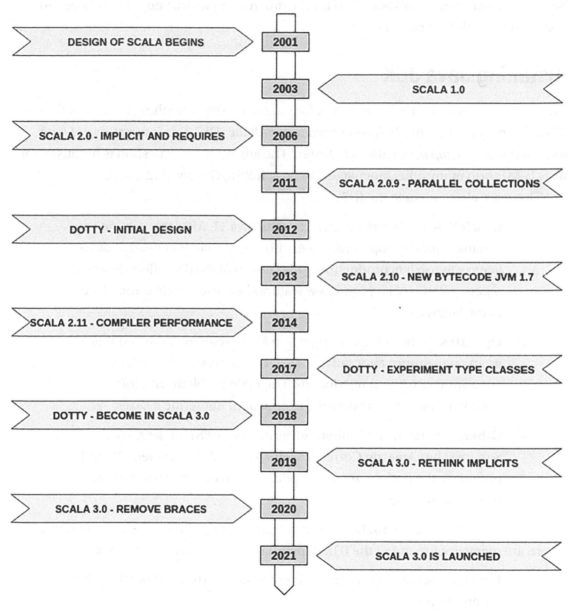

Figure 1-1. *The evolution of Scala*

Installing Scala Tools

Before you start to read this book and try the different topics that appear, you need to install some tools for Scala to work.

Installing Java JDK

The first thing that you need to install before starting to try something in Scala is the Java JDK. You may be thinking *"Why do I need to install the JDK? This is something of Java and I want to develop applications in Scala."* The answer to this question is because Scala uses JVM, as do many other languages like Java, Kotlin, Groovy, and Clojure.

There are alternatives to the JDK:

- **OracleJDK**[8]**:** This version was free until Java 11. After this version you can use it for development/test environments, but you need to pay a license to use it in production. This version of the JDK offers the most recent patches of bugs and new features because Oracle is the owner of the language.

- **OpenJDK**[9]**:** When Oracle bought Sun Microsystems, it created this as an open-source alternative that all developers can use in any environment without restrictions. The main problem with this version is the patches take time to appear in non-critical cases.

- **Others:** There are many alternatives to JDK. AWS (Amazon Web Services) has Amazon Corretto[10], which extends from OpenJDK and optimizes the performance of applications in the environments of this cloud provider.

In this book, we use **OpenJDK** but you can choose any alternative that you want. There are many ways to install the JDK depending on the operating system:

- For Mac OS/Linux, you can use brew, which is a tool to install/update different things.

  ➔   ~ brew install openjdk

---

[8] www.oracle.com/java/technologies/
[9] https://openjdk.java.net/
[10] https://aws.amazon.com/es/corretto/?nc1=h_ls

- For Windows platforms, you have two possibilities:

  - The first option is to install brew[11] and run the same command as Mac OS/Linux.

  - The second option is to install AdoptOpenJDK[12], which lets you download OpenJDK for different platforms. In the case of Windows, you can download a MSI file, which makes the installation so easy.

After finishing the installation of the JDK, check if the version of Java is available on your system. To do this, type the following:

```
➜  ~ java -version
OpenJDK version "11.0.9.1" 2020-11-04
OpenJDK Runtime Environment AdoptOpenJDK (build 11.0.9.1+1)
OpenJDK 64-Bit Server VM AdoptOpenJDK (build 11.0.9.1+1, mixed mode)
```

Scala 3 works with JDK 8 or 11, but in future versions of this language support for JDK 8 will disappear and the minimum will become 11. For that reason, it is recommended that you install JDK 11 or up. Also, JDK 11 offers improvements related to performance, such as changing the default garbage collector to G1[13], which reduces the pause times in general.

Last but not least, if you have installed SBT, the minimum version that supports Scala 3.x.x is SBT 1.5.0.

Installing Scala

There are a lot of ways to install Scala on your machine depending on your preferences. Some include the installation of the JDK, Scala, and SBT. The following two methods let you use the command line of Scala, but if you want to use it exclusively in your IDE, you can skip this step and install only the SBT, which is a tool to create and compile Scala projects.

---

[11] https://brew.sh/
[12] https://adoptopenjdk.net/releases.html
[13] https://openjdk.java.net/jeps/248

Using Brew

You can use brew as an option to install the compiler of Scala because it has support on Mac/Linux. You can now use it on Windows too with some extra steps to install it. To install Scala, run the following command:

➜   ~ `brew install lampepfl/brew/dotty`

After finishing with the installation, check if Scala is installed on your system. To do this, run the following command:

➜   ~ `scala -version`
`Scala compiler version 3.0.0 -- Copyright 2002-2021, LAMP/EPFL`

Using Coursier

As an alternative to installing using brew, you can use Coursier[14], which is a dependency resolver of Scala libraries. This tool helps you install the things required to use Scala 3, but one of the problems of using this tool is all the commands related to the console change a little.

To install this tool, follow the steps on this page[15], which explain how to do it depending on your operating system. You can also install this tool using brew.

When you finish installing Coursier on your system, run the following commands:

➜   ~ `cs setup`
➜   ~ `cs install scala3-repl`
➜   ~ `cs install scala3-compiler`

After finishing the installation, check if Scala is installed on your system. To do this, run the following command, which opens the console with the REPL of Scala 3:

➜   ~ `cs launch scala3-repl`
`scala>`

---

[14] https://get-coursier.io/
[15] https://get-coursier.io/docs/cli-installation

Installing SBT

SBT[16] is the de facto build tool to use Scala on your machine. This tool needs at least JDK 8 to work, but if you install JDK 11 on your machine, you will not have any problems. You will see more details about the things you can do with this tool in Chapter 11, so for now just focus on installing it.

There are some different ways to install this tool depending on your operating system:

- For Mac OS/Linux, you can use brew, which is a tool to install/update different things.

  → `~ brew install sbt`

- For Windows platforms, you can download the MSI installer from the official page[17].

After you've finished with the installation of the SBT, check if everything is installed on your system. To this, run the following command:

```
→  ~ sbt --version
sbt version in this project: 1.5.2
sbt script version: 1.5.2
```

SBT lets you run a specific part of your application, considering the version of Scala that you previously configured.

```
→  ~ sbt
[info] welcome to sbt 1.5.2 (Homebrew Java 16.0.1)
[info] loading global plugins from /Users/user/.sbt/1.0/plugins
[info] loading project definition from /Users/user/project
[info] set current project to codigo (in build file:/Users/user/)
[info] sbt server started at local:///Users/user/.sbt/1.0/server/
b5ec50d5e016a82e5659/sock
[info] started sbt server
sbt:user> console
scala>
```

---

[16] www.scala-sbt.org/

[17] www.scala-sbt.org/download.html

Installing the IDE

There are some IDEs that add support for Scala 3. Each has several pros/cons, which are out of the scope of this book. Two options are IntelliJ[18] or Visual Studio Code[19], which introduced support a long time ago when the first milestone appeared and fixed some problems with the plugins to validate the syntax.

You can see the instructions to install both IDEs on their official pages, which mention the minimum resources and operating system options. In both cases, support for Scala is not enabled by default, so you need to install it by doing the following step, depending on the IDE:

- **IntelliJ**: Go to IntelliJ IDEA ➤ Preferences ➤ Plugins and find and install Scala (see Figure 1-2).

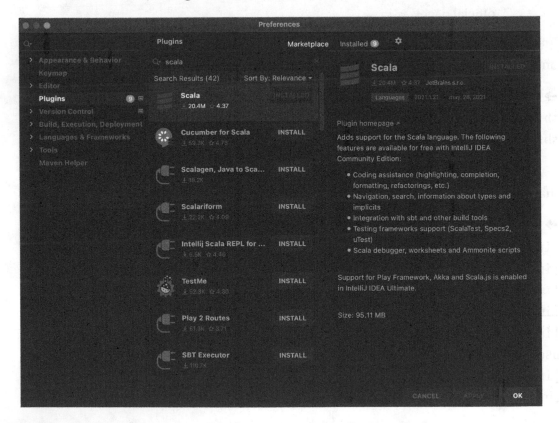

Figure 1-2. *The different IntelliJ plugins available for installation*

---

[18] www.jetbrains.com/idea/
[19] https://code.visualstudio.com/

- **Visual Studio Code:** Go to Code ➤ Preferences ➤ Extensions, and find and install Scala Metals, which offers support for Scala 2 and 3 (see Figure 1-3).

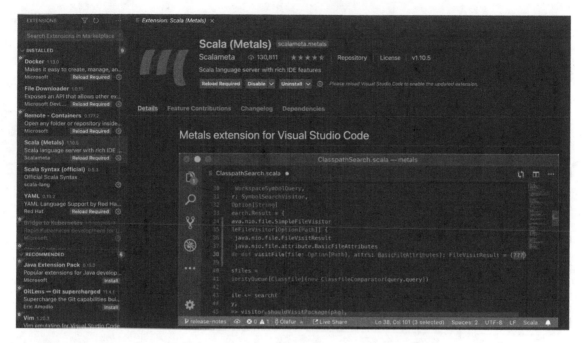

Figure 1-3. *The Scala plugin, which introduces support for version 3.x.x*

If you use these IDEs, check if you have the latest version because some of the plugins/extensions do not work well with old versions.

Running Code Examples

After finishing the installation of all the tools related to Scala, you can run some fragments of the code without opening an IDE by using the REPL (Read Eval Print Loop), which is the command line of Scala.

Using an IDE

Using an IDE is the best way to develop in any language, and Scala is no exception to this rule. A good way to create a project agnostic of the IDE that you choose to use is to create a project using SBT, which you installed in the previous section.

SBT has a specific command to create a project that uses Scala 3, which is different from the common command to create any Scala project. The following command will create a project with the latest version of Scala 3:

```
➜   ~ sbt new scala/scala3.g8
```

After the execution of this command, you'll see a lot of logs that show you the steps. Some part of the process will ask you the name of the project.

```
[info] welcome to sbt 1.5.2 (Homebrew Java 16.0.1)
[info] loading global plugins from /Users/user/.sbt/1.0/plugins
[info] set current project to new (in build file:/private/var/folders/2b/
kp4ljsm95ds2n78p6b77ppbw9f_rkf/T/sbt_155ffd12/new/)

A template to demonstrate a minimal Scala 3 application

name [Scala 3 Project Template]: scala3-test

Template applied in /Users/user/./scala3-test
```

If everything finishes without error, you can access the directory and see something like this:

```
➜   ~ scala3-test ls
README.md build.sbt project    src        target
```

With the project created using SBT, you can import it into your preferred IDE (IntelliJ or Visual Studio Code), and when the compilation of the files finishes, you can run it.

The following is the output to run `Main.scala` in Visual Studio Code but the same happens if you run it in IntelliJ:

```
Hello world!
I was compiled by Scala 3. 💻
```

Manually Using the REPL

To use the REPL, you need to open your console and type the following command:

```
➜   ~ scala
scala>
```

A possible use of the REPL is to do little experiments when you don't want to create an entire class or project to test them.

Running Little Blocks

Now you can start typing different blocks of code and see what happens. The REPL validates and compiles each block of code that you write. For example, if you try to *print* the value of a variable that does not exist, the REPL will show you an error:

```
scala> print(number)
1 |print(number)
  |       ^
  |       Not found: number
```

Modify the previous block of code by defining a variable with the name `number` and try to *print* the value to see what happens now:

```
scala> val number = 10
val number: Int = 10
scala> print(number)
10
```

Note that if you don't assign the value to a variable with a name, the REPL creates its variable with a name using the prefix `resX` (X is a number that starts from 0) and you can use it as in the previous example.

```
scala> "Hello World"
val res0: String = Hello World
scala> print(res0)
Hello World
```

As with any IDE, you can use the Tab key to complete the sentence or find possible names of variables or keywords in Scala.

```
scala> val number = 2
val number: Int = 2

scala> n
native     ne        nn         noinline   notify    notifyAll   number
```

Another good feature of the REPL is you can import common packages to use it, such as the util library to obtain the current date.

```
scala> import java.util._

scala> val date = Date()
val date: java.util.Date = Sun May 30 18:19:06 ART 2021
```

Finally, when you finish with your test and want to close the REPL, you have two alternatives:

- Press Ctrl + any key.

- Use the quit command.

  ```
  scala> :quit
  ➜  ~
  ```

One thing to consider after closing the REPL is all the blocks of code that you define will be lost, so if you need to test something, you will need to create it again to use it.

Compiling and Running Files

When blocks of code are too complex to write in the REPL, a good option is to write a file with the extension scala for the compiler to validate the correct format. After you create your file, you need to compile it before running the code.

To represent these steps, create a file with the name Color.scala and add the following code inside:

```
enum Color extends Enum[Color]:
  case RED, BLUE, GREEN;

@main def main = {
  val color = Color.valueOf("BLUE")
  print(color)
}
```

After you have created your file, you compile the content using the scalac command. You can compile a list of files just by adding one space between each file.

```
➜  ~ scalac Color.scala
```

If you have any doubt about how to execute the scalac command or the possible options that exist, use the help option.

```
→ ~ scalac --help
Usage: scalac <options> <source files>
where possible standard options include:
-P                      Pass an option to a plugin, e.g. -P:<plugin>:<opt>
-X                      Print a synopsis of advanced options.
-Y                      Print a synopsis of private options.
-bootclasspath          Override location of bootstrap class files.
-classpath              Specify where to find user class files.
                        Default: ..
-color                  Colored output
                        Default: always.
                        Choices: always, never.
-d                      Destination for generated classfiles.
a long list of options...
```

When the compilation process ends, you can run the code using the command scala with the name of the file:

```
→ ~ scala Color.scala
BLUE
```

Check that your code works fine. It's a good idea to see what happens in the directory where your file exists. If you execute the ls command, you will see a list of files that contain all the compiled code:

```
→ ~ ls
Color$$anon$1.class   Color$package$.class
Color$package.tasty   Color.scala
main.class            Color$.class        Color$package.class   Color.class
Color.tasty           main.tasty
```

Say you want to know the final format of your code. In previous sections, you read that Scala uses JVM to run the code. For that reason, you can use the command javap to decompile and see the final format of your file.

```
→  ~ javap Color
Compiled from "Color.scala"
public abstract class Color extends java.lang.Enum<Color> implements scala.
reflect.Enum {
  public static final Color RED;
  public static final Color BLUE;
  public static final Color GREEN;
  public static Color fromOrdinal(int);
  public static Color valueOf(java.lang.String);
  public static Color[] values();
  public Color(java.lang.String, int);
  public scala.collection.Iterator productIterator();
  public java.lang.String productPrefix();
  public java.lang.String productElementName(int);
  public scala.collection.Iterator productElementNames();
}
```

As you can see, the only methods that appear in the console with this command are public. If you want to see the private methods too, add the option -private.

```
→  ~ javap -private Color
```

Note   Behind the scenes, each IDE invokes the compiler and does the same operation on all files. Obviously you don't see this kind of magic in the console or any place in your IDE, but it is a good way to validate or see what is happening with a very strange case.

Online Tools

Other online tools offer the same functionality of running fragments of code without having Scala on your machine. For example, Scastie[20] lets you switch between multiple versions of Scala to test your code. Also, Scastie lets you share your code with anyone or embed it in a webpage. See Figure 1-4.

---

[20] https://scastie.scala-lang.org/

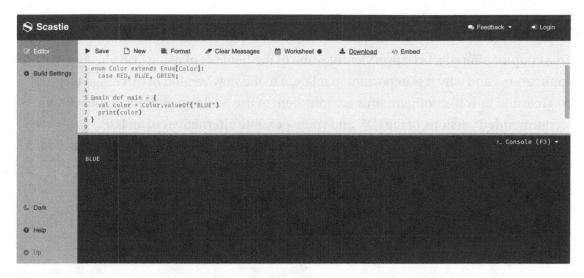

Figure 1-4. *The Scastie web page, which has a simple interface*

Another option to run Scala code is ScalaFiddle[21], which offers a lot of libraries. The main problem with this tool is that it works with version 2.x.x. See Figure 1-5.

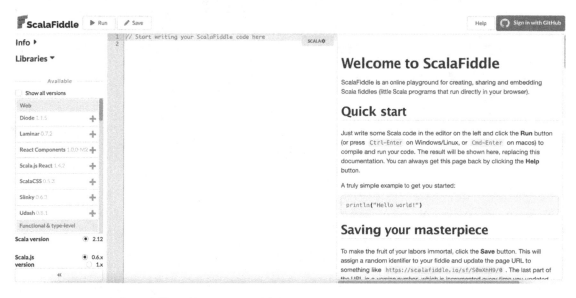

Figure 1-5. *ScalaFiddle offers several libraries*

---

[21] https://scalafiddle.io/

Summary

This chapter offered a brief overview of some of the benefits of using Scala in your applications and why it is important to migrate to the new version of this language. You learned how to configure your environment to use Scala on your machine with the recommended versions of the JDK and some possible alternatives of an IDE.

Most of the topics that appear in this chapter appear in the following chapters with a lot of details and some good practices.

CHAPTER 2

Basics of Scala

Scala offers the chance to combine different paradigms with a lot of incredible features. Some of these features are new to Scala 3, which removes the complexity of common operations. But before going deeply into these features, you need to know the basics of the language.

Over the course of this chapter, you will learn:

- How to define and use different types of variables

- How to use each of the control structures

- How to declare comments

- How run a block of code without using REPL

- Some of the reserved keywords

Variables

You can think of a variable as a space of memory where you can save some value in a particular scope for a period of time. Some variables are defined and accessible in one particular block (`if/try/catch`) and others are accessible in all of the methods of one class.

In Scala, there are three ways to declare a variable: `var`, `val`, or `lazy`. The language does not have a specific constraint about which you have to use but there are some suggestions:

- Use `val` when you are sure that the value cannot mutate. This way of declaring a variable is only for read-only access. Use this type of variable to reduce any possible side effects of changing the value of the variable.

21

© David Pollak, Vishal Layka, and Andres Sacco 2022
D. Pollak et al., *Beginning Scala 3*, https://doi.org/10.1007/978-1-4842-7422-4_2

- Use var when the content could be changed in the following lines of code.

- Use lazy when you don't need this part of code evaluated in the declaration.

To see the variables, open a terminal to use REPL or your IDE to play with some concrete examples.

```
scala> val number = 2
val number: Int = 2
```

You can think of this expression as an equivalent of declaring a variable with the modifier final in Java.

```
final Integer number = 2;
```

Now that you can define a variable with one particular value and name, you can use it to do certain operations, such as printing the value in the console.

```
scala> println("Number value is " + number)
Number value is 2
```

You can do certain mathematical operations like multiply or subtract with numeric variables.

```
scala> number - 1
val res0: Int = 1
```

In this particular case, you didn't define the name of the variable to save the result of the operation, so Scala assigns one particular name, which always has the prefix res. You can use this type of variable in the same way as the variables for which you choose the name, but you need to consider that all variables are only for reading access.

```
scala> res0 + number
val res1: Int = 3
```

Now that you have defined some immutable variables, it's time to declare some where you can change the value at any moment.

```
scala> var mutableNumber = 5
var mutableNumber: Int = 5
```

As you can see, there is almost no difference from the previous example. The only thing that changes is the val to var. Let's do a modification of the value and see what happens.

```scala
scala> mutableNumber = 10
mutableNumber: Int = 10
```

If you print the value of this variable, you can see that the new value is correct.

```scala
scala> println("Mutable number value is " + mutableNumber)
Mutable number value is 10
```

Now create a variable that has a particular type and try to assign a different type, such as a number with decimals.

```scala
scala> mutableNumber = 99.99
1 |mutableNumber = 99.99
  |                ^^^^^
  |                Found:    (99.99d : Double)
  |                Required: Int
```

These types of errors could happen in the console but also in the IDE. Of course, your IDE reduces the risk of doing this kind of thing because it shows an error before you run the application.

The last way to declare a variable is using lazy, which is only calculated the first time the variable is accessed. You can only use val with lazy variables because the value does not change.

```scala
scala> lazy val lazyNumber = 2;
lazy val lazyNumber: Int
```

```scala
scala> println("Lazy number value is " + lazyNumber)
Lazy number value is 2
```

As you can see, when you declare the variable, lazy does not appear, which is the value. The value only loads when you call the method print, which is the first access to the variable.

Variable without defining the type	Variable defining the type
scala> val numberWithoutType = 3; val numberWithoutType: Int = 3;	scala> val numberWithType : Int = 3; val numberWithType: Int = 3;

Scala Type Hierarchy

Scala does not have language primitives types of values, unlike Java or C++, which have the chance to use int, double, and float. Instead, all the types are objects with methods to manipulate the values or do some kind of operation in Scala. Figure 2-1 shows the hierarchy of the different types that exist in Scala.

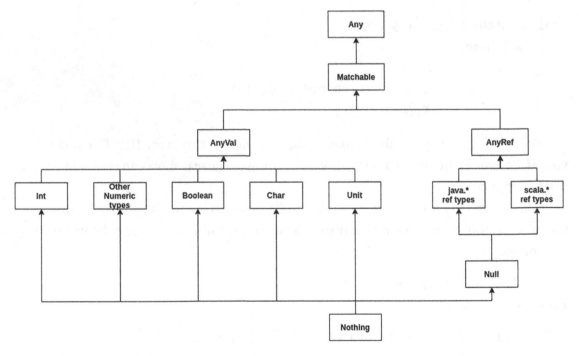

Figure 2-1. *Hierarchy of types in Scala*

In the following sections, you will see the definitions and some operations that support each of them. Just to clarify, on the right side of the figure appears "All java.*/ scala.* ref types." This means objects like collections (e.g., List and Map), Optional, String, Date, and others. You'll explore these objects in more detail in future chapters.

Any, AnyVal, and AnyRef Types

Any is an abstract class and the root class in the Scala hierarchy, so all classes directly or indirectly inherit from it. You can think of this class as the Object class in Java. From this root class, there are two subclasses, AnyVal and AnyRef, which contain all the classes that you can use in Scala for different purposes. AnyVal contains all the types that contain a value, such as Double or Int, which is a final abstract class that extends from AnyVal. AnyRef contains references to non-value Scala classes and is user defined.

Numeric Types

The numeric types in Scala are represented by Byte, Short, Int, Long, and Char, which are known as integral numbers because you can use an integer to represent the value. The types Double and Float are constituted and are not related directly to the previous types.

Types and Range

Table 2-1 shows the different types and the range of values that each of them supports.

Table 2-1. *Types and Their Value Ranges*

Numeric type	Description	Range
Char	16-bit unsigned value	0 to 65,535
Byte	8-bit signed value	-128 to 127
Short	16-bit signed value	-32,768 to 32,767
Int	32-bit signed value	-2,147,483,648 to 2,147,483,647
Long	64-bit signed value	-2^{63} to 2^{621}
Float	32-bit single precision	1.40129846432481707e-45 to 3.40282346638528860e+38
Double	64-bit double precision	4.94065645841246544e-324d to 1.79769313486231570e+308d

You don't need to memorize the ranges because Scala provides methods to obtain this information. If you write the numeric type and invoke the methods `MinValue` or `MaxValue`, you can obtain the values.

```
scala> Int.MinValue
val res0: Int = -2147483648

scala> Int.MaxValue
val res1: Int = 2147483647
```

Conversion

Scala has the ability to automatically convert numbers from one type to another following this particular order: Byte ➤ Short ➤ Int ➤ Long ➤ Float ➤ Double. The following is an example of creating a Byte and assigning it to a Short. You explicitly declare the type in the REPL.

```
scala> val byteNumber: Byte = 1
val byteNumber: Byte = 1

scala> val shortNumber: Short = byteNumber
val shortNumber: Short = 1
```

As an alternative to converting one type to another by assigning the value in a variable, you can use the methods that provide each type. This alternative is useful when you need to compare two variables that have different types, and it's a safe way to convert any type to another, such as Float to Short. If you want to see the methods to convert from one type to another, you can type the name of the variable with `to` and press the Tab key.

```
scala> byteNumber.to
toByte    toChar    toDouble    toFloat    toInt    toLong    toShort    toString
```

This great feature of converting one type into another does not work in the reverser order, so if you try to convert a Float into an Int, an exception will appear.

```
scala> val otherByteNumer : Byte = shortNumber
1 |val otherByteNumer : Byte = shortNumber
  |                            ^^^^^^^^^^^
  |                            Found:    (shortNumber : Short)
  |                            Required: Byte
```

Scala offers the ability to declare big/complex numbers using underscores, and the compiler traduces this in the common format.

```
scala> val longNumber : Long = 1_250_000
val longNumber: Long = 1250000
```

Format

Converting into another format is a great feature but sometimes you only need to convert a numeric type as a String to save it in another place, add the currency symbol, or just print in the console/log.

To do this, you need to import a particular class that contains all the logic to do this conversion. In the following example, you create a format to print a number with the currency symbol:

```
scala> import java.text.NumberFormat
scala> val formmater = NumberFormat.getCurrencyInstance
scala> println(formmater.format(999.99))
$999.99
```

Not all of the types and formats that this class contains are solutions for your problems, so if you want to create a custom format outside those defined in the NumberFormat class, you can use DecimalFormat.

```
scala> import java.text.DecimalFormat
scala> val formatter = DecimalFormat("0.##")
scala> println(formatter.format(99.1221))
99.12
```

Boolean

The Boolean type is used to indicate variables that can only have two possible values, true or false, such as *the flight is international* or *the product is refurbished*.

```
scala> val booleanType = true
val booleanType: Boolean = true
```

27

Also, you can negate a Boolean to obtain the opposite value, which is extremely useful in a block of control like if, for, or while.

```
scala> val negateBooleanType = !booleanType
val negateBooleanType: Boolean = false
```

Char

Char types are written with single quotes to indicate that the content is just one character (any character at all but just one). The main differences from the String type are that with a String type you can have multiple characters inside and you need to use the double quotes to declare or assign the content to a variable.

```
scala> val charType = 'X'
val charType: Char = X
```

In this type, you can use methods to obtain certain information about the content of the variable. isLetter and isLetterOrDigit are two methods that you can use to verify the content.

```
scala> charType.isLetter
val res0: Boolean = true
```

Unit

The Unit type is used to represent the logic, method, or variable. It does not return anything. You can think of it as a void in Java or C++.

```
scala> val empty = ()
empty: Unit = ()
```

Strings

In any language, you will need to manipulate strings that contain certain information like an address or the full name of a person. The main difference from a Char type is that a String type can contain a certain number of characters and you need to use double quotes to declare the content.

```
scala> val stringType = "This variable is a string"
val stringType: String = This variable is a string
```

Also, you can define a String over multiples lines. To use a double quote to declare the start or the finish of this type, you need to use """.

```
scala> val multiLine = """This string
     | contain multiples
     | lines"""
val multiLine: String = This string
contain multiples
lines
```

Interpolation

Interpolation is a mechanism that allows you to combine strings and values defined in variables. To use this feature, start the declaration with s and follow with the string to use; it can be a variable or you can declare the string in the same place. The main thing is to import the variables to use. To do so, you need to declare the variables with the dollar symbol and round by {}.

```
scala> val fullName = "John Q"
val fullname: String = John Q
scala> print(s"Hello ${fullname}")
Hello John Q
```

Compare

In some languages, like Java, it is not recommended to use == to compare Strings, but in Scala, it is permitted.

```
scala> val nameOne = "Martin"
scala> val nameTwo = "Martin"
scala> print(nameOne == nameTwo)
true
```

There are some methods (equalsIgnoreCase) to compare Strings and ignore lowercase and uppercase. This is a great alternative when you don't care if the letters are in a certain case.

```
scala> val nameOne = "Martin"
scala> val nameTwo = "martin"
scala> print(nameOne.equalsIgnoreCase(nameTwo))
true
```

Split

Separating a String into an array is a common practice to iterate the content of a group or count the number of occurrences of some word. You can combine it with other methods, like replacing a part of the content.

```
scala> val splitText = "This is a test to split the text"
scala> splitText.split(" ")
val res0: Array[String] = Array(This, is, a, test, to, split, the, text)
```

Replace

String provides a set of methods to replace part of the content with another value. If the value you want to find in the String exist, nothing will happen.

```
scala> val replaceText = "This is a test to explit the test"
scala> replaceText.replace("explit", "split")
val res0: String = This is a test to split the test
```

The method finds the first occurrence of this condition and replaces the content but does not look for more possible occurrences. If you want to replace all occurrences, you need to use the method replaceAll.

Special Characters

Inside the String type, you can use special characters to indicate tabulation, a new line, or a simple quote. Table 2-2 lists some of the most common escape characters.

Table 2-2. *Common Escape Characters*

Character	Description	Example
\b	Backspace	scala> val commonString = "test\bspecial" val commonString: String = tesspecial
\t	Tabulation	scala> val commonString = "test\tspecial" val commonString: String = test special
\n	Newline	scala> val commonString = "test\nspecial" val commonString: String = testspecial
\'	Single quote (')	scala> val commonString = "this test isn\'t special" val commonString: String = this test isn't special

Other Methods

Table 2-3 lists some methods that you can use in a String, plus descriptions and examples.

Table 2-3. *Other Methods Available in the String Class*

Method	Description	Example
charAt	Returns the value of one particular position	scala> val commonString = "Test" scala> print(commonString.charAt(3)) t
indexOf	Returns the index of a character. If it does not exist, it returns -1.	scala> val commonString = "Test" scala> print(commonString.indexOf("s")) 2
toLowerCase	Converts all characters into lowercase	scala> val commonString = "Test" scala> print(commonString.toLowerCase) test
toUpperCase	Converts all characters into upper case	scala> val commonString = "Test" scala> print(commonString.toUpperCase) TEST

Date

The Date type is not directly available to use in Scala without importing anything. To use it, you need to import the different classes related to the manipulation of dates that are available in Java. Since Java 11, a lot of common problems with the use and manipulation of dates can be solved without including any external dependency, such as adding or subtracting days from one particular date. Before doing anything, you need to import the class associated with the type of data that you want to use.

```scala
scala> import java.util.Date;
scala> val actualDate =  Date()
val actualDate: java.util.Date = Sun Jun 13 19:59:11 ART 2021
```

In the case of the class Date, several methods are deprecated in version 11 of Java. This means that in future versions of the JDK they will disappear. For more information, check out the official documentation on the Oracle webpage[1].

Table 2-4 contains alternatives to Date.

Table 2-4. *Different Classes That Contain Some Format of the Date*

Class	Description
LocalDate	A date (day, month, and year) without anything related to the time
LocalTime	A time (hour, minute, seconds) that does not contain references to a particular date
LocalDateTime	A combination of the two previous classes
Period	To represent a period of time
ZoneId	Defines the different time zones
Instant	Represents a point in time expressed in nanoseconds

As a recommendation, use LocalDateTime or LocalDate instead of Date because they offer a lot of methods. Some methods are static in these classes. For example, to instantiate a new date, you have the static method now().

---

[1]https://docs.oracle.com/en/java/javase/11/docs/api/java.base/java/util/Date.html

```
scala> import java.time.LocalDateTime
scala> val actualDate = LocalDateTime.now()
val actualDate: java.time.LocalDateTime = 2021-06-13T20:12:49.342185
```

Say you want to subtract ten days from the actual date. LocalDateTime provides a specific method to remove days, months, years, and all the different segments related to the time.

```
scala> actualDate.minusDays(10)
val res2: java.time.LocalDateTime = 2021-06-03T20:12:49.342185
```

The same situation happens when you want to add something to a particular date. You have the same structure of names as in the case of subtracting but change the word minusXX to plusXX.

```
scala> actualDate.plusMonths(1)
val res3: java.time.LocalDateTime = 2021-07-13T20:12:49.342185
```

To see more information about all of the methods of LocalDateTime, please go to https://docs.oracle.com/en/java/javase/11/docs/api/java.base/java/time/LocalDateTime.html.

Format

As you saw in the previous section, the classes related to dates contain a lot of methods but don't directly include a way to format the value into a readable format for humans. To solve this particular problem, you can use the class DateTimeFormatter, which lets you specify any possible format, such as only showing the day and month of one date.

```
scala> import java.time.LocalDateTime
scala> val actualDate = LocalDateTime.now()
scala> import java.time.format.DateTimeFormatter
scala> val formatter = DateTimeFormatter.ofPattern("dd/MM")
scala> actualDate.format(formatter)
val res0: String = 13/06
```

Table 2-5 shows the most common values that you can use in the method ofPattern in the DateTimeFormatter.

Table 2-5. *Symbols to Specify the Format of a Date*

Symbol	Description	Example
Y	Year	yyyy = 2004 ; yy = 04
D	Day of year	189
M	Month of year	MM = 07 ; M = 7
D	Day of month	10
E	Day of week	Tue; Tuesday; T
H	Clock hour of am pm (1-12)	11
H	Hour of day (0-23)	18
M	Minute of hour	45
S	Second of minute	20
A	Millisecond of day	1234
N	Nanosecond of second	123454321
V	Time zone ID	America/Buenos_Aires; Z; –03:00
Z	Time zone name	Pacific Standard Time; PST
Z	Zone offset	+0100; –0300; –05:00;

Arrays

An array is a common structure that contains several elements from the same type (such as Int, Double, Float, and Date) and has an index (which means the position of the element). You always need to define the size of an array and you have two alternatives:

- Declaring the size without any value inside:

```
scala> var names = Array[String](3)
var names: Array[String] = Array(null, null, null)
```

- Inferring the size by the number of elements that it receives:

```
scala> var names = Array("John", "Anna", "Isabel")
var names: Array[String] = Array(John, Anna, Isabel)
```

There are some operations that you can do with an array:

- If you know the index, you can directly access the position that contains the value.

```
scala> print(names(0))
John
```

- If you try to set one element in a position that does not exist in the array, an exception will appear.

```
scala> names(4) = "Francesca"
java.lang.ArrayIndexOutOfBoundsException: Index 4 out of bounds
for length 3
    ... 28 elided
```

- You can find the size of the array using the size/length methods.

```
scala> names.length
val res0: Int = 3
```

- You can combine two different arrays into a new one.

```
scala> var italianNames = Array("Pietro", "Giovanni", "Renzo")
scala> var argentinanNames = Array("Martin", "Luis", "Jorge")
scala> argentinanNames.concat(italianNames)
val res0: Array[String] = Array(Martin, Luis, Jorge, Pietro,
Giovanni, Renzo)
```

- You can iterate in the reverse order.

```
scala> var italianNames = Array("Pietro", "Giovanni", "Renzo")
scala> italianNames.reverse
val res15: Array[String] = Array(Renzo, Giovanni, Pietro)
```

- You can filter for a specific value and create a new array.

```
scala> var names = Array("John", "Anna", "Isabel")
scala> name.filter(_ == "John")
val res0: Array[String] = Array(John)
```

Lists

Lists are similar to arrays because both can only contain elements of the same type, but there are some important differences:

- The first difference is that Lists are immutable, so when you add or remove an element, a new List is created with the new size and all the elements are copied from one List to another. Also, connected with this difference, you cannot change the value of any position.

- The second difference is that all Lists are LinkedLists, so each position has a pointer to the next element.

You can declare a List using any of the alternatives that appear in the Array section. If you create an empty List and start to add elements, a new List is created each time. As a recommendation, every time that you can create the List with all the elements, do it.

```
scala> val italianNames = List("Pietro", "Giovanni", "Renzo")

val italianNames: List[String] = List(Pietro, Giovanni, Renzo)
```

There is an alternative way to declare the elements without using the keyword `List` but the compiler will infer the type and created.

```
scala> val italianNames = "Pietro" :: "Giovanni" :: "Renzo" :: Nil
val italianNames: List[String] = List(Pietro, Giovanni, Renzo)
```

As in the case of an Array, a List has some methods to interact with the contents of the List and obtain more information. See Table 2-6.

Table 2-6. *Methods to Obtain Different Elements of a List*

Method	Description	Example
head	Returns the first element	scala> italianNames.head val res0: String = Pietro
tail	Returns the last element	scala> italianNames.tail val res0: String = Renzo
isEmpty	Returns a Boolean with the value of true if the list is empty	scala> italianNames.isEmpty val res0: Boolean = false
reverse	Returns a list in the inverse order	scala> italianNames.reverse val res0: List[String] = List(Renzo, Giovanni, Pietro)
contains	Iterates the List and checks if a value exists	scala> italianNames. contains("Pietro") val res0: Boolean = true

Null

Null is a subtype of the AnyRef types, including custom classes, to save any null references. This type does not contain methods or fields. If you try to invoke any method from Any, you will receive an exception.

```
scala> val nullType = null
val nullType: Null = null
scala> nullType.toString
java.lang.NullPointerException
    ... 28 elided
```

Nothing

Nothing is a subtype of all the other types (AnyVal and AnyRef), and you can use it to provide a compatible return type for operations that produce abnormal termination, such as methods that throw an exception.

Functions

Functions can appear in any place in the source file, and you can assign them inside a variable. These are two of the main differences from the methods that are similar but only exist inside the classes. The way to declare a function is by using the keyword def followed by the name and the parentheses.

```
scala> def printSomething() = println("Hello")
def printSomething(): Unit
scala> printSomething()
Hello
```

As you can see, after declaring the function, the way to call it is by using the name with the parentheses. Now let's change the example to receive a parameter and print it. You can do this by adding the definition of the function in the name and the type of variable that the function receives.

```
scala> def printSomething(s:String) = println(s)
def printSomething(s: String): Unit
scala> printSomething("Hello everyone!!!")
Hello everyone!!!
```

Also, functions can support multiple parameters separated by commas.

```
scala> def printSomething(s:String, name:String) = println(s.concat("
").concat(name))
def printSomething(s: String, name: String): Unit
scala> printSomething("Hello", "Martin")
Hello Martin
```

Functions can return the result of some operation. In this case, it is not necessary to indicate the type of value to return.

```
scala> def concatValues(s:String, name:String) = s.concat(" ").concat(name)
def concatValues(s: String, name: String): String
scala> concatValues("Hello", "Martin")
val res0: String = Hello Martin
```

Control Structures

Scala, like many other languages, provides some way to control the flow of the application. This feature is important for handling decisions or iterating elements. The following are some of the control structures: if/then/else expressions, for loops, while loops, try/catch/finally blocks, and match expressions.

if/then/else Expressions

These expressions are used to branch the logic in different parts depending on if the condition is true or not.

```
scala> val age = 18
scala> if age > 18 then
     |        println("You can have a driver license")
     | else
     |        println("You need authorization from your parents")
     |
You need authorization for your parents
```

The syntax of this expression has changed since Scala 2, and it introduces the keyword then to indicate what the code needs to do if the condition is true. Also, the parentheses and the braces disappear. The following is the previous block of code but with the syntax of Scala 2:

```
scala> if (age > 18) {
     |        println("You can have a driver license")
     | } else {
     |        println("You need authorization from your parents")
     | }
```

You won't always have just one condition to solve a problem. Perhaps you need to validate different scenarios; you can use a new if block next to the else to add a new condition.

```
scala> val age = 16
scala> if age > 18 then
     |        println("You can have a driver license")
     | else if age > 16 && age < 18 then
     |        println("You need authorization from your parents")
```

```
|  else
|      println("You can't drive")
You need authorization for your parents
```

The conditional operators that you see in the previous blocks of code are valid not just for the case of `if` expressions. You can use them in `for`/`while` loops and in other places that accept the use of conditions. For that reason, it's important that you know the most important operators. See Table 2-7.

Table 2-7. *Operators for Using if/else Structures*

Operator	Operation	Example
&&	And	scala> val age = 16 scala> println(age > 10 && age < 18) true
||	Or	scala> val age = 16 scala> println(age > 10 || age < 16) true
>	Greater than	scala> val age = 16 scala> println(age > 16) false
>=	Greater than or equal to	scala> val age = 16 scala> println(age >= 16) true
<	Less than	scala> val age = 16 scala> println(age < 16) false
<=	Less than or equal to	scala> val age = 16 scala> println(age <= 16) true

(*continued*)

Table 2-7. (*continued*)

Operator	Operation	Example
==	Equal to	scala> val age = 16 scala> println(age == 16) true
!=	Not equal to	scala> val age = 16 scala> println(age != 19) true

for Loops

The for loops are used to iterate different types of elements like arrays or any collection of elements as a List. The structure is simple: you need to indicate the start element/ position and the condition to finish the loop. The following is an example that iterates an array of elements until (not including) the size of the array:

```scala
scala> val names = Array("John", "Anna", "Isabel")
scala> for i <- 0 until names.size do
     |      println(names(i))
John
Anna
Isabel
```

This structure shows the improvement of Scala 3. The following code is written in Scala 2:

```scala
scala> for(i <- 0 until names.size) {
     |      println(names(i))
     | }
John
Anna
Isabel
```

You can think of this as a way to iterate an array. A collection could produce an error because you need to remember to use until instead of to and remember which letter accesses that particular index. There is another way to iterate, which is clearer:

```
scala> for(name <- names)
     |       println(name)
John
Anna
Isabel
```

Another alternative to iterate an array is to use the method `foreach` which is present in the collections and the array of elements.

```
scala> names.foreach(name => println(name))
John
Anna
Isabel
```

Say you need to iterate an array/collection and all the elements that satisfy a condition need to be saved in a new array. Scala offers a way to solve this particular problem. You need to add the condition and use the keyword `yield` to indicate that each iteration that satisfies the condition needs to be saved in something like a buffer, and when the `for` loop finishes, it will return the array with the elements.

```
scala> val shortNames = for name <- names if name.size <=4  yield name
val shortNames: Array[String] = Array(John, Anna)
```

while Loops

There is another way to iterate an array/collection of elements where the loop continues until the condition becomes false. Always use a condition that in some moment becomes false because some of the common problems of iterations are related to the condition never changing.

```
scala> val names = Array("John", "Anna", "Isabel")
scala> var i = 0
scala> while i < names.size do
     |       println(names(i))
     |       i += 1
John
Anna
Isabel
```

match Expressions

If expressions are a great solution when the number of conditions is not a big number, but what happens when this number increases? In this situation, the code will run into serious problems of maintainability and may not be easy to read for some developers. For these reasons, the expression match exists, which is similar to switch in Java.

```scala
scala> val month = 3
scala> month match
     |   case 1 => println("January")
     |   case 2 => println("February")
     |   case 3 => println("March")
     |   case _ => println("Invalid month") //This works as the default
March
```

In the previous example, all the cases print different strings, but imagine the case where you must execute the same logic for some cases. You can solve this problem by concatenating the cases using |.

```scala
scala> val month = 2
scala> month match
     |   case 1 | 2 => println("Winter")
     |   case 6 | 7 => println("Summer")
     |   case _ => println("Invalid month") //This works as the default
Winter
```

Also, you can return a value to save it inside a particular variable.

```scala
scala> val month = 2
scala> val season = month match
     |   case 1 | 2 => "Winter"
     |   case 6 | 7 => "Summer"
     |   case _ => ""
var season: String = Winter
```

A good way to optimize this type of expression is to use the annotation @switch in the match condition. You will see more about this structure in Chapter 5. Also, this annotation gives you some information related to the compilation errors.

```
scala> import scala.annotation.switch
scala> val month = 2
scala> (month: @switch) match
     |   case 1 | 2 => println("Winter")
     |   case 6 | 7 => println("Summer")
Winter
```

In some cases, you can have a method/function that receives different types and returns a specific value. The match expression gives you the chance to use it not with some specific type. You can combine multiple types like Strings, numbers, and Booleans.

```
scala> val strange : Any = true
scala> val option = strange match
     | case "test" => "String"
     | case true =>"Boolean"
val option: String = Boolean
```

try/catch/finally Blocks

This type of block is helpful to solve problems related to any type of exceptions in a block of code. The correct way to use this block is to declare all of the logic that can produce an exception inside the try section. The logic to do something with the exception goes inside the catch block, and the finally block is logic that is always executed (occurs or not an exception). Inside the catch block you can use the keyword case to execute a specific action for each exception.

```
scala> val nullType = null
scala> try
     |        println(nullType.toString)
     | catch
     |        case e: NullPointerException => println("Exception")
     | finally
     |        println("Execute the last part of the block")
Exception
Execute the last part of the block
```

A common use of the `finally` block is to close certain resources like files or a connection with a database.

Comments

Comments in Scala are very similar to those in other languages like Java or C++. You have two ways to create them:

- **Multiline:** Use /* to start the block that contains the comment and */ to finish the block. Inside this block, you can use as many lines of text that you consider necessary to explain something.

```
/*
I decided to define this value with 1 because I want to test part
of the logic of one method.
*/
val number = 1
```

- **Single line:** Use // to start the comment. Note that with this type of comment you can put the description on only one line.

```
val number = 1 // I define this value with one to test the logic
```

In cases where the name of the class/method/variable is clear, it is not necessary to add a comment to explain the idea of that block of code. Instead, when the logic is so complex or you add a hardcoded class/method/variable for some specific reason, add a comment with a lot of detail for any developer who will access the code later.

Running Code Without the REPL

Everything looks fine when you use the REPL, but there are some cases where it is too complex to do it. For that reason, an alternative is to create a file with the extension `.scala`. You can use your favorite IDE to do it. After that, you need to create a `@main` object, which runs all the logic of your application. You can think of this concept as the `main` method in Java, which most developers learn as the first step, or run the application using a framework like Spring Boot.

```scala
@main def main() =
    //Here you can put all your code
    print("Main method")
```

This code is a little different from the previous versions of Scala when you needed to define an object that extended from App.

```scala
object MyApp extends App {
    println("Main method")
}
```

If you want to run the code in the file using the console, you need to compile the file and then run the code.

```
~ scalac MyApp.scala
~ scala MyApp.scala
Main method
```

If you want to pass some parameters to change the behavior of your application, you need to modify your main to receive the parameters, separated by comma.

```scala
@main def main(message: String, second_message: String) =
    //Here you can put all your code
    print(message)
    print(second_message)
```

To run this piece of code and pass the parameters, the process is similar to the previous example, but you need to add the values of the parameters separated by one space and in the same order that appear in the main.

```
~ scalac MyApp.scala
~ scala MyApp.scala "hello"
Hello
```

Keywords

Each language has a certain number of exclusive keywords to indicate some kind of instruction. You cannot use most of them as a name of a variable or class. The list in Table 2-8 gives you an overview of some keywords. Most of them appear in this chapter and the following chapters.

Table 2-8. *Important Keywords in Scala*

Word	Description
abstract	Makes a method or class abstract, which means that you cannot instantiate directly; you need to use a concrete class.
case	Each of the possible options of one match block. Also used to declare a concrete case when you have an abstract class.
catch	To catch an exception that appears in the try block and do something
class	Defines a new class that can contain methods and variables
def	Starts the declaration of a method
do	An alternative way to iterate a collection or range
else	Connected with the keyword if. When the condition is false, this block of code is executed.
end	Used to indicate the end of one particular block, such as in one if/else
Enum	Exclusively used to declare an enumeration
extends	Indicates that the class or trait has a supertype
false	One of the possible values of a Boolean variable
final	You can use this word to indicate that one class/method/variable cannot be overridden.
finally	This block of code is connected with the try/catch block and is always executed after the execution of the logic of the try/catch operation.
for	Declares the beginning of an iteration

(continued)

Table 2-8. (*continued*)

Word	Description
given	Declares a block of code eligible to be used in another part. It is connected with the keyword `using`.
if	Starts the declaration of a conditional block
implicit	Refers to the old way of declaring and using the keywords `given` and `using`
import	Used to include in the actual scope of one or more methods or classes
lazy	Used to defer the evaluation of a variable
match	Means a block of code with multiple alternatives depending on one value. You can see this as `switch` in other languages like Java or C++.
new	Creates a new instance of a class. The use of this word is optional in Scala 3
null	Used to indicate that one variable does not have a specific value
object	To declare a class that has only one instance. You can think of this as a Singleton.
override	You can use this keyword to override a method that is not marked as final.
package	Declares the name of one package which contains some classes/enum/files
private	Restricts the visibility of the declaration. Only the logic in the same class can access it directly.
protected	Restricts the visibility of a declaration. Only the logic in the same class or subclasses can access it directly.
return	To indicate the return of a method
super	Refers to a method or part of the logic that exists in the superclass
then	In the `if` structure, this keyword replaces the curly braces {} and is executed only when the condition is true.
this	Refers to using a method or variable declared in the same class
throw	Throws an exception
trait	Indicates the declaration as an abstract type. You can see this keyword as an equivalent of *interfaces* in Java.

(*continued*)

Table 2-8. (*continued*)

Word	Description
true	One of the possible values of a Boolean variable
try	Declares the beginning of a block that can produce an exception during the execution
using	It's an alternative for implicit clauses.
val	Declares a variable as immutable and just read-only.
var	Declares a variable as mutable, so you can read or write in this variable.
while	This is another way to iterate a collection or range of values.
with	Used to include a specific *trait*
=	Used to assign the values in one variable
@	Marks the beginning of one annotation

Summary

In this chapter, you learned how to define and use the common structures and variables of Scala. These aspects are the keys to understanding the rest of the book because most of them appear in different chapters to explain a particular feature. The following are some of the most important points from this chapter:

- You can create variables as read-only with the keyword val. If you want to create a variable that needs to modify the content, use var.

- Strings are several characters that reside in one place. This type offers you a great number of methods to manipulate the value in different ways.

- Using the classes provided by Java, you can manipulate dates using different formats and with different levels of precision.

- Array and List are two ways to create a structure that contains a number of elements, all of the same type.

- `if/else` expressions are ideal for creating branching in your code depending on one or more conditions. If the number of `if/else` expressions becomes complex, consider using `match` expressions.

- There are different ways to iterate an array or collection, such as `for` or `while` loops. In the case of a `while` loop, the condition to validate the loop in some moment needs to be false.

- `Try/catch` blocks are ideal to mitigate problems associated with any exception that can appear in your code.

- Comments are a great way to give more detail about a block of complex code. There are two types of comments: multiline or single line.

- When you have complex blocks of code or an entire application, you need to use `@main` to execute the code.

CHAPTER 3

Object-Oriented Modeling

Many languages offer different ways to model using structures to represent the solution to a particular problem in the real world. With Scala, you can use two methods of modelling: object-oriented programming (OOP) and functional programming (FP). They share some structures with different meanings but the idea is to define attributes and behavior. As you read in the previous chapter, languages like Java, JavaScript, Python, C++, C#, Ruby, and PHP use OOP as the default modelling option or paradigm.

Concepts of OOP

OOP can be summarized by four different aspects, which differentiate from other paradigms:

- **Abstraction**: This concept represents the complexity of a problem using objects, fields, and methods. You can have all the logic for solving a situation in one structure without sharing the details of the implementation. You can imagine these concepts as one part of your car. You know the expected behavior when you turn on the lights, but you don't know what happens inside. Another example is the power button on a machine. You know that the button starts the machine and connects with other pieces of your machine, but you don't know all the things that exist inside the button.

  ```scala
  scala> class Light():
       |     def turnOn() = print("Turn on the lights")
  // defined class Light
  ```

  When you invoke the method turnOn, you don't know what happens inside because you can only see the *signature* of the method.

© David Pollak, Vishal Layka, and Andres Sacco 2022
D. Pollak et al., *Beginning Scala 3*, https://doi.org/10.1007/978-1-4842-7422-4_3

- **Encapsulation**: This aspect lets you restrict access to the internal attributes/fields inside an object and only access that information using specific methods. To do this, Scala provides three modifiers (public, private, and protected), which you will see in later sections of this chapter. This is important because you don't want someone to modify a variable that you are using in some of your methods.

```scala
scala> class Light:
     |    private val bulb = 75 // private restrict the access
     |    def turnOn() = print("Turn on the lights of " + bulb)
// defined class Light
```

If you try to access the bulb attribute, this will appear:

```scala
scala> val light = Light()
scala> light.bulb
1 |light.bulb
  |^^^^^^^^^^
  |value bulb cannot be accessed as a member of (light : Light)
    from module class rs$line$8$.
```

- **Inheritance**: This aspect lets you reuse or extend some part of the logic that you previously defined in another object that shares the same idea. Imagine that you have an object that contains all the logic to create a file and save a piece of information, but you need to define the format of data. A possible solution is to define one object per format that you want to save, which extends the logic to create and saves the information. Figure 3-1 illustrates an example.

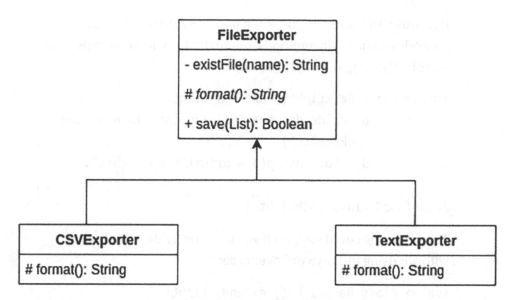

Figure 3-1. *Both exporters have concrete logic but share common logic to create a file*

Another example is in a car. The backlights have an extra behavior: when you press the brakes, an extra light turns on.

```scala
scala> class Light():
     |   def turnOn() = print("Turn on the lights")
scala> class BackLight() extends Light:
     |   def turnOnStop() = print("Stop lights")
```

- **Polymorphism**: This is the ability of an object to take on many forms. There are two types of polymorphism:

  - **Static**: You see this type when you need a method with the same name but with a different number of parameters or different types.

    ```scala
    scala> class Light:
         |     def turnOn() = print("Turn on the lights")
         |     def turnOn(message : String) = print(message)
    ```

53

- **Dynamic**: You see this type when one class inherits another and overrides some of the methods, but to do this you need to declare it explicitly using the override method.

```scala
scala> class BackLight() extends Light:
     |       override def turnOn() = print("Turn on the
           backlights")
     |       def turnOnStop() = print("Stop lights")
     |
// defined class BackLight
```

The following could happen if you try to override a method without using the keyword override:

```scala
scala> class BackLight() extends Light:
     |       def turnOn() = print("Turn on the backlights")
     |       def turnOnStop() = print("Stop lights")
     |
   2 |     def turnOn() = print("Turn on the backlights")
     |         ^
     |         error overriding method turnOn in class Light of
             type (): Unit;
     |           method turnOn of type (): Unit needs `override`
             modifier
```

From Concepts to Concrete Things

The concepts in the previous section are great, but you need to see them implemented in the real world. In Scala, the concepts of OOP come in four different things:

- **Classes**: You can think of a class as a blueprint that contains methods and attributes but no reference to any position of memory, so you can't use it to store any value or execute any method. The only way to use it is to create an instance of each class that knows it as an object.

```scala
scala> class Engine: //Define the structure of the class
     |   def start() = print("Start the engine")
scala> val engine = Engine() //Create an instance of the class
val engine: Engine = Engine@432c0f1
scala> engine.start() //Invoke the method to start the engine
Start the engine
```

- **Traits**: Traits are reusable components that have definitions of methods and attributes that all classes need in order to implement some part of the logic. You can think of them as a contract that all classes need to implement or follow and not change the name/parameters or return.

```scala
scala> trait AbstractLight:
     |   def turnOn() : Unit
scala> class Light extends AbstractLight:
     |   override def turnOn() = print("Turn on the lights")
```

There are a lot of features related to traits, such as extending the functionality of a trait in another trait and implementing multiple traits, which you will see in the following chapters.

Another way to think of a trait is as the equivalent of an `interface` in Java:

```java
public interface AbstractLight {
    void turnOn();
}
```

- **Enums**: Enums are a new feature in Scala 3. They help you define/reuse constants that have certain elements or values in common, such as the gender of a person (male, female, other) or type of flight (one way or round-trip). This type of structure is helpful when you want to have certain information in your class but you don't want anyone to enter a wrong value. An enum helps reduce the possible problems and provides a way to reuse the constant across different part of the code.

```scala
scala> enum LightType:
     |   case Big, Medium, Small
// defined class LightType
```

This topic will appear in more detail in Chapter 6 when you will see all the possible applications of the enum.

- **Objects**: An object is a way to create a static structure that you can access without instantiating a particular class. Another way to see this concept is as a Singleton because this structure only allows one instance.

```scala
scala> object Logger:
     |    def info(message: String) = print(s"INFO: $message")
scala> Logger.info("test")
INFO: test
```

Classes

As you read in the previous section, a class is a blueprint where you store certain values in fields/attributes and define certain behaviors of the methods. The only constraint with the use of this type of structure is that you need to define an instance that is assigned in the JVM position in the memory so you can reference it in parts of your application.

To define a class, you need to use the keyword `class` followed by the name. A good practice is to use camel case for the names, which means that each word of the name needs to have the first letter in a capital case. For more information, you can check the official documentation[1]. Also, don't use an underscore (_) in any part of the name. (These practices are the same in Java.) Table 3-1 lists bad options for a name.

Table 3-1. *Examples of Poor Class Names*

Class name	Wrong or correct?
_light	Wrong
Light	Wrong
AbstractLight	Correct
abstract_light	Wrong
Abstractlight	Wrong

---

[1] https://docs.scala-lang.org/style/naming-conventions.html

Now it's time to create your first class. For this example, create a class without any logic inside.

```
scala> class Book //Define a empty class only with constructor
// defined class Book
```

A good way to see what happens when you create a class is to decompile it. To do this, create a file named Book.scala and put the declaration of the class in it. After that, compile the class using the command scalac Book.scala and the compiler will create the file Book.class, which you can decompile using the command javap -c Book.class.

```
$ javap -c  Book.class
Compiled from "Book.scala"
public class Book {
  public Book();
    Code:
       0: aload_0
       1: invokespecial #9                // Method java/lang/Object."<init>":()V
       4: return
```

As you can see, there are no constructors, methods, or variables inside the class, just the definition. Now you've created your first class, but you need to instantiate it to use it. There two ways to do so, but the second is the best option in Scala 3.

Scala 2	Scala 3
scala> val book = new Book()val book: Book = Book@50a7c72b	scala> val book = Book()val book: Book = Book@50a7c72b

One last thing with creating an instance of a class: If you don't assign the new class in any variable, the compiler will assign a name.

```
scala> Book()
val res0: Book = Book@bf2aa32
```

Fields

Fields are a type of variable that let you store certain values related to one instance of a class. Valid types are anything that extends from Any, so you can store the status of custom objects or simple values like Strings.

The way to declare a field in Scala is very simple. You only need to indicate the type of variable with a name and add if the variable is immutable or not (var or val).

```scala
scala> class Book():
     |    var quantity = 0
// defined class Book
```

You need to consider something before declaring a variable in this way. If you don't explicitly indicate that the variable has restricted access, anyone can modify the value and you can lose control. Of course, many cases justify that a variable can be accessed directly but be aware that there are other options.

To continue with the previous idea, three access control modifiers give you a different level of access to the fields, as shown in Table 3-2.

Table 3-2. *Access Control Modifiers*

Modifier	Description	Example
private	With this the modifier, only the methods in the class can access the fields but you can create a custom method to return the value.	scala> class Book(): | private var quantity = 0 // defined class Book
protected	With this modifier, only the methods in the class and the class that extends from this one can access the value.	scala> class Book(): | protected var quantity = 0 // defined class Book
public	Anyone can access and modify the values stored in the fields.	scala> class Book(): | public var quantity = 0 // defined class Book
Nothing	In this case, it is the same as public.	scala> class Book(): | var quantity = 0 // defined class Book

When you create fields inside a class, use a name that defines the meaning of the field, such as *salary* or *quantity*. It is not a good practice to have fields with names like *a*, *b*, and *aux* because it is difficult for other developers to understand the meaning of those fields and it decreases the maintainability of the code.

Constructors

A constructor is a way to send parameters to your class at the same moment that you instantiate them. The main difference from other languages like Java, where the constructor appears in the body of the class, is that Scala gives you the advantage of declaring all parameters in the same definition of the class and internally they become the constructors. Another thing to consider is that if the class does not have parameters, Scala does not create a specific constructor; it uses the default constructor.

The constructor does a combination of things that you need to consider in order to understand how it works: it accepts the parameters that you define, creates fields in the class, assigns the values of the variables with the same name, and you can add some logic inside. To create a constructor, you need to pass the parameters one by one, separated by a comma.

```scala
scala> class Book(val name : String, val isbn : String)
// defined class Book
```

As in the previous section, you can decompile the code by saving this line in a file, compiling it, and executing the command `javap -c Book.class`.

```
public class Book {
  public Book(java.lang.String, java.lang.String);
    Code:
       0: aload_0
       1: aload_1
       2: putfield      #12          // Field name:Ljava/lang/String;
       5: aload_0
       6: aload_2
       7: putfield      #14          // Field isbn:Ljava/lang/String;
      10: aload_0
      11: invokespecial #17          // Method java/lang/Object."<init>":()V
      14: return
```

```
public java.lang.String name();
  Code:
     0: aload_0
     1: getfield        #12                    // Field name:Ljava/lang/String;
     4: areturn

public java.lang.String isbn();
  Code:
     0: aload_0
     1: getfield        #14                    // Field isbn:Ljava/lang/String;
     4: areturn
}
```

You can see that this is more code than in the previous sections. This is because Scala uses the modifier of the parameters to determine if it is necessary to create set/get methods for each attribute.

Visibility of the Fields

In the previous section, you saw one example of passing parameters to the constructor in the definition of the class. Scala uses the field modifiers to define which methods need to create them. You can see the meaning of each of them in Table 3-3.

Table 3-3. *Different Field Modifiers*

Type	Description	Example
val	This means that you can only access the information in the fields, so Scala only creates the get method.	scala> class Book(val name : String, val isbn : String) // defined class Book
var	In this case, Scala assumes the fields can be accessed and modified by anyone so it creates the methods set and get.	scala> class Book(var name : String, var isbn : String) // defined class Book
non defined	When you don't indicate which type is the field, Scala assumes that no one can access the fields, only the methods of the class.	scala> class Book(name : String, isbn : String) // defined class Book

These concepts and examples are great but how can you access them? This depends on the way you declare your parameters in the constructors. In the case of var/val, you can access them using the name of the instance and the parameter.

```scala
scala> class Book(var name : String, var isbn : String)
scala> val book = Book("ET", "S2323")
scala> print(book.name)
ET
```

The only case where you can assign a new value to a parameter is when you declared it as var so Scala creates a set method to modify the stored value.

```scala
scala> class Book(var name : String, var isbn : String)
scala> val book = Book("ET", "S2323")
scala> print(book.name)
ET
scala> book.name = "ET II"
scala> print(book.name)
ET II
```

Auxiliary Constructors

Scala lets you create extra constructors where you define which parameters receive but in all cases you need to indicate what to do with the parameters that receive tk. The best approach to this problem is to invoke the primary constructor, which receives all of the parameters and puts a default value in the parameters that the constructor does not receive.

The way to do make this happen is simple. You need to create a method named def this and add the parameters that you want.

```scala
scala> class Book(var name : String, var isbn : String):
    |       def this(name : String) =
    |           this(name, "default")
    |
    |       def this() =
    |           this("", "default")
```

Using the auxiliary's constructors is not complex. You need to create an instance of the class and pass only the parameters that you want. Scala checks for the correct constructor to invoke.

```scala
scala> val bookOne = Book("ET")
scala> print(bookOne.isbn)
default
```

Providing Default Values

Defining an auxiliary constructor is a good way to reduce possible problems when someone does not indicate all of the parameters but there is an alternative. You can put a default value in some or all the parameters so when someone does not specify the value, Scala uses the default value. This reduces the risk of something going wrong.

It's simple to implement this. After the definition of each type of parameter, add = with the value.

```scala
scala> class Light(val bulb: Int = 75)
scala> var light = Light()
scala> print(light.bulb)
75
```

Private Constructor

It's very uncommon to see a private constructor in the code of an application but it's possible. You can create a primary constructor as private so no one can create an instance. There are two uses of this approach: to create a class that only has constants or to combine it with an object to create a Singleton of the class. The way to do it is simple. Just add the access modifier private after the name of the class.

```scala
scala> class Light private ()
scala> val light = Light()//This will happen when you try to instantiate
1 |val light = Light()
  |            ^^^^^
  |            method apply cannot be accessed as a member of Light.type
  |            from module class rs$line$6$.
```

Methods

Methods are the way to assign behaviors to your classes. Of course, when you create a class that only stores values, behind the scenes it creates certain methods to access the information, but the idea is to show you how to create explicit methods in your classes.

Each method starts with the keyword def followed by the name, the parameters that it receives, and optionally the return type.

```scala
scala> class Light(val bulb: Int, val status: Boolean):
    |    def isWorking() : Boolean = if bulb >0 then true else false
scala> val light = Light(75, true)
scala> println(light.isWorking())
true
```

As you saw in previous sections, you can add access modifiers to restrict the possibility of accessing certain methods.

```scala
scala> class Light(val bulb: Int, val status: Boolean):
    |    private def isWorking() : Boolean = if bulb >0 then true
else false
scala> val light = Light(75, true)
scala> println(light.isWorking())
1 |println(light.isWorking())
    |        ^^^^^^^^^^^^^^^^
    |        method isWorking cannot be accessed as a member of (light :
            Light) from module class rs$line$15$.
```

Order

There is no constraint related to the order of methods and access modifiers but try to group all methods with the same modifiers in one part of the class. This will help you understand which ones are accessible outside the class. A possible approach that most Java developers follow is all private methods first, followed by the protected ones, and then the public ones.

Invoking Methods

To invoke a method internally in a class, you need to use the keyword this followed by the name of the method with the parameters. This is optional and in most cases is not necessary because the compiler infers which method you are calling but it is a good practice because it reduces the complexity in the code for other developers.

```scala
scala> class Light(val bulb: Int, val status: Boolean):
     |     private def isWorking() : Boolean = if bulb >0 then true
         else false
     |     def turnOn() : Unit = if this.isWorking() then print("Turn on
         the lights") else print("It's impossible to turn on the lights")
scala> var light = Light(75, true)
scala> light.turnOn()
Turn on the lights
```

Override Default Methods

Scala, like Java, gives you a set of default methods in each class that contain the default implementation but in some cases, it is necessary to override them to get a certain behavior.

toString

This method could give you some information about the values that exist in the class but, by default, most classes only give some information about the position of the memory that hold the class.

```scala
scala> class Light(val bulb: Int, val status: Boolean)
scala> val light = Light(75, true)
val light: Light = Light@4196a44a
scala> println(light)
rs$line$24$Light@4196a44a
```

To get a method that gives valuable information, you need to override the method. The way to do this is to add the keyword override and the logic of the method.

```
scala> class Light(val bulb: Int, val status: Boolean):
    |     override def toString() : String = s"The bulb has a potency of
        $bulb and the status is $status"
scala> val light = Light(75, true)
scala> println(light)
The bulb has a potency of 75 and the status is true
```

equals

This method allows you to compare two different instances and check if they are the same or not. The default behavior of this method compares the position of the memory, so in many cases this is not useful so you need to override the default method. You need to put the keyword override before the entire declaration of the method.

Note that the equal method receives the parameter Any so you need to validate before doing something that is the correct type. A good way to do it is to use match.

```
scala> class Light(val bulb: Int, val status: Boolean):
    |         override def equals(that: Any): Boolean =
    |             that match
    |                 case that: Light => that.isInstanceOf[Light] && this.
                    bulb == that.bulb && this.status == that.status
    |                 case _ => false
// defined class Light
```

After declaring the new method equals, you can create two instances of the class and assign the same values and see what happens when you try to compare them.

```
scala> val lightOne = Light(75, true)
scala> val lightTwo = Light(75, true)
scala> lightOne == lightTwo
val res0: Boolean = true
```

Inheritance

Inheritances are a common way to refer tk when you extend the functionality from another class or trait. Scala, like Java, does not support multiple inheritances but you can extend from multiple traits. In Java, you can implement multiple interfaces.

The way to extend from another class is by using the keyword extends followed by the name of the class.

```scala
scala> class Light(val bulb: Int, val status: Boolean):
     |        protected def isWorking() : Boolean = if bulb >0 then true
            else false
     |       def turnOn() : Unit = if this.isWorking() then print("Turn on the
            back lights") else print("It's impossible to turn on the lights")
scala> class BackLight(bulb: Int, status: Boolean) extends
Light(bulb, status)
scala> val backLight = BackLight(75, true)
scala> backLight.turnOn()
Turn on the lights
```

As you saw in previous sections, you define the behavior and override in the subclass using the keyword override.

```scala
scala> class BackLight(bulb: Int, status: Boolean) extends Light(bulb, status):
     |       override def turnOn(): Unit = if this.isWorking() then
            print("Turn on the back lights") else print("It's impossible to
            turn on the back lights")
scala> val backLight = BackLight(75, true)
scala> backLight.turnOn()
Turn on the back lights
```

In some cases, you want to override the entire logic. Perhaps you want to extend the functionality of the principal class. The correct way to invoke the logic in the main class is by using the keyword super followed by the name of the method to invoke.

```scala
scala> class BackLight(bulb: Int, status: Boolean) extends Light(bulb, status):
     |       override def turnOn(): Unit =
     |           super.turnOn()
     |           if this.isWorking() then print("Turn on the back lights")
            else print("It's impossible to turn on the back lights")
scala> val backLight = BackLight(75, true)
scala> backLight.turnOn()
Turn on the lights Turn on the back lights
```

Inner Classes

Scala and Java let you define inner classes (a class inside another class). The main difference from Java is that in Scala the inner classes are accessible from the outside. Each instance of a class can contain an instance of the inner classes. For example, create a class that contains a playlist of books you want to read. Each playlist has a name and a list of books.

```scala
scala> class Playlist(var name : String):
     |     var books : List[Book] = Nil
     |     def addBook(book : Book) : Unit =
     |         books = book :: books
     |     class Book(var name : String, var isbn : String)
scala> val playlist = Playlist("Horror")
scala> playlist.addBook(playlist.Book("ET", "sdsd"))
scala> print(playlist.books.size)
1
```

Note that you can only pass to the method addBook that books creates using the same instance of the class Playlist. If you use another instance, an exception will appear on your console.

Value Classes

Scala provides a way to decrease possible problems that can occur when a class, method, or object receives multiple parameters because it can be easy to make a mistake in the order of them. You can think of a value class as a wrapper that contains one and only one parameter, and the compiler will help you check that your methods receive only this type. If you have some experience with Java, you can think of this type of class as an *Integer*, which is a wrapper of *int* but adds some methods.

Here are some examples of a value class:

- Imagine that you have a phone number as a string and you need to have the string but you also need the ability to decompose the number into the country code or area code or number.

- Imagine that you have the ISBN of a book with a prefix ("I-") and you need to remove this special character.

Let's take the last example and put it in the class Book in the wrong order and see what happens.

```scala
scala> class Book(val name : String, val isbn : String)
scala> val book = Book("ISBN", "NAME")
```

As you can see, nothing happens if you make a mistake. Now it's time to define your first value class, which contains the ISBN with one method that removes the prefix.

```scala
scala> class ISBNumber(val isbn: String) extends AnyVal:
     |      def shortNumber = isbn.replace("I-", "")
scala> print(ISBNumber("I-122345").shortNumber)
122345
```

You have a value class but you don't modify your Book class, so now let's introduce the modifications and try to instantiate the class and pass two strings.

```scala
scala> class Book(val name : String, val isbn : ISBNumber)
scala> val book = Book("ISBN", "NAME")
1 |val book = Book("ISBN", "NAME")
  |                        ^^^^^^
  |                        Found:    ("NAME" : String)
  |                        Required: ISBNumber
```

When you try to create a new instance of the class with the new definition, an exception appears, but if you create it using the new type, everything works and you can access the internal methods.

```scala
scala> val book = Book("NAME", ISBNumber("I-TEST"))
scala> print(book.isbn.shortNumber)
TEST
```

There are some constraints when creating value classes:

- They need to be extended from AnyVal.

- They can only have one parameter and can't be declared using val. If you are using var or indicate nothing, Scala will show you an exception.

- You can't define an inner class inside.

- You can't define variables in the class. You can only define methods that can contain variables.

- They can't be extended by another class.

- You can't define a method named hashcode or equals.

Packages and Imports

Packages are used to contain in one place all the logic related to one module or certain types of logic, such as classes with database access. This is ideal for preventing possible collisions with names of classes because the package name is the differentiator. You can think of these concepts in this way: the name of the class is like the first name of a person because it could be someone else with the same name but the package declaration is like your surname so the combination of these things is different in each class.

To do this, you need to use the keyword package followed by the name of the package. As a good practice, don't use an underscore (_) or any special character.

```
package com.behindcodeline.model

class Book(var name : String, var isbn : String)
```

You cannot use this type of feature in the REPL because it is not possible. The only way to do this is to create a class in your IDE or a file and compile it in the console. In previous sections, you saw the use of the annotation @main. This is a good alternative to test this type of feature.

```
@main def main =
    val book = Book("ET", "test")
    println(book.name)
```

Now that you can define packages to import them, you need to use the keyword import with the entire name of the package, such as com.behindcodeline.model.Book. This is valid for the classes that you create and for the classes that exist in any library of Scala or Java.

Multiple Imports

When you have more than one class from the same package, you have three ways to import them:

- Import all classes of the package.

  ```
  import java.util.*
  ```

  This is not recommended because many of the classes may be unnecessary.

- Do one import per line.

  ```
  import java.util.LinkedList
  import java.util.Date
  ```

  This approach makes more sense because you only import the classes that you need but it looks bad if you have several classes from the same package.

- Do one import with multiple classes.

  ```
  import java.util.{LinkedList, Date}
  ```

  This approach is the best way to reduce the number of code lines in your application. Many developers know this approach as an *import selector clause*; it exists in a library of JavaScript named React[2].

Exclude Class

Everything looks great but say you don't want to use a specific class. Scala is different from Java because it provides an easy way to do this.

```
import java.util.{ArrayList => _}
```

With this import, when anyone who instantiates a class of the type ArrayList will receive an error.

---

[2] https://en.wikipedia.org/wiki/React_(JavaScript_library)

```
scala> import java.util.{ArrayList => _}

scala> val list = ArrayList()
1 |val list = ArrayList()
  |           ^^^^^^^^^
  |           Not found: ArrayList
```

Objects

The first time you heard the word "object," you might have thought it was an instance of a class. This is true in languages like Java or C++, but in Scala it has a different meaning. You can think of an object as an instance of a class, but it also means that you can create a Singleton with static methods that you can access without creating an instance. To create a unique instance, you need to use the keyword object followed by the name and the logic inside, in the same way as in the classes.

A simple example that most developers who use Scala 2 use when they start programming is the main method, which runs the entire application.

```
object MyApp extends App { //Only one instance of the application run
    println("Main method")
}
```

Defining Singletons

In the previous section, you saw a simple example, but imagine that you want to have something that contains methods with the common logic that you need to use across the entire application. In Java, you can create a class with static methods and with a private constructor so you can't instantiate many times, but in Scala, it is simpler. Let's create an object that creates a new file in a directory and prints a message.

```
scala> object FileUtil:
     |     def create(directory : String, name : String) : Unit =
     |         println(s"File $name created in the directory $directory")
// defined object FileUtil
scala> FileUtil.create("/test/", "test.txt")
File test.txt created in the directory /test/
```

You can see that after defining the object you can invoke a method directly without creating an instance. Another example of the use of objects is to create custom methods to parse a string or validate if it is empty.

Companion Objects

In Java, you can have a class with static methods or attributes like constants and use it from outside or inside the class, but in Scala, this is not possible in the same way. Scale offers the companion object instead. A companion object is when you create an object and a class in the same file with the same name and you can refer to the same name without any problem with the compiler.

To see how this feature works, first create a file named Book.scala and enter the following code:

```scala
class Book(val name : String, val isbn : String)

object Book:
    val PREFFIX = "I-"
```

After that, you can create a new file with the main method, or you can use the REPL but first you need to compile the file in the console and then import it in the REPL using :load.

```scala
scala> :load Book.scala
// defined class Book
// defined object Book
scala> val book = Book("ET", Book.PREFFIX + "Test")
scala> print(book.isbn)
I-Test
```

One important thing with the companion object is that both object and class can directly access private fields or methods without any restriction because the compiler considers them as one object. However, another class or object cannot access the private methods or fields.

Static Factory

If you want to have the creation of one class in one place, the best way to do so is to transform the constructor to `private` and create a particular method in the object that receives some parameters invoke to the private constructor and return the new instance of the class.

A possible use of this type of feature is to validate the parameters before creating an instance and, if something is wrong, return an exception.

```
class Book private (val name : String, val isbn : String)

object Book:
    val PREFFIX = "I-"
    def apply(name : String, isbn : String) = new Book(name, isbn)
```

To use this new way of instantiating a class, you need to do the following:

```
scala> :load Book.scala
// defined class Book
// defined object Book
scala> val book = Book.apply("name", "isbn")
val book: Book = Book@4fa5cc73
```

Opaque Types

Scala 3 offers a new feature called opaque types. They let you create a certain type of abstraction without any overhead. This means that you can create a type that from outside appears like a new type. You can use this type as a parameter in a method or an `if/else` condition.

This feature is similar to value classes. The main difference is that you can internally use the opaque type or the real type. You can create an opaque type in a class or an object, but if you create it inside an object, you can use or reference it in any part of the code because you take advantage of the object, instead of in the case of a class where you can only see the opaque type when you instantiate it.

To see this feature in action, create an object that contains the domain id and a method that translates the common types into opaque types.

```
object DomainIds:
    opaque type BookId = Int
    object BookId:
        def apply(id: Int): BookId = id
```

In this case, the apply method is executed as a "constructor" on a class so you can invoke a BookId and pass a number and return an opaque type with the value. To use this opaque type, you can create a main method and import all domain ids.

```
@main def main =
    //Import the domain objects.
    import DomainIds._

    val bookId = BookId(1)
    print(bookId)
```

Everything looks fine, but what happens if you want to extract the value of this BookId? By default, you don't have any methods but you can modify the code to include an extension that receives a BookId and returns the Int.

```
object DomainIds:
    opaque type BookId = Int
    object BookId:
        def apply(id: Int): BookId = id
    extension (bookId: BookId)
        def value: Int = bookId
```

Now change the main method to compare elements and print the result.

```
@main def main =
    //Import the domain objects.
    import DomainIds._

    val bookId = BookId(1)
    print(bookId.value == 1)
```

You can also define it inside a class and use it as the return type. This particular use is called an opaque type member. The following example shows how to implement it:

```scala
class Book (val name : String, val isbn : String)

class BookService:
    opaque type BookId = Int
    def getIdByName(name: String) : BookId = 1
```

To run the example, use the command load to access these new types that appear in one file.

```scala
scala> :load MyApp.scala
scala> val bookService = BookService()
scala> bookService.getIdByName("sad")
val res0: bookService.BookId = 1
```

These are the main considerations for using opaque types:

- They offer an easy way to define new types.

- They don't support pattern matching.

- They don't have the default methods implemented, like equals, hashcode, and toString.

Export Clauses

Export clauses appear in Scala 3 and let you expose a method inside another class or object as part of another. Sometimes you have a class that contains another class, like a composition of classes, and if you want to expose one method or class, you need to create a specific method. With this approach, you can create some kind of inheritance for some methods.

In the following example, BookService has an instance of the repository to obtain information about a book.

```scala
class Book (val name : String, val isbn : String)

class BookRepository:
    def getBook() = new Book("test", "test")

class BookService:
    private val bookRepository = new BookRepository()
    export bookRepository.getBook //Use export to expose the method
```

As you can see, if you want to expose a method of the repository, you need to create a specific method. However, you can use an export clause in the service, so for the rest of the world the method getBook appears as part of BookService. Note that you won't create an instance of a repository in all cases. There are other mechanisms to instantiate safely, but for this example it works well. To check if everything works, you can create a main method and call the method getBook.

```
@main def main =
    val bookService = BookService()
    val book = bookService.getBook()
    print(book.name)
```

There are some rules to consider when creating an export clauses:

- All exports are final so any subtype cannot override the logic.

- You cannot expose a constructor.

- You can exclude some methods, so if the repository has an apply method and you want to exclude, you need to change the actual line for export bookRepository.{*, apply => _}.

Summary

In this chapter, you saw how different aspects of OOP and Scala reduce code complexity or improve performance. Most of these concepts are connected in some way with the next chapter, which describes the different aspects of functional programming. The following are the highlights of this chapter:

- In OOP, you need to follow four principles: abstraction, encapsulation, inheritance, and polymorphism.

- OOP has a structure to represent its principles: classes, enums, traits, and objects.

- Classes are a structure that represents a model of a real solution for a problem and contains all the logic inside including methods and fields.

- The package separates or groups the classes, enum, and traits in some way, which helps to prevent collisions of names.

- Opaque types offer a way to create new types simply and reduce the possible complexity of the code.

- Export clauses let you expose methods that exist in another class as part of the actual class.

- An object is a representation of something that only has an instance, like a Singleton. You can use an object to contain methods to parse a String or create a connection to a database.

CHAPTER 4

Functional Programming

In the non-fiction work *Old Times on the Mississippi*, Mark Twain wrote, "When I was a boy of 14, my father was so ignorant I could hardly stand to have the old man around. But when I was 21, I was astonished at how much the old man had learned in seven years." Functional programming is the old man who comes to the rescue when writing robust concurrent software. Functional programming treats computation as the evaluation of mathematical functions and avoids state and mutable data. It is a declarative programming paradigm, in which programming is done with expressions. The imperative style of programming emphasizes a sequence of operations characterized by iteration with loops, mutating data in place, and methods with side effects where the order of side effects is critical for the right effect. The basic constructs in an imperative language, such as Java, are imperative statements that change the state of a program, as illustrated here:

```
x = x + 1
```

The functional style of programming emphasizes the results, characterized by passing function values into looping methods, immutable data, and methods with no side effects where the order in which operations occur is of no importance. In a functional language such as Scala, the basic constructs are declarative, as seen here, and there are no side effects:

```
f(int x){return x + 1}
```

In a functional language, the computation proceeds primarily by evaluation expressions. As a language that supports functional programming, Scala encourages an expression-oriented programming (EOP) model.

Martin Odersky, the creator of Scala, said the essence of the language is a fusion of functional and object-oriented programming in a typed setting: functions for the logic and objects for the modularity. For this reason, you need to understand both paradigms to use all the power of this language.

© David Pollak, Vishal Layka, and Andres Sacco 2022
D. Pollak et al., *Beginning Scala 3*, https://doi.org/10.1007/978-1-4842-7422-4_4

What Is Functional Programming?

When someone encounters the term *functional programming*, they may think that it is something that appeared recently, but the truth is some languages implemented this idea in the past. Most of these languages are not very popular nowadays.

One example of an old functional language is Lisp, which was born in 1958. Another example is Haskell, which appeared in 1990. These languages were very popular in academic settings but most developers did not use them in their professional life. This does not mean that the paradigm was bad or difficult to understand. Sometimes some languages or paradigms find new importance in a different era. Imagine that someone in the 1990s wanted you to create the entire back end of an application using JavaScript. You might have considered that person as crazy because JavaScript at that time was used to do certain validations or effects in HTML. Today, JavaScript is used on many platforms to create microservices using NodeJs[1] and other technologies.

To answer the question that appears in the title of this section, there are many definitions of this paradigm but one summarizes the entire idea in a simple way:

> *Functional code is characterized by one thing: the absence of side effects. It doesn't rely on data outside the current function, and it doesn't change data that exists outside the current function. Every other "functional" thing can be derived from this property. Use it as a guide rope as you learn.*

Mary Rose Cook

Another writer of many books about functional programming said:

> *Functional programming is a way of writing software applications using only pure functions and immutable values.*

Alvin Alexander

Both definitions have something in common. They mention the importance of immutability because it removes all the problems of coordinating the concurrency or sharing access to certain variables. Of course, you can create variables using the keyword `var` but the essence or spirit of the paradigm is to use tk inside the functions. When you

---

[1] https://nodejs.org/es/

pass parameters to a function, you can't change the values inside, following the principle of immutability. Instead, you need to create a new variable and return the value.

To see immutability with an example, let's create a function that removes the prefix in one string. First, try to reassign the result of the operation to the same variable and see what happens.

```scala
scala> def removePreffix(name : String) =
     |     name = name.replace('T', ' ')
     |
2 |     name = name.replace('T', ' ')
     |     ^^^^^^^^^^^^^^^^^^^^^^^^^^^^^^
     |     Reassignment to val name
```

The correct way to follow the principle of immutability is something like this:

```scala
scala> def removePreffix(name : String) =
     |     name.replace('T', ' ')
def removePreffix(name: String): String
```

This means that the function takes one string, replaces the prefix, and returns a new value without changing the value of the original parameter.

Pure Functions

In mathematics, functions are nothing short of pure, in that they lack side effects. Consider the classic functions in (x):

```
y = sin(x)
```

Regardless of how many times $sin(x)$ gets called, $sin(x)$ does not modify the state of the variable. Such a function is called a pure function and is oblivious to the context.

Now, sometimes your function doesn't just do mathematical operations, so the following are rules for making a pure function:

- They are functions that do not modify the value of the parameters; instead, they return a new value with the result.

- They are functions that do not modify the context of the application.

- They only depend on the parameters that the function receives.
  They don't access external resources like databases, files, or other
  applications using the network.

Side Effects

Following the definition of a pure function, side effects refer to the idea that the
execution of a function does not affect the rest of the application or external resources
like a database. Imagine that you have a function which, depending on the parameters
it receives, throws an exception or calls another function that is not pure. These are
examples of side effects that can affect parts of your application.

Referential Transparency

An expression is referentially transparent if it can be substituted by its resulting value,
without changing the behavior of the program, regardless of where the expression is
used in the program. For instance, you can assign the expression of two immutable
variables x and y to a third variable z, like this:

```
val z = x + y
```

So anywhere the expression x + y is used throughout the given scope of your
program, you can substitute it with z within that scope without affecting the result of
the program. As stated, functional programming gives you the right foundation to think
about concurrency. The three keystones of this foundation are referential transparency,
higher-order function, and immutable value. Understanding these key elements is
crucial to understanding functional programming. In functional programming, a pure
function with one or more input parameters does not mutate the input parameters and
always returns the same value for the same input.

Note   A pure function is referentially transparent and has no side effects.

A pure function is free of side effects. However, a function that never causes side
effects would be useless. A language that does not sanction side effects would be useless,
as input and output are essentially the ramifications of side effects.

We have introduced enough theory for you to begin to explore Scala functions. In Chapter 2, you learned the basic syntax of Scala functions and how you can declare, define, and call functions. Before continuing with the sections that follow in this chapter, we recommend you skim through the Scala functions introduced in Chapter 2.

Now we will get started with a basic functional construct in Scala: the function literal.

Expression-Oriented Programming

In expression-oriented programming, every statement is an expression. To understand EOP, you have to understand the difference between a statement and an expression. A statement executes code but does not return any value, for example:

```
customer.computeDiscount()
```

An expression returns a value. Expressions are blocks of code that evaluate to a value.

```
val discount = computeDiscount(customer)
```

Note   An expression-oriented programming language is a programming language where every construct is an expression and thus evaluates to a value.

In Scala, the following expression returns a result:

```
scala> 2 + 2
res0: Int = 4
```

The strength of expression-oriented programming is more discernible from an if/ else expression, which also returns a value in Scala.

```
val test = if (3 > 2) "true" else "false"
```

This if clause checks a conditional expression and returns one expression or another, depending on the value of the conditional expression. An if block in Java does not evaluate a value. The code illustrated here is illegal in Java, in contrast to Scala, because the if clause in Java is a statement, not an expression.

```
boolean test = if (3 > 2) "true" else "false"
```

To accomplish the same effect shown in the Scala if clause, you must use the ?: syntax in Java, as illustrated here:

```
boolean test = 3 > 2 ? true : false ;
```

In Java, there is a difference between if and ?: where if is a statement while ?: is an expression. The if clause in Scala is much more like ?: in Java than the if clause in Java. Scala has unified the concept of ?: with its if blocks and so Scala doesn't have a ?: syntax.

Note   As mentioned, every construct in Scala is an expression where the order in which operations occur is of no importance and therefore these expressions can be executed in any order. This simple concept has a deep implication in concurrency in multicore programming where you can execute expressions in parallel.

Functions, Lambdas, and Closures

Some of these terms do not exist in the previous versions of Scala or change meaning in this version, so before going more in depth, you need to understand the basic idea of each term.

- **Function**: This operation can have a name where the code is not evaluated until it's called for someone. This operation may or may not have variables. The following is an example of a function that calculates the area:

  ```
  scala> def calculateArea(height: Int, width: Int) =
  height*width
  def calculateArea(height: Int, width: Int): Int
  ```

- **Lambda**: This is an anonymous function that may or may not have variables in the definition.

  ```
  (height: Int, width: Int) => height*width
  ```

  Languages like Java or Python use the term *lambda function,* but in Scala, most developers use the terms *anonymous function* or *function literal* to describe the idea of lambda.

- **Closure:** This is a function, anonymous or named, which use one or more free variables to return a new value. The idea of free variables is to have variables in the scope of the function and it's not necessary passing to the function as parameters.

```scala
scala> var count = 0
scala> val incrementCount = (number:Int) => count + number
scala> incrementCount(1)
val res1: Int = 1
```

Function Literal/Anonymous Function

A literal is the simplest form of an expression. A literal is a notation for representing a fixed value in the source code. Almost all programming languages have notations for atomic values such as integers, floating-point numbers, strings, and so on. Literals are often used to initialize variables. In the following, 1 is an integer literal:

```
int x = 1;
```

Scala allows you to express functions as literals. Function literals allow you to have an expression of a function type that you can write in a short format without declaring a name for it. A function type could be one of the following:

- The type of a variable or parameter to which a function can be assigned

- An argument of a higher-order function, which you will see in detail in Chapter 10, taking a function parameter

- The result type of higher-order function returning a function

The syntax for a function literal starts with a parenthesized, comma–separated list of arguments followed by an arrow and the body of the function. A function literal is also called an *anonymous function*, that is, a function without any name specified with the function literal syntax. Consider an add function:

```scala
val add = (x: Int, y: Int) => x + y
```

Using the function literal, you can define the add function as illustrated here:

```scala
(x: Int, y: Int) => x + y
```

A function literal is instantiated into an object called a function value. A function value is a function object, and you can invoke the function object in the same manner as you invoke any other function. The function object extends one of the FunctionN traits, such as Function0, Function1, and so on up to Function22. Depending on the number of arguments in the function, the corresponding FunctionN trait is chosen by the compiler. For a function with two arguments, the compiler will elect Function2 as the underlying type. For a function with three arguments, the compiler will choose Function3; for a function with four arguments, Function4; and so on.

Because the function value is an object, it can be stored in a variable and it can be invoked using parentheses in the function call, as illustrated here:

```
scala> val add = (a: Int, b: Int) => a + b
add: (Int, Int) => Int = <function2>
scala> add(1, 2)
res0: Int = 3
```

The invocation of this function is converted to a call to the apply method of the function class instance, which is assigned to the variable.

From these kinds of function literals, the Scala compiler generates a function object that mixes in one of the FunctionN traits. So the left side of the → becomes the parameter list and the right side becomes the implementation of the apply method. Every function that you define in Scala becomes an instance of an implementation that features a certain FunctionN trait ranging from Function1 up to Function22.

Now, to take a deeper look into Function traits, you first write a function that calculates the area of a rectangle as illustrated here:

```
val areaOfRectangle:(Int, Int) => Int = (width:Int, height:Int) =>
width*height
```

When you run this function in REPL, you will see that the compiler elects and chooses the Function2 trait for this function. Why? Because there are two arguments to this function.

```
scala> val areaOfRectangle:(Int, Int) => Int = (width:Int, height:Int) =>
width*height
areaOfRectangle: (Int, Int) => Int = = Lambda$1475/0x000000080121504
0@712594f4
```

You can invoke this function as seen here:

```
scala> areaOfRectangle(5,3)
res0: Int = 15
```

Now, let's look at traits in Scala. Function2 in the Scala package looks like this:

```
trait Function2[-T1, -T2, +R] extends AnyRef {
    ...
abstract def apply( v1 :T1, v2 :T2 ) : R
    ...
}
```

This shows only the apply method. The two type parameters, T1 and T2, in the apply method take the type of the arguments, while the type parameter R represents the function's return type.

For every function that you define in Scala, the compiler will come up with an instance of the appropriate Function trait, where the type parameters are parameterized with the given types of the arguments and the return type of the function.

In the areaOfRectangle function defined earlier, the type of areaOfRectangle function is

```
(Int, Int)  =>Int
```

This is the same as illustrated here:

```
Function2[Int,Int,Int]
```

So you could have defined your add function this way:

```
 val areaOfRectangle:  Function2[Int,Int,Int]  = (width:Int, height:Int) =>
{ width*height }
```

You can test this in the REPL as seen here:

```
scala> val areaOfRectangle:  Function2[Int,Int,Int]  = (width:Int,
height:Int) => { width*height }
val areaOfRectangle: (Int, Int) => Int = Lambda$1502/0x000000080122804
0@61c0fb12
```

Now you can explicitly call the method to apply on a given function as illustrated:

```
areaOfRectangle.apply(5,3)
```

You can test this in the REPL as illustrated here:

```
scala> val area = areaOfRectangle.apply(5,3)
area: Int = 15
```

You can go a step further and define a function by implementing an appropriate Function trait and define its required apply method. Let's do this for the areaOfRectangle function:

```
val areaOfRectangle :(Int, Int) => Int = new Function2[Int, Int, Int]{
    def apply(width:Int, height:Int):Int = width*height
}
```

You can test this in the REPL as seen here:

```
scala> areaOfRectangle(5,3)
res18: Int = 15
```

Now that you have learned function values and function types, you will see how to use a function literal to pass it into a method that takes a function or assigns it to a variable. We will discuss this in detail in the following section.

First-Class Functions and Higher-Order Functions

One of the key factors in Scala that beautifully blends the functional paradigm with the object-oriented paradigm is that functions are objects. In functional programming, functions are first-class citizens. A first-class function is a function that can be

1. Assigned to variables,

2. Passed as an argument to the other function, and

3. Returned as values from the other function.

The other function emphasized in point 2 that takes a function as an argument and the other function emphasized in point 3 that returns a function are called higher-order functions. In the sections that follow, you will learn about all three aspects of a first-class function.

> **Note** In functional programming, functions are first-class citizens, meaning functions can be assigned to variables, functions can be passed to other functions, and functions can be returned as values from other functions. And such functions, which take functions as arguments or return a function, are called higher-order functions.

Functions as Variables

Just as you pass Strings, Ints, and other variables around in OOP, you can pass a function around like a variable. You can define a function literal as you saw in the previous section, and then assign that literal to a variable. The following code defines a function literal that takes an Int parameter and returns a value that is twice the amount of the Int that is passed in:

```
(i: Int) => { i * 2 }
```

You can now assign that function literal to a variable.

```
scala> val doubler = (i: Int) => { i * 2 }
val doubler: Int => Int = Lambda$1503/0x0000000801229040@689eab53
```

The variable `doubler` is an instance of a function, known as a function value. You can now invoke `doubler` as illustrated here:

```
scala> doubler(2)
res25: Int = 4
```

Under the hood, `doubler` is an instance of the function1 trait, which defines a function that takes one argument. In terms of implementation, `doubler` is a function created using the keyword `val` and assigned to a variable. To define `doubler` as a method instead of as a function, you must define the `doubler` method in a class and use the keyword `def` to define a method.

Beyond just invoking `doubler`, you can also pass it to any function (or method) that takes a function parameter. We will discuss this in the following section.

Functions as Parameters

You can create a function or a method that takes a function as a parameter. For this, first define a method that takes a function as a parameter.

```scala
scala> def operation(functionparam:(Int, Int) => Int)
= println(functionparam(4,4))
def operation(functionparam: (Int, Int) => Int): Unit
```

The operation method takes one parameter named functionparam, which is a function. The functionparam function takes two Ints and returns an Int. The operation method returns a Unit that indicates that the operation method returns nothing.

Next, define a function that matches the expected signature. The following add function matches that signature because it takes two Int arguments and returns an Int:

```scala
val add = (x: Int, y:Int) => { x + y }
```

Now you can pass an add function into the operation method.

```scala
scala> operation(add)
8
```

Any function that matches this signature can be passed into the operation method. Let's define two new functions named subtract and multiply that take two Ints and return an Int.

```scala
val subtract = (x: Int, y:Int) => { x - y }
val multiply = (x: Int, y:Int) => { x*y }
```

Now you can pass these functions into your operation method.

```scala
scala > operation(subtract)
0

scala> operation(multiply)
16
```

Returning a Function

You can return a function from a function or method. In order to do this, first define an anonymous function. The following code declares an anonymous function that takes a String argument and returns a String:

```
(name: String) => { "hello" + " " + name }
```

Now define a method that returns the anonymous function that you just defined.

```
def greeting() = (name: String) => {"hello" + " " + name}
```

On the left side of the = symbol you have a normal method declaration.

```
def greeting()
```

On the right side of the = is a function literal (an anonymous function).

```
scala> def greeting() = (name: String) => {"hello" + " " + name}
greeting: ()String => String
```

Now you can assign `greeting()` to a variable.

```
scala>  val greet= greeting()
val greet: String => String = Lambda$1261/0x000000080114c840@769b0752
```

The greet function is now equivalent to your anonymous function `(name: String) => {"hello" + " " + name}`. Because the anonymous function takes a String parameter name, you can pass it a name.

```
scala> greet("Reader")
res0: String = hello Reader
```

Closure

A closure is a function whose return value depends on the value of one or more variables declared outside this function. Consider the following multiplier function:

```
 val multiplier = (x:Int) => x * 3
```

In the `multiplier` function, y is the variable used in the function body. x is defined as a parameter to the function. Now let's modify the multiplier function as illustrated here:

```
val multiplier = (x: Int) => x * y
```

Because x is a formal parameter to the function, it is bound to a new value each time `multiplier` is called. However, y is not a formal parameter. Let's further modify the multiplier function as illustrated:

```
var y = 3
val multiplier = (x: Int) => x * y
```

Now y has a reference to a variable outside the function but in the enclosing scope.

```
scala> var y = 3
y: Int = 3
scala> val multiplier = (x: Int) => x * y
multiplier: Int => Int = <function1>
```

Now you can invoke the `multiplier` function as illustrated here:

```
scala> multiplier(3)
res37: Int = 9
```

The `multiplier` function references y and reads its current value each time. The Scala compiler creates a closure (closes over) that encompasses the variable in the enclosing scope.

Partially Applied Functions

In functional programming languages, when you call a function that has parameters, you are said to be applying the function to the parameters. When all parameters are passed to the function, you have fully applied the function to all the parameters.

A simple add function:

```
scala> val add = (x: Int, y: Int) => x + y
add: (Int, Int) => Int = <function2>
```

<function2> indicates it is a function of two parameters.

```
scala> add(1,2)
res01: Int = 3
```

But when you give only a subset of the parameters to the function, the result of the expression is a partially applied function.

```
val partiallyAdd = add(1, _:Int)
```

Because you haven't provided a value for the second parameter, the variable partiallyAdd is a partially applied function. You can see this in the REPL.

```
scala> val partiallyAdd = add(1, _:Int)
partiallyAdd: Int => Int = <function1>
```

The output in the REPL shows that partiallyAdd is a function that implements the Function1 trait. Implementing a Function1 trait indicates that the partiallyAdd function takes one argument. When you give partiallyAdd an Int value 2, you get the sum of the Int number passed into the add and partiallyAdd functions:

```
scala> partiallyAdd(2)
res02: Int = 3
```

The first argument, 1, was passed into the original add function and the new function named partiallyAdd was created, which is a partially applied function. Then the second argument, 2, was passed into partiallyAdd. When you provide all the parameters, the original function is executed, yielding the result.

Curried Functions

Currying converts a function with multiple parameters, creating a chain of functions, each expecting a single parameter.

Let's look at a simple add function that adds two Int parameters, a and b, as illustrated here:

```
scala> val add = (x: Int, y: Int) => x + y
add: (Int, Int) => Int = <function2>
scala> add(3,3)
res38: Int = 6
```

In Scala, curried functions are defined with multiple parameter lists, as follows:

```
def add(x: Int)(y: Int) = x + y
```

You can also use the following syntax to define a curried function:

```
def add(x: Int) = (y: Int) => x + y
```

As you can see, instead of one list of two Int parameters, you apply the curried add function to two lists of one Int parameter. Thus, the curried add function looks like this:

```
scala> def curriedAdd(a: Int)(b: Int) = a + b
curriedAdd: (a: Int)(b: Int)Int
scala> curriedAdd(2)(2)
res1: Int = 4
```

You could define more than two parameters on a curried function. Your add function that takes two arguments is transformed into its curried equivalent.

Function Compositions

In functional programming, you can compose functions from other functions, such a $\tan(x) = \sin(x)/\cos(x)$. An implication of composability is that functions can be treated as values. So far, you've created simple functions and manipulated the function instances. However, you can also build functions from other functions. The functionalTo composition provides the basis for a lot of cool things in Scala, including the parser combinator, which you will explore in Chapter 8. But for now, let's see the difference between interpreting a series of commands and "compiling" a function that interprets them. First, let's define the grammar. We have expressions, which can be constant values or named variables. Expressions can also be the addition or multiplication of other expressions. Here's a collection of case classes that describes the grammar (recall that we covered case classes in Chapter 3):

```
sealed trait Expr
case class Add(left: Expr, right: Expr) extends Expr
case class Mul(left: Expr, right: Expr) extends Expr
case class Val(value: Int) extends Expr
case class Var(name: String) extends Expr
```

We can build expressions like 1 + 1, Add(Val(1), Val(1)), 3 * (1 + 1),
Mul(Val(3),
Add(Val(1), Val(1)), and a * 11, Mul(Var("a"), Val(11)).

You can evaluate an expression by interpreting the expression.

```
def calc(expr: Expr, vars: Map[String, Int]): Int = expr match {
    case Add(left, right) => calc(left, vars) + calc(right, vars)
    case Mul(left, right) => calc(left, vars) * calc(right, vars)
    case Val(v) => v
    case Var(name) => vars(name)
}
```

Let's look at how this method works. expr is the expression to evaluate, and vars is a
Map that contains the variables. You use pattern matching, which you will see in the next
chapter, to determine what to do based on the case class. If expr is an Add, you extract
the left and right parameters, which are themselves Exprs. You call calc to calculate the
value of the left and right parameters and add the results. If expr is Mul, you do the same
thing (except you multiply things rather than add them). If expr is Val, you simply extract
the value and return it. If expr is Var, you extract the name and return the lookup of the
name in the vars Map. You can turn this from a method call into a function. Having a
function allows you to pass around the logic that the expression represents. It also means
that you don't have to interpret the tree of Exprs each time. Let's see how to compose a
function based on the Expr.

```
def buildCalc(expr: Expr): Map[String, Int] => Int = expr match {
    case Add(left, right) =>
        val lf = buildCalc(left)
        val rf = buildCalc(right)
        m => lf(m) + rf(m)
    case Mul(left, right) =>
        val lf = buildCalc(left)
        val rf = buildCalc(right)
        m => lf(m) * rf(m)
    case Val(v) => m => v
    case Var(name) => m => m(name)
}
```

The buildCalc method returns a function that can be passed to other functions. Also, the JVM can optimize the composed functions so that they perform better than the interpreted version. The performance of the composed function is better because there is no overhead associated with pattern matching each element. The function is evaluated by repeatedly calling the function's apply method. Thus, the cost of each node is one or two method dispatches rather than the cost of the pattern matching. Let's turn to other ways that functions can help improve performance and readability.

Function Error Handling

When you write code that follows the OOP paradigm, you can use a mechanism to catch the exceptions and do something with the error. In functional programming, you can't return an exception because it follows the idea that it always needs to return something (pure functions). Scala provides some mechanisms to solve this situation:

- **Option/Some/None**: Option is the same idea as Optional in Java, so the function can return two possible values: an integer (Some) or nothing (None). This approach is great because you reduce the number of blocks if/else to check by null.

  The following example takes a String and tries to transform it into an Int:

```scala
scala> def transformToInt(number:String) : Option[Int] =
     |     try
     |         Some(Integer.parseInt(number))
     |     catch
     |         case e: NumberFormatException => None
def transformToInt(number: String): Option[Int]
```

  Now check what happens when you pass a correct value to the function:

```scala
scala> transformToInt("1")
val res1: Option[Int] = Some(1)
```

  Let's see if you send something that is not a number:

```scala
scala> transformToInt("a")
val res0: Option[Int] = None
```

- **Try/Success/Failure**: This trio of classes has the same idea as the previous one but has some features like `Failure`, which contains which exception causes the error, and `Try`, which has an easy way to catch all possible exceptions in the function.

```scala
scala> import scala.util.{Try, Success, Failure}
scala> def transformToInt(number: String): Try[Int] =
Try(Integer.parseInt(number))
def makeInt(number: String): util.Try[Int]
```

Now check what happens when you pass to the function a correct value:

```scala
scala> transformToInt("1")
val res2: util.Try[Int] = Success(1)
```

Let's see if you send something that is not a number:

```scala
scala> transformToInt("s")
val res3: util.Try[Int] = Failure(java.lang.
NumberFormatException: For input string: "s")
```

Tail Calls and Tail Call Optimization

A recursive function may invoke itself. Recursion plays a crucial role in functional programming because it offers a way to iterate over data structures using mutable data since each function call has its stack for storing function parameters. One classic example of recursion can be seen in the implementation of `factorial` as shown:

```scala
scala> def factorial(number:Int) : Int = {
     |       if (number == 1)
     |           return 1
     |       number * factorial (number - 1)
     | }
factorial: (number: Int)Int
```

You can call this function as shown here:

```scala
scala> println(factorial(3))
6
```

One problem associated with using recursive functions is that invoking a recursive function too many times leads to a stack overflow error. The Scala compiler can optimize recursive functions with tail recursion so that recursive calls do not use all the stack space and therefore won't run into a stack overflow error. Tail recursion is a specific kind of recursion that occurs when a function calls itself in its final operation. With tail recursion-optimized functions, recursive invocation doesn't create a new stack but instead uses the current function's stack. Only functions whose last statement is the recursive invocation can be optimized for tail recursion by the Scala compiler.

Next is the implementation of factorial, calculated with tail-call recursion. To facilitate tail-call optimization, Scala provides an annotation available to mark a function to be optimized for tail recursion. A function marked with the tail recursion function annotation causes an error at compilation time if it cannot be optimized for tail recursion. To mark a function to be optimized for tail recursion, add @annotation. tailrec before the function definition.

Now mark the factorial function shown earlier with @annotation.tailrec to instruct the Scala compiler that this function must be optimized for tail recursion and that if an annotated function cannot be optimized for tail recursion, the compiler should treat it as an error.

```
scala> @annotation.tailrec
     | def factorial(number:Int) : Int = {
     |     if (number == 1)
     |         return 1
     |     number * factorial (number - 1)
     | }
<console>:12: error: could not optimize @tailrec annotated method
factorial: it contains a recursive call not in tail positionnumber *
factorial (number - 1)^
```

As you can see, the Scala compiler throws an error. The factorial method can't be optimized because the recursive call is not the last statement in the function; the factorial calls itself and then performs multiplication with the result, so actually, multiplication is the last statement in the function, not the recursive call. A function can't be optimized for tail recursion if the result of invoking itself is used for anything but the direct return value.

The `factorial` method marked with `@annotation.tailrec` will not compile successfully until recursion is the final operation. So you need to perform the multiplication operation before invoking the `factorial` method for which you use the accumulator argument to hold the computation in progress. This argument is computed with a multiplication before the recursive call. Thus, recursion is the final operation.

```scala
scala> @annotation.tailrec
     | def factorial(accumulator: Int, number: Int) : Int = {
     |   if(number == 1)
     |     return accumulator
     |   factorial(number * accumulator, number - 1)
     | }
factorial: (accumulator: Int, number: Int)Int
```

A successful compile guarantees that the function will be optimized with tail recursion so that each successive call will not add new stack frames.

```scala
scala> println(factorial(1,3))
6
```

Call-by-Name, Call-by-Value, and General Laziness

In Java programs, when you call a method with parameters, the value of the parameters is calculated before the method is called. Thus, in

```
foo(1 + 1, "A String".length());
```

the expressions `1 + 1` and `"A String".length()` are both evaluated before the call to `foo` is made. This is usually what you want. However, there are some cases when you want parameters to be optionally evaluated or repeatedly evaluated. In these cases, Scala provides the call-by-name mechanism. There's no syntactic difference to the caller for call-by-name parameters.

The first use of call-by-name is passing an expression that takes a long time to evaluate that may not be evaluated. The second use for call-by-name is a situation where you want to evaluate the expression many times in the target method, such as if you want to evaluate an expression until some condition is met. That condition could be until the expression returns false or until the expression returns null.

The first example for call-by-name is the logging example. It's computationally costly to calculate log messages simply to discard them if the message is not going to be logged. This is very common in Java code.

```
if (logger.level().intValue() >= INFO.intValue()) {
    logger.log(INFO, "The value is "+value);
}
```

In this code, you must push the decision to evaluate `logger.log(INFO, "The value is "+value);` into the place where you call `logger`. This means you need to wrap the call to `logger` in an `if` statement. It's much better from a coding perspective if the cost of evaluating the String to be logged is incurred only if the String is going to be logged and if the current log level is known to and tested by the code inside `logger` rather than in the call to `logger`. Call-by-name gives you the ability to delay the evaluation of the String to log only if that String will be logged.

In Scala, you can define a `log` method that takes the thing to log as call-by-name:

```
def log(level: Level, msg: => String) =
if (logger.level.intValue >= level.intValue) logger.log(level, msg)
```

And you call this code:

```
log(INFO, "The value is "+ value)
```

The Scala version passes `"The value is "`+ value as a function that is evaluated each time it is accessed in the `log` method. The `log` method will access it only if the log message is going to be printed. Your code is cleaner because you don't have to repeatedly test the log level, but it performs as well as the previous Java code that has the inline test. To make something call-by-name, just put => before the type. So, `foo(s: String)` is call-by-value, and `foo(s: => String)` is call-by-name.

You may be wondering how the code can perform as well if a function object is being created and handed off to the `log` method. In the JVM, the cost of creating an object that never escapes the current thread and is very short-lived is zero or very near zero. The JVM may also inline the `log` method such that the test is performed without an actual method call. The result is that your code will run as quickly with the Scala code as it will with the Java code that has the repeated test for the log level. For example, you could collect all Strings returned from an expression until you encounter a null.

```scala
def allStrings(expr: => String): List[String] = expr match {
    case null => Nil
    case s => s :: allStrings(expr)
}
```

You can test this method.

```scala
scala> import java.io._
import java.io._
scala> val br = new BufferedReader(new FileReader("foo.txt"))
br: java.io.BufferedReader = jaferedReva.io.Bufader@2bfa91
scala> allStrings(br.readLine)
res0: List[String] = List(import scala.xml._, , object Morg {,...)
```

Each time the call-by-name parameter, expr, is accessed, it is applied. If it is passed
as a parameter that is also call-by-name, it will be passed without evaluation. In the
previous code, your pattern matches against the application of expr. If it's null, it returns
an empty List, a Nil. If it's not null, it returns a List that is the current String and the result
of allStrings(expr).

Functional Structures

Scala offers structures to solve particular problems. Some of these structures exist in
other languages like Java or C++. This section is a little introduction to the meaning of
each of them, but the following chapters offer more in-depth coverage.

Sequence

A sequence in Scala are a very general interface for different data structures with
a defined order. Some examples that you can consider a sequence of elements are
Lists, Arrays, Vectors, or Ranges, which contain certain methods like apply, iterator,
and length.

```scala
scala> val elements: Seq[Int] = Seq(1,2,3,4,5)
val elements: Seq[Int] = List(1, 2, 3, 4, 5)
```

The following are some examples of what you can do using different methods:

```scala
scala> println(elements.reverse) // Invert the order of the sequence
List(5, 4, 3, 2, 1)
scala> println(elements(1)) // Obtain the value of the second position
2
scala> println(elements.sorted) //Sort all the elements
List(1, 2, 3, 4, 5)
```

When you use this type of structure, the big-O is O(N), in the worst case where N is the number of elements.

To add elements in this type of structure, one possible approach is to create the variable as mutable using the keyword var.

```scala
var elements: Seq[Int] = List(1, 2, 3, 4, 5)
scala> elements = elements.appended(6)
elements: Seq[Int] = List(1, 2, 3, 4, 5, 6)
```

Maps

Maps are collections used to save information using a key and a value associated to it. You can think of the key as the index or the id in a database to find a particular row and the value as the information that is connected with the key.

```scala
scala> val movies: Map[String, String] = Map()
val movies: Map[String, String] = Map()
```

There are some ways to add information to a Map:

- Using -> to indicate that in the left part is the key and the right is the value.

  ```scala
  scala> val movies: Map[String, String] = Map("ET" ->
  "Science fiction", "Saw" -> "Horror")
  val movies: Map[String, String] = Map(ET -> Science
  fiction, Saw -> Horror)
  ```

- Using parentheses and commas to separate the different rows in a Map.

```scala
scala> val movies: Map[String, String] = Map(("ET",
"Science fiction"), ("Saw", "Horror"))
val movies: Map[String, String] = Map(ET -> Science
fiction, Saw -> Horror)
```

- Using + to add a new key value in an existing Map.

```scala
scala> movies + ("Rocky IV" -> "Action")
val res6: Map[String, String] = Map(ET -> Science fiction,
Saw -> Horror, Rocky IV -> Action)
```

The main problem with this approach is you create a new variable with the original information and the new information. This is not a problem because in the previous chapter you saw that the idea of Scala is to create immutable variables most of the time but imagine that you for some reason add an element in the same Map. The correct way to do it is

```scala
scala> var movies: Map[String, String] = Map("ET" ->
"Science fiction", "Saw" -> "Horror")
var movies: Map[String, String] = Map(ET -> Science
fiction, Saw -> Horror)
scala> movies += ("Rocky IV" -> "Drama")
```

Note that if you add the same key two times but with different values in the Map, only one key will exist with the last value.

```scala
scala> val movies: Map[String, String] = Map("ET" ->
"Science fiction", "Saw" -> "Horror", "Saw" -> "Drama")
val movies: Map[String, String] = Map(ET -> Science
fiction, Saw -> Drama)
```

One last thing: If you need to remove an element from the Map, you can use - or the method removed and the name of the key.

```scala
scala> var movies: Map[String, String] = Map("ET" -> "Science fiction",
"Saw" -> "Horror")
var movies: Map[String, String] = Map(ET -> Science fiction, Saw -> Horror)
scala> movies -= ("ET")

scala> println(movies)
Map(Saw -> Horror)

scala> movies = movies.removed("Saw")
movies: Map[String, String] = Map()
```

Sets

A set is a structure that contains unordered elements, like a List. The main difference is that this structure only contains values, no duplicates.

```scala
scala> val countries: Set[String] = Set()
val countries: Set[String] = Set()
```

There are some ways to add information to a set:

- In the constructor, separated by commas.

  ```scala
  scala> val countries: Set[String] = Set("Italy", "Spain",
  "France", "Germany")
  val countries: Set[String]
  ```

- Using + to add a new value in an existing set.

  ```scala
  scala> countries + ("Russia")
  val res10: Set[String] = HashSet(Spain, Russia, Italy,
  France, Germany)
  ```

  With this approach, the same as with Map, each time you add an element using +, you create a new instance of a set with all the values. A possible approach to modify the actual values of the set is to create the variables as mutable and use += to add a new element to the existing set.

```
scala> var countries: Set[String] = Set("Italy", "Spain",
"France", "Germany")
var countries: Set[String] = Set(Italy, Spain, France,
Germany)
scala> countries += ("Russia")
scala> print(countries)
HashSet(Spain, Russia, Italy, France, Germany)
```

When you change the values that a set contains, Scala changes the
type of structure to a concrete class like HashSet.

To remove an existing value in the set, you can use - and the value to remove it. If the
value does not exist, nothing happens.

```
scala> var countries: Set[String] = Set("Italy", "Spain", "France",
"Germany")
scala> countries -= ("Italy")
scala> print(countries)
HashSet(Spain, France, Germany)
```

Tuples

Scala provides a structure named tuple to save information that has different types. You
can think a tuple as a custom object but without defining all the attributes.

For example, let's create a tuple that contains certain information about a movie.

```
scala> val moviesReproductions = Tuple2("ET", 2)
val moviesReproductions: (String, Int) = (ET,2)
```

To access the value of one position, you only need to indicate the position.

```
scala> moviesReproductions._1
val res19: String = ET
```

If you put the values in the wrong order, you can change them using the
method swap.

```
scala> moviesReproductions.swap
val res20: (Int, String) = (2,ET)
```

The tuple can support multiple elements, not just two. If you type *tuple* and press the Tab button, many options appear.

```
scala> Tuple
Tuple      Tuple10    Tuple12    Tuple14    Tuple16    Tuple18    Tuple2
Tuple21    Tuple3     Tuple5     Tuple7     Tuple9
Tuple1     Tuple11    Tuple13    Tuple15    Tuple17    Tuple19    Tuple20
Tuple22    Tuple4     Tuple6     Tuple8
```

Options

As you read in the section "Functional Error Handling," Options help developers reduce the condition that checks if something is null or not. This is a great way to prevent null pointer exceptions that appear to check if a variable is null or not.

This structure, which appears in Scala 2.13.x, has several things in common with the class Optional, which appears in Java 8.

This structure is used in operations like map, flatMap, and filter, which you will see in detail in the next section. There are some structures like Maps that return an Option in some methods like get.

```
scala> val movies = Map("ET" -> "Science fiction")
val movies: Map[String, String] = Map(ET -> Science fiction)
```

The following is the behavior when you try to obtain the value of something that exists and does not exist in a Map:

```
scala> movies.get("ET")
val res1: Option[String] = Some(Science fiction)
scala> movies.get("ET II")
val res2: Option[String] = None
```

Instantiating

To instantiate an Option type there are some different alternatives:

- Using Option and passing the value. With this approach, the compiler checks if the value is null or not and creates the correct class.

  ```
  scala> val instantiateOption : Option[Int] =  Option(1)
  val instantiateOption: Option[Int] = Some(1)
  ```

- Define the result using Some or None. With this approach, you eliminate one step because the compiler assigns to the variable the class that you indicate.

```
scala> val instantiateOption : Option[Int] =  None
val instantiateOption: Option[Int] = None
scala> val instantiateOption : Option[Int] =  Some(1)
val instantiateOption: Option[Int] = Some(1)
```

Chained Methods

Say you have a method that returns an Option with None but you need your logic to always have a value or do something. An Option provides a method named orElse, which is executed only when it has a None value.

```
scala> def returnNoneFunction() : Option[String] = None
def returnNoneFunction(): Option[String]
scala> def returnSomeFunction() : Option[String] = Some("Your logic works")
def returnSomeFunction(): Option[String]
scala> val obtainInformation = returnNoneFunction() orElse returnSomeFunction()
val obtainInformation: Option[String] = Some(Your logic works)
```

Functional Operations

Scala, like many other languages, lets you use a set of operations with the collections.

Traversing

Traversing is the most common operation in the collection of elements because you can iterate all elements of the collection to do a specific operation.

```
scala> val countries: Set[String] = Set("Italy", "Spain", "France", "Germany")
scala> countries.foreach(println)
Italy
Spain
France
Germany
```

Mapping

The Map structure is very useful when you need to iterate each element and create an output, which can be the same type or not.

Let's imagine that you need to iterate a set of countries and calculate the length of each of them.

```scala
scala> val countries: Set[String] = Set("Italy", "Spain", "France", "Germany")
scala> val nameSize = countries.map(country => (country, country.length))
val nameSize: Set[(String, Int)] = Set((Italy,5), (Spain,5), (France,6),
(Germany,7))
```

Another possibility is to concatenate to the actual value a suffix.

```scala
scala> println(countries.map(_ + " - Europe"))
Set(Italy - Europe, Spain - Europe, France - Europe, Germany - Europe)
```

Filtering

Filtering is one of the most important operations because it lets you iterate, filter the elements, and return a new structure only with the elements that return true.

```scala
scala> val countries: Set[String] = Set("Italy", "Spain", "France", "Germany")
scala> countries.filter(country=>country.startsWith("I"))
val res21: Set[String] = Set(Italy)
```

You can combine all operations to reduce the complexity of your code, such as filtering the countries that start with I and printing the result.

```scala
scala> countries.filter(country=>country.startsWith("I")).foreach(println)
Italy
```

This section is just an overview of all the operations you can do. You will see more details in the following chapters.

Summary

You saw Scala functions in action in Chapter 2 when you declared, defined, and called functions. As a continuation to the brief introduction in Chapter 2, this chapter provided a detailed treatment of functional programming in Scala, introducing several functional constructs. In the next chapter, you will learn pattern matching with Scala.

CHAPTER 5

Pattern Matching

So far, you've explored some of the basic functional cornerstones of Scala: immutable data types and the passing of functions as parameters. The third cornerstone of functional programming is pattern matching. Pattern matching provides a powerful tool for declaring business logic in a concise and maintainable way. Scala blends traditional functional programming pattern matching with object-oriented concepts to provide a very powerful mechanism for writing programs. In this chapter, you're going to explore the basics of pattern matching. Then you're going to see how Scala's case classes bridge object-oriented data encapsulation and function decomposition. Next, you'll see how Scala's pattern-matching constructs become functions that can be passed around and composed. Let's look at a simple example first.

Basic Pattern Matching

Pattern matching allows you to make a programmatic choice between multiple conditions, such as if Boolean x is true, print a "true" message, and if x is false, print a "false" message. However, don't let this simple example beguile you into underestimating the true power of Scala's pattern matching. Scala's pattern matching allows your cases to be far more complex than merely a case of whether x is true or false. In Scala, your cases can include types, wildcards, sequences, regular expressions, and so forth.

```scala
scala> def printNum(int: Int) =
         int match
             case 0 => println("Zero")
             case 1 => println("One")
             case _ => println("more than one")
def printNum(int: Int): Unit
```

© David Pollak, Vishal Layka, and Andres Sacco 2022
D. Pollak et al., *Beginning Scala 3*, https://doi.org/10.1007/978-1-4842-7422-4_5

Now execute the object with different parameters and check what happens with the results.

```scala
scala> printNum(0)
Zero
scala> printNum(1)
One
scala> printNum(2)
more than one
```

As you can see, there are no big ideas in the previous block of code. It just prints *zero*, *one*, or *more than one*. However, notice the last case with the underscore (_) wildcard. It matches anything not defined in the cases above it, so it serves the same purpose as the default keyword in Java and C# switch statements. If you are unfamiliar with the switch statement in Java or C#, don't worry. It just means that if you try to put a case _ before any other case clauses, the compiler will throw an unreachable code error on the next clause, as shown in the example below, because nothing will get past the case _ clause so case _ serves as a default.

```scala
scala> def printNum(int: Int) =
           int match
               case _ => println("more than one")
               case 0 => println("Zero")
               case 1 => println("One")
```

When you try to create that object, some errors appear in your console.

```
def printNum(int: Int): Unit
4          case 0 => println("Zero")
               ^
           Unreachable case
5          case 1 => println("One")
               ^
           Unreachable case
                 ^
```

Now see what happens in following code when your pattern matching does not have a default value and you pass a value that does not have a case:

```
scala> def printNum(int: Int) =
          int match
              case 0 => println("Zero")
              case 1 => println("One")
scala> printNum(2)
scala.MatchError: 2 (of class java.lang.Integer)
  at rs$line$9$.printNum(rs$line$9:4)
  ... 28 elided
```

Scala not only offers _ to define the default behavior in a pattern matching expression, but you can also use any other word that does the same. Look the example below with the use of default instead of _:

```
scala> def printNum(int: Int) =
          int match
              case 0 => println("Zero")
              case 1 => println("One")
              case default => println("more than one")
def printNum(int: Int): Unit
scala> printNum(2)
more than one
```

Pattern matching, at its core, is a complex set of if/else expressions that lets you select from several alternatives. At first glance, if we are allowed to unabashedly assume that you are from a Java background, pattern matching looks a lot like Java's switch statement, but you will notice several key differences in even Java's simplest case. Let's analyze this by writing one example using both Scala's pattern matching and Java's switch statement. The following block illustrates an example of calculating Fibonacci numbers:

```
scala> def fibonacci(in: Int): Int =
          in match
              case 0 => 0
              case 1 => 1
              case n => fibonacci(n - 1) + fibonacci(n - 2)
def fibonacci(in: Int): Int
```

Let's write the same code in Java:

```java
public int fibonacci(int in) {
  switch (in) {
    case 0:
     return 0;
    case 1:
     return 1;
    default:
     return fibonacci(in - 1) + fibonacci(in - 2);
  }
}
```

You will notice the following differences between the two examples:

- There's no break statement between cases in Scala, whereas you need to break or return at the end of the case in Java.

- The last case in Scala assigns the default value to the variable n. Pattern matching in Scala is also an expression that returns a value.

We just pointed out several key differences in the Fibonacci example written using both Scala's pattern matching and Java's switch statement. Take into consideration that the latest version of Java has some features that Scala has offered since version 2.12.x.

We will now show that it gets even better with Scala's pattern matching by modifying the above code.

Scala allows guards to be placed in patterns to test particular conditions that cannot be tested in the pattern declaration itself. Thus, you can write your Fibonacci calculator to return 0 if a negative number is passed in, like so:

```scala
def fib2(in: Int): Int =
    in match
        case n if n <= 0 => 0
        case 1 => 1
        case n => fib2(n - 1) + fib2(n - 2)
```

case n if n <= 0 => 0 is the first test in the pattern. The test extracts the value into the variable n and tests n to see whether it's zero or negative and returns 0 in that case. Guards are very helpful as the amount of logic gets more complex. Note that the case statements are evaluated in the order that they appear in the code. Thus, `case n if n <= 0 =>` is tested before `case n =>`. Under the hood, the compiler may optimize the pattern and minimize the number of tests, cache test results, and even cache guard results.

One last thing to consider is that you can have multiple values with the same behavior, so you don't need to define much time the same block of code. Instead, you can combine all the logic in one case using tk. Check the following block of code, which has a behavior when receiving -1 or -2:

```scala
scala> def printNum(int: Int) =
        int match
            case 0 => println("Zero")
            case 1 => println("One")
            case -1  -2 => println("less than zero")
            case _ => println("more than one")
scala> printNum(-2)
less than zero
```

Matching Any Type

Let's consider a list of any type of element, containing a String, a Double, an Int, and a Char:

```scala
val anyList = List(1, "A", 2, 2.5, 'a')
```

You decide to let the user know of the Int, String, and Double type from the List using the following code:

```scala
scala> for (m <- anyList)
        m match
            case i: Int => println("Integer: " + i)
            case s: String => println("String: " + s)
            case f: Double => println("Double: " + f)
            case other => println("other: " + other)
```

In the console of the REPL appears something like this:

```
Integer: 1
String: A
Integer: 2
Double: 2.5
other: a
```

This code deep implications, as you will learn in the section that follows.

Testing Data Types

Let's write a method that tests an incoming Object to see whether it's a String, an Integer, or something else. Depending on what type it is, different actions will be performed as illustrated in the following example:

```
def test2(in: Any) =
    in match
        case s: String => "String, length "+s.length
        case i: Int if i > 0 => "Natural Int"
        case i: Int => "Another Int"
        case a: AnyRef => a.getClass.getName
        case _ => "null"
```

The first line tests for a String. If it is a String, the parameter is cast into a String and assigned to the s variable, and the expression on the right of the => is returned. Note that if the parameter is null, it will not match any pattern that compares to a type. On the next line, the parameter is tested as an Int. If it is an Int, the parameter is cast to an Int, assigned to i, and the guard is tested. If the Int is a natural number (greater than zero), "Natural Int" will be returned. In this way, Scala pattern matching replaces Java's test/cast paradigm. Now to fully appreciate the power of pattern matching in Scala, let's see the Java equivalent of the previous block of code:

```
public String test2(Object in) {
    if (in == null) {
        return "null";
    }
```

```
    if (in instanceof String) {
        String s = (String) in;
        return "String, length " + s.length();
    }
    if (in instanceof Integer) {
        int i = ((Integer) in).intValue();
        if (i > 0) {
            return "Natural Int";
        }
        return "Another Int";
    }
    return in.getClass().getName();
}
```

In the Java equivalent code of the previous code, there is a separation between the instance of test and the casting operation. This often results in bugs when a block of test/cast code is copied and pasted. There's no compiler check that the instance of test matches the cast, and it's not uncommon to have a mismatch between the test and the cast in Java code that's been copied and pasted. The same code in Scala is shorter, and there's no explicit casting. Pattern matching is a powerful way to avoid explicit casting.

Pattern Matching in Lists

Scala's pattern matching can also be applied to Lists. Scala's List collection is implemented as a linked list where the head of the list is called a cons cell.

Note   The naming of the cons cell traces its roots back to Lisp and came from the act of constructing a list. One constructs a list by linking a cons cell to the head of the list.

It contains a reference to its contents and another reference to the tail of the list, which may be another cons cell or the Nil object. Lists are immutable, so the same tail can be shared by many different heads. In Scala, the cons cell is represented by the : : case class. Perhaps you have just said, "Ah hah!"

Creating a List in Scala is as simple as this:

```
1 :: Nil
```

:: is the name of the method and the name of a case class. By keeping the creation method, ::, and the case class name the same, you can construct and pattern match Lists in a syntactically pleasing way. And as you've just seen, case classes can be used in pattern matching to either compare or extract values. This holds for Lists as well and leads to some very pleasing syntax.

You construct a List with

```scala
scala> val x = 1
x: Int = 1

scala> val rest = List(2,3,4)
rest: List[Int] = List(2, 3, 4)

scala> val list = x :: rest
val list: List[Int] = List(1, 2, 3, 4)

scala> def printNumbers(list : List[Int]) : Unit =
         list match
            case head :: tail => println(head); printNumbers(head)
            case Nil => println("")
def printNumbers(list: List[Int]): Unit

scala> printNumbers(list)
1
2
3
4
```

Then you can extract the head (x) and tail (rest) of the List in pattern matching.

Pattern Matching and Lists

Pattern matching and Lists go hand in hand. You can start off using pattern matching to sum up all the odd Ints in a List[Int].

```scala
def sumOdd(in: List[Int]): Int =
    in match
        case Nil => 0
        case x :: rest if x % 2 == 1 => x + sumOdd(rest)
        case _ :: rest => sumOdd(rest)
```

If the List is empty, Nil, then you return 0. The next case extracts the first element from the List and tests to see whether it's odd. If it is, you add it to the sum of the rest of the odd numbers in the List. The default case is to ignore the first element of the List (a match with the _ wildcard) and return the sum of the odd numbers in the rest of the List.

Extracting the head of a List is useful, but when pattern matching against a List, you can match against any number of elements in the List. In the following example, you replace any number of contiguous identical items with just one instance of that item:

```scala
def noPairs[T](in: List[T]): List[T] =
    in match
        case Nil => Nil
        case a :: b :: rest if a == b => noPairs(a :: rest)
        // the first two elements in the list are the same, so we'll
        // call noPairs with a List that excludes the duplicate element
        case a :: rest => a :: noPairs(rest)
        // return a List of the first element followed by noPairs
        // run on the rest of the List
```

Let's run the code and see whether it does what you expect:

```scala
scala> noPairs(List(1,2,3,3,3,4,1,1))

res6: List[Int] = List(1, 2, 3, 4, 1)
```

Pattern matching can match against constants as well as extract information. Say you have a List[String] and you want to implement a rule that says that you discard the element preceding the "ignore" String. In this case, you use pattern matching to test as well as extract:

```scala
def ignore(in: List[String]): List[String] =
    in match
        case Nil => Nil
        case _ :: "ignore" :: rest => ignore(rest)
        // If the second element in the List is "ignore" then return the ignore
        // method run on the balance of the List
        case x :: rest => x :: ignore(rest)
        // return a List created with the first element of the List plus the
        // value of applying the ignore method to the rest of the List
```

You've seen how to use pattern matching and Lists with extraction and equality testing. You can also use the class test/cast mechanism to find all the Strings in a List[Any].

```scala
def getStrings(in: List[Any]): List[String] =
    in match
        case Nil => Nil
        case (s: String) :: rest => s :: getStrings(rest)
        case _ :: rest => getStrings(rest)
```

However, the paradigmatic way of filtering a List[Any] into a List of a particular type is by using a pattern as a function. You'll see this in the "Pattern Matching as Functions" section.

In this section, you've explored how to do pattern matching. You've seen extraction and pattern matching with Lists. It may seem that a List is a special construct in Scala, but there's nothing special about a List in Scala.

Compiler Optimization

Since Scala 2.x.x, there has been a way to optimize the pattern matching expression with the annotation @switch. When the annotation is present, the compiler checks if the expression is valid or not to introduce some optimizations. Behind the scenes, this annotation tells the compiler to not transform a simple conditional expression (if/else). Instead, the compiler tries to become a branch table that is faster than the other expressions.

```scala
scala> import scala.annotation.switch //You need to import this annotation
scala> def printNum(int : Int) =
          (int: @switch) match //You indicate to Scala to use the optimization
              case 0 => println("Zero")
              case 1 => println("One")
              case _ => if int > 0 then println("More than one") else
              println("Less than zero")
def printNum(int: Int): Unit
scala> printNum(3)
More than one
```

Everything works fine with this new annotation but behind the scenes, this code is transformed into two different structures depending on the type of case. The structures are called tableswitch and lookupswitch.[1]

Tableswitch

Most of the time the compiler uses tableswitch when the values are contiguous or there is a little gap between the different values. This approach has an O(1) so you can directly access the block of code connected with one specific key; this happens because the value is used as an index.

```
import scala.annotation.switch

def print(int : Int) =
    (int: @switch) match
        case 0 => println("Zero")
        case 1 => println("One")
        case 2 => println("Two")
        case 3 => println("Three")
        case 4 => println("Four")
        case _ => println("More than four")
```

Lookupswitch

When the values are not contiguous and there's a big gap between the different values of the structure, lookupswitch is used. The compiler sorts all the keys, and when someone tries to obtain the logic of one case, the compiler does a binary search. For that reason, the complexity of the algorithm is O(log n).

```
import scala.annotation.switch

def print(letter : Char) =
    (letter: @switch) match
        case 'A' => println("Animal")
        case 'B' => println("Bank")
```

---

[1] https://docs.oracle.com/javase/specs/jvms/se7/html/jvms-3.html#jvms-3.10

```
case 'D' => println("Dance")
case 'E' => println("Elephant")
case _ => println("Is not a letter")
```

Considerations

You need to consider some things when you include this annotation in your code:

- The pattern matching needs to have more than two cases. If you don't have more than two cases, the code compiles but the performance benefit is not included.

- The value of the different cases needs to be literals, not reference values, because it is the only way that the compiler knows which structure it needs to use (tableswitch or lookupswitch).

- The different cases don't need to contain any conditions like the ones shown above.

Pattern Matching with the Matchable Trait

Scala 3 introduces the trait Matchable. Remember that a trait is like an interface in another language and it controls the ability to do pattern matching. This new trait does not have members in version 3.0.x of Scala, but the idea of the developers that are in charge of introducing new features on Scala is to add this particular feature which is more or less similar to that the last version of Java.

The classes AnyVal and AnyRef extend from two different things now, Any and Matchable.

```
abstract class Any:
    def isInstanceOf
    def getClass
    //and more methods.

trait Matchable extends Any

class AnyVal extends Any, Matchable

class AnyRef extends Any, Matchable
```

Now imagine that you need to create a method that receives a sequence of elements and, depending on the type of element, you will do something in particular. The way to do this is to indicate that your method will receive something (T does not indicate a particular type) which is Matchable (use <: to indicate that the type extends from Matchable).

```scala
scala> val seq = Seq("one", 2, 3.5)
val seq: Seq[Matchable] = List(one, 2, 3.5)
scala> def check [T <: Matchable](seq: Seq[T]) =
         seq.map {
               case i: Int => println(s"Int $i")
               case s: String => println(s"String $s")
               case f: Float => println(s"Float $f")
               case other => println(s"Other $other")
         }
def check[T <: Matchable](seq: Seq[T]): Seq[Unit]

scala> check(seq)
String one
Int 2
Other 3.5
```

Pattern Matching and Case Classes

Case classes are classes that get toString, hashCode, and equals methods automatically. It turns out that they also get properties and extractors[2], which you will see in Chapter 8. Case classes also have properties and can be constructed without using the new keyword.

Let's define a case class.

```scala
case class Person(name: String, age: Int, valid: Boolean)
```

Let's create an instance of Person.

```scala
scala> val p = Person("David", 45, true)
p: Person = Person(David,45,true)
```

---

[2]https://docs.scala-lang.org/tour/extractor-objects.html#inner-main

You may use new to create a Person as well.

```
scala> val m = new Person("Martin", 44, true)
m: Person = Person(Martin,44,true)
```

Each of the Person instances has properties that correspond to the constructor parameters.

```
scala> p.name
res0: String = David
scala> p.age
res1: Int = 45
scala> p.valid
res2: Boolean = true
```

By default, the properties are read-only, and the case class is immutable.

```
scala> p.name = "Fred"
<console>:7: error: reassignment to val
p.name = "Fred"
```

You can also make properties mutable.

```
scala> case class MPerson(var name: String, var age: Int)
defined class MPerson
scala> val mp = MPerson("Jorge", 24)
mp: MPerson = MPerson(Jorge,24)
scala> mp.age = 25
scala> mp
res3: MPerson = MPerson(Jorge,25)
```

So far, this is just some syntactic sugar. How, you ask, does it work with pattern matching?

Pattern matching against case classes is syntactically pleasing and very powerful. You can match against your Person class, and you get the extractors for free.

```
def older(p: Person): Option[String] =
    p match
        case Person(name, age, true) if age > 35 => Some(name)
        case _ => None
```

Your method matches against instances of Person. If the valid field is true, the age is extracted and compared against a guard. If the guard succeeds, the person's name is returned; otherwise, None is returned. Let's try it out:

```
scala> older(p)
res4: Option[String] = Some(David)
scala> older(Person("Fred", 73, false))
res5: Option[String] = None
scala> older(Person("Jorge", 24, true))
res6: Option[String]
```

Nested Pattern Matching in Case Classes

With previous versions of Scala, you could create case classes that contained other case classes and you could use pattern matching, but in the latest version of Scala (2.13.1), this feature was deprecated and removed. The following code shows what happens when you try to create a case class that extends from another:

```
scala> case class MarriedPerson(override val name: String,
        override val age: Int,
        override val valid: Boolean,
        spouse: Person) extends Person(name, age, valid)
1 |case class MarriedPerson(override val name: String,
          ^
           Cannot extend sealed class Person in a different source file
4 |spouse: Person) extends Person(name, age, valid)
                   ^^^^^^^^^^^^^^^^^^^^^^^^^^
                   case class MarriedPerson has case ancestor class
                   Person, but case-to-case inheritance is prohibited.
                   To overcome this limitation, use extractors to
                   pattern match on non-leaf nodes.
```

Pattern Matching as Functions

Scala patterns are syntactic elements of the language when used with the `match` operator. However, you can also pass pattern matching as a parameter to other methods. Scala compiles a pattern match down to a `PartialFunction[A,B]`, which is a subclass of `Function1[A,B]`. So a pattern can be passed to any method that takes a single parameter function. This allows you to reduce

```
list.filter(a => a match {
    case s: String => true
    case _ => false
})
```

to

```
list.filter {
    case s: String => true
    case _ => false
}
```

Because patterns are functions and functions are instances, patterns are instances. In addition to passing them as parameters, they can also be stored for later use.

In addition to `Function1`'s `apply` method, `PartialFunction` has an `isDefinedAt` method so you can test to see whether a pattern matches a given value. If you try to apply a `PartialFunction` that's not defined for the value, a `MatchError` will be raised. How is this useful?

If you're building a web application, you might have particular URLs that need special handling while others get handled in the default manner. The URL can be expressed as a `List[String]`. You can do the following:

```
def handleRequest(req: List[String])(exceptions:
PartialFunction[List[String], String]): String =
    if (exceptions.isDefinedAt(req)) then
        exceptions(req)
    else
        "Handling URL " + req + " in the normal way"
```

So, if the partial function exceptions (the pattern) match the request `req` according to the `isDefinedAt` method, then you allow the request to be handled by the `exceptions` function. Otherwise, you do default handling. You can call `handleRequest` and handle any "`api`" requests by a separate handler.

```
handleRequest("foo" :: Nil) {
  case "api" :: call :: params => doApi(call, params)
}

def doApi(call: String, params: List[String]): String =
    "Doing API call "+ call
```

Partial functions can be composed into a single function using the `orElse` method. So, you can define a couple of partial functions.

```
val f1: PartialFunction[List[String], String] =
    case "stuff" :: Nil => "Got some stuff"
```

```
val f2: PartialFunction[List[String], String] =
    case "other" :: params => "Other: " + params
```

And you can compose them.

```
 val f3 = f1 orElse f2
```

And you can pass them into the `handleRequest` method.

```
handleRequest("a" :: "b" :: Nil)(f3)
```

In this way, Scala gives you a very nice, declarative way of handling complex filtering tasks. Partial functions can match on data and can be passed around like any other instance in Scala. Partial functions replace a lot of the XML configuration files in Java because pattern matching gives you the same declarative facilities as a configuration file, but they are type-safe, high performance, and they can have guards and generally take advantage of any method in your code. Here's an example of using pattern matching to dispatch REST requests in the ESME[3] code:[4]

---

[3] ESME is the Enterprise Social Messaging Experiment (`http://blog.esme.us`).

[4] This code will not compile without the rest of the ESME code, but it serves as an illustration of using pattern matching as an alternative to XML configuration files or annotations.

```
def dispatch: LiftRules.DispatchPF = {
  case Req("api" :: "status"   :: Nil, "", GetRequest) => status
  case Req("api" :: "messages" :: Nil, "", GetRequest) => getMsgs
  case Req("api" :: "messages" :: "long_poll" :: Nil, "", GetRequest) =>
    waitForMsgs
  case Req("api" :: "messages" :: Nil, "", PostRequest) =>
    () => sendMsg(User.currentUser.map(_.id.is), S)

  case Req("api" :: "follow"    :: Nil, _, GetRequest) =>
      following(calcUser)
  case Req("api" :: "followers" :: Nil, _, GetRequest) =>
      followers(calcUser)
  case Req("api" :: "follow"    :: Nil, _, PostRequest) =>
      performFollow(S.param("user"))
}
```

Pattern Matching on Regular Expressions

You can combine pattern matching with regular expressions to extract information that a String or another type contains. Let's imagine that you have a sequence that contains different multimedia elements with their information and you need to print it.

First, define the sequence of elements with the information that you need to extract.

```
val multimedia = Seq(
    "Photography: author=Richard Avedon, place=New York",
    "Movie: name=Casablanca, director=Michael Curtiz",
    "Music: name=Fly on the moon, author=Fran Sinatra");
```

Now create two extractors, one to obtain the information of the photographs and another for the movies.

```
val PhotographyExtractorRE = """Photography: author=([^,]+),
\s+place=(.+)""".r
val MovieExtractorRE = """Movie: name=([^,]+),\s+director=(.+)""".r
```

Last but not least, you need to define the conditions to map each of the elements in the sequence to a specific case.

```
multimedia.map {
    case PhotographyExtractorRE(author, place) => println(s"Phography -
    Author: $author - Place: $place")
    case MovieExtractorRE(name, director) => println(s"Movie - Name:
    $name - Director: $director")
    case unknown => println(s"Unknown entry $unknown")
}
```

The output that you will obtain after executing this code looks like this:

```
Phography - Author: Richard Avedon - Place: New York
Movie - Name: Casablanca - Director: Michael Curtiz
Unknown entry Music: name=Fly on the moon, author=Fran Sinatra
```

The explanation of how to create regular expressions is out of the scope of this book but you can find several pages like RegExr to create and test each possible case.[5]

Object-Oriented and Functional Tensions

At this point, the hard-core object-oriented designer folks may be somewhat unhappy about Scala `case` class's exposure of lots of internal information. Data hiding is an important part of OOP's abstraction. But in fact, most of the Java classes we define have getters and setters, so data is exposed in OOP. However, there is a tension between the amount of internal state that's exposed in our program and the amount of state that's hidden. In this section, you'll explore OOP and functional programming (FP) patterns for data hiding and exposure.

Another tension in OOP is how to define methods in class and interface hierarchies. Where does a method definition belong? What happens when a library is deployed but it's necessary to add new functionality to subclasses? How do you retrofit the defined-in-stone library classes to add this functionality? Put more concretely, if you have a library of shapes (circle, square, and rectangle) that each have an `area` method but hide all other data, how do you add a `perimeter` method to the shapes? Let's explore the tension and the tools Scala and FP offer to address the tension.

---

[5] https://regexr.com/

Shape Abstractions

If you have a collection of shapes that derive from the common trait OShape that has an area method in it, your object definitions will look something like the following if you use a traditional OOP approach:

```
trait OShape:
  def area: Double

class OCircle(radius: Double) extends OShape:
   def area = radius * radius * Math.PI

class OSquare(length: Double) extends OShape:
   def area = length * length

class ORectangle(h: Double, w: Double) extends OShape:
   def area = h * w
```

Let's compare this with the pattern-matching implementation:

```
trait Shape
    case class Circle(radius: Double) extends Shape
    case class Square(length: Double) extends Shape
    case class Rectangle(h: Double, w: Double) extends Shape

object Shape:
    def area(shape: Shape): Double =
        shape match
            case Circle(r) => r * r * Math.PI
            case Square(l) => l * l
            case Rectangle(h, w) => h * w
```

In the pattern-matching example, all the logic for calculating the area is located in the same method, but the fact that the method exists is not obvious from looking at the Shape trait. So far, the OOP methodology seems to be the right answer because it makes it obvious what shapes can do.

However, if you have a shape library and you want to calculate the perimeter of each of the shapes, there's a benefit to pattern matching.

```
def perimeter(shape: Shape) =
    shape match
        case Circle(r) => 2 * Math.Pi  * r
        case Square(l) => 4 * l
        case Rectangle(h, w) => h * 2 + w * 2
```

In this case, the open data makes implementing the perimeter method possible. With the OOP implementation, you would have to expose data to make the perimeter method possible to implement. So your OOP implementation would look like

```
trait OShape:
    def area: Double

class OCircle(radius: Double) extends OShape:
    def area = radius * radius * Math.PI
    def getRadius = radius

class OSquare(length: Double) extends OShape:
    def area = length * length
    def getLength = length

class ORectangle(h: Double, w: Double) extends OShape:
    def area       = h * w
    def getHeight = h
    def getWidth  = w
```

In a broader sense, the designer of an object hierarchy rarely implements all the methods that a library consumer is going to need.

The visitor pattern is a design pattern that allows you to add functionality to a class hierarchy after the hierarchy is already defined. Let's look at a typical visitor pattern implementation. The following is the interface that defines the visitor. The code contains circular class references and will not work in the REPL. So, first the code, and then a walk-through of the code.

```
trait OCarVisitor:
    def visit(wheel: OWheel): Unit
    def visit(engine: OEngine): Unit
    def visit(body: OBody): Unit
    def visit(car: OCar): Unit
```

```
trait OCarElement:
    def accept(visitor: OCarVisitor): Unit

class OWheel(val name: String) extends OCarElement:
    def accept(visitor: OCarVisitor) = visitor.visit(this)

class OEngine extends OCarElement:
    def accept(visitor: OCarVisitor) = visitor.visit(this)

class OBody extends OCarElement:
    def accept(visitor: OCarVisitor) = visitor.visit(this)

class OCar extends OCarElement:
    val elements = List(new OEngine, new OBody, new OWheel("FR"),
                    new OWheel("FL"), new OWheel("RR"), new OWheel("RL"))

    def accept(visitor: OCarVisitor) = (this :: elements).foreach
    (_.accept(visitor))
```

The library author must think about extensibility and implementing the visitor pattern. Note also that the class hierarchy is fixed in the visitor because the visitor must implement an interface that defines all the possible classes that the visitor can handle.

```
trait OCarVisitor:
    def visit(wheel: OWheel): Unit
    def visit(engine: OEngine): Unit
    def visit(body: OBody): Unit
    def visit(car: OCar): Unit
```

Each element derives from a trait that creates a contract, which requires that the class implements the accept method.

```
trait OCarElement:
    def accept(visitor: OCarVisitor): Unit
```

You implement each subclass and implement the accept method.

```
class OWheel(val name: String) extends OCarElement:
    def accept(visitor: OCarVisitor) = visitor.visit(this)

class OEngine extends OCarElement:
    def accept(visitor: OCarVisitor) = visitor.visit(this)
```

```scala
class OBody extends OCarElement:
    def accept(visitor: OCarVisitor) = visitor.visit(this)
```

```scala
class OCar extends OCarElement:
    val elements = List(new OEngine, new OBody, new OWheel("FR"),
                        new OWheel("FL"), new OWheel("RR"), new OWheel("RL"))

    def accept(visitor: OCarVisitor) = (this :: elements).foreach
    (_.accept(visitor))
```

That's a lot of boilerplate.[6] Additionally, it violates the data-hiding principles of OOP because the visitor has to access some of the data in each element that it visits. Let's compare the pattern-matching version:

```scala
trait CarElement:
    case class Wheel(name: String) extends CarElement
    case class Engine() extends CarElement
    case class Body() extends CarElement
    case class Car(elements: List[CarElement]) extends CarElement
```

The code is cleaner because there's no boilerplate accept method. Let's see what you do when you want to traverse the object hierarchy:

```scala
def doSomething(in: CarElement): Unit =
    in match
        case Wheel(name) =>
        case Engine() =>
        case Body() =>
        case Car(e) => e.foreach(doSomething)
```

Take into consideration that all the code related to the explanation of the visitor patterns needs to be executed in the REPL in the same order. If you close and open it again, you will lose all the declarations and the example may not work. If you use Scastie or another online tool, you only need to add all the code in the same editor.

---

[6] Here is where a unity ped language such as Ruby or Python has a material advantage over a static language such as Java. In Ruby, you don't need all the boilerplate and the class hierarchy is not fixed at the time the OCarVisitor interface is defined.

Summary

In this chapter, you explored pattern matching and saw how pattern matching provides a powerful declarative syntax for expressing complex logic. Pattern matching provides an excellent and type-safe alternative to Java's test/cast paradigm. Pattern matching used with case classes and extraction provides a powerful way to traverse object hierarchies and is an excellent alternative to the visitor pattern. And because patterns are functions and objects, they can be passed as parameters and used wherever functions are used.

In the next chapter, you'll explore Collections. The Scala collections library is the most noteworthy library in the Scala ecosystem.

CHAPTER 6

Scala Collections

The collections class in Scala is a high-performance and type-parameterized framework with support for mutable and immutable type hierarchies. These distinct and independent mutable and immutable type hierarchies make switching between mutable and immutable implementations much simpler. Scala's object-oriented collections also support functional higher-order operations such as `map`, `filter`, and `reduce`, which let you use expression-oriented programming in collections. You can access and use the entire Java Collections library from your Scala code because Scala is a JVM language, but this is not recommended because higher-order operations are not available with the Java Collections library. Scala has a rich collection library. This chapter gives you a tour of the most used collection types and operations, showing just the types you will use most frequently. The goal of this chapter is to guide you through the myriad options to find the solutions you need.

One thing to take into consideration is that Scala 3 has not introduced a lot of changes in this topic since the latest version of Scala 2, which is 2.13. However, some of the features that are deprecated in version 2.13 are removed in version 3.x.x.

Note   If you have an application that uses a version previous to Scala 2.13 and you want to migrate to Scala 3, the most recommended approach is to migrate first to version 2.13 or up and solve all the possible problems or conflicts and later migrate to Scala 3.x.x.[1]

---

[1] Migrate a project to Scala 2.13's collections `https://docs.scala-lang.org/overviews/core/collections-migration-213.html`

D. Pollak et al., *Beginning Scala 3*, https://doi.org/10.1007/978-1-4842-7422-4_6

Scala Collection Hierarchy

Most collection classes needed by client code exist in three different packages, which appear in Table 6-1. In this section, you will explore the three main packages of the collection framework and see how to use the general and most prevalent features.

Table 6-1. *Packages That Contain All Things Related to the Scala Collection*

Package	Description
scala.collection	This package defines all the traits or objects that will be extended for the rest of the packages.
scala.collection.immutable	This package defines most of the collections that are immutable so you can change the values inside.
scala.collection.mutable	This package contains all the collections that can modify the values that have one instance of an object inside.

There are other packages that cover specific situations. Table 6-2 shows some of them.

Table 6-2. *Packages for Specific Situations*

Package	Description
scala.collection.concurrent	This package contains only two things: a Map trait and a TrieMap, which has lock access to the operations.
scala.collection.convert	This package defines the types to wrap Scala to Java collections and vice versa.
scala.collection.generic	This package defines things that are reusable in the entire collection package.
scala.collection.parallel	This package contains versions of the collection that support parallelism.

The scala.collection Package

This package is composed of all high-level abstract classes or traits, which generally have mutable as well as immutable implementations. Figure 6-1 shows the collections in package `scala.collection`.

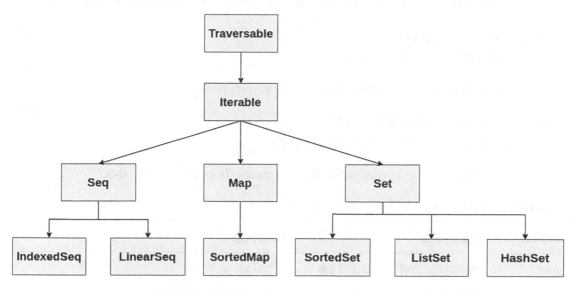

Figure 6-1. scala.collection package

The types in the `scala.collection` package shown in Figure 6-1 are implemented in two different ways in the Scala libraries based on whether the implementations are immutable or mutable. To keep these different implementations separate, there are packages called `scala.collection.immutable` and `scala.collection.mutable`.

Note   All types in the `scala.collections` package are implemented in different ways in the Scala libraries based on whether the implementations are immutable or mutable. To keep these different implementations separate, there are packages called `scala.collection.immutable` and `scala.collection.mutable`.

Sequences

Sequences store a number of different values in a specific order. Because the elements are ordered, you can ask for the first element, second element, and so on.

As shown in Figure 6-1, sequences branch off into two main categories: indexed sequences and linear sequences. By default, Seq creates a List, as shown here:

```
scala> val x = Seq(1,2,3)
val x: Seq[Int] = List(1, 2, 3)
```

By default, IndexedSeq creates a Vector, as shown here:

```
scala> val x = IndexedSeq(1,2,3)
val x: IndexedSeq[Int] = Vector(1, 2, 3)
```

This type of collection contains the default methods listed in Table 6-3.

Table 6-3. *Common Methods of Sequences*

Method	Description	Example
head	Returns the first element of the collection	scala> x.head val res48: Int = 1
tail	Returns an iterable that contains all the elements without the first element	scala> x.tail val res50: Seq[Int] = List(2, 3)
isEmpty	Returns a Boolean expression where the value is true when the Set is empty	scala> x.isEmpty val res47: Boolean = false
contains	Returns a Boolean expression where the value is true when the element exists in the collection	scala> x.contains(2) val res53: Boolean = true
length	Returns an Int with the number of elements that contain the collection	scala> x.length val res52: Int = 3
reverse	Return a new collection with the inverse order of the elements	scala> x.reverse val res51: Seq[Int] = List(3, 2, 1)

Sets

A Scala Set is a collection of unique elements. The common Set classes are shown in Figure 6-1. By default, Set creates an immutable Set, as shown here:

```
scala> val x = Set(1,2,3)
val x: Set[Int] = Set(1, 2, 3)
```

Note   While the `collection.immutable` package is automatically added to the current namespace in Scala, the `collection.mutable` package is not.

This type of collection contains the default methods shown in Table 6-4.

Table 6-4. *Common Methods in a Set*

Method	Description	Example
head	Returns the first element of the collection	scala> x.head val res48: Int = 1
tail	Returns an iterable that contains all the elements without the first element	scala> x.tail val res50: Set[Int] = Set(2, 3)
isEmpty	Returns a Boolean expression where the value is true when the Set is empty	scala> x.isEmpty val res47: Boolean = false

Map

Scala Map is a collection of key/value pairs where all the keys must be unique. The most common Map classes are shown in Figure 6-1. When you just need a simple, immutable Map, you can create one without requiring an import, as shown here:

```
scala> val map = Map(1 -> "a", 2 -> "b", 3 -> "c")
val map: Map[Int, String] = Map(1 -> a, 2 -> b, 3 -> c)
```

This type of collection contains the default methods shown in Table 6-5.

Table 6-5. *Common Methods in a Map*

Method	Description	Example
keys	Returns an iterable that contains all the keys that exist in the Map	scala> map.keys val res45: Iterable[Int] = Set(1, 2, 3)
values	Returns an iterable that contains all the values that exist in the Map	scala> map.values val res46: Iterable[String] = Iterable(a, b, c)
isEmpty	Returns a Boolean expression where the value is true when the Map is empty	scala> map.isEmpty val res47: Boolean = false

The scala.collection.immutable package

The scala.collection.immutable package stores various types of collections that are all immutable. The main classes and traits in this package are shown in Figure 6-2, Figure 6-3, and Figure 6-4 for Seq, Set, and Map, respectively. The top part of the hierarchy looks the same as that shown in Figure 6-1 for the scala.collection package. It begins with Traversable and Iterable, and then has three main subtypes in the form of Set, Seq, and Map. The difference is that there are many more subtypes.

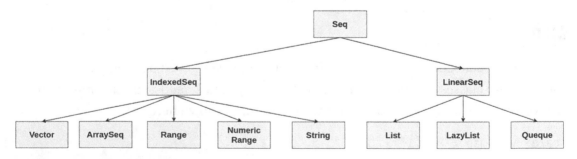

Figure 6-2. *Immutable Seq*

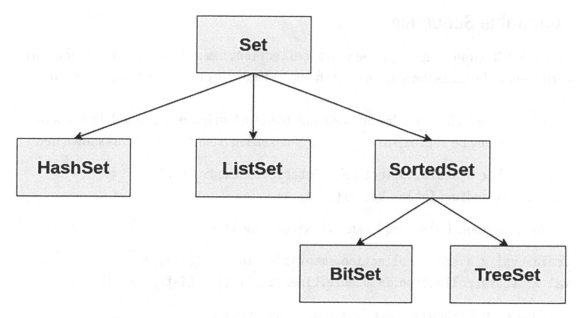

Figure 6-3. Immutable Set

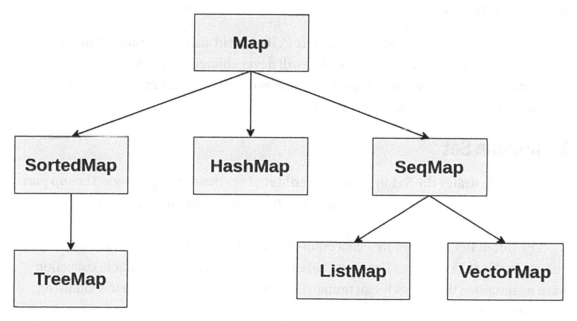

Figure 6-4. Immutable Map

Immutable Sequence

Figure 6-2 illustrates the Seq in the scala.collection.immutable package. The top part of the hierarchy looks the same as that shown in Figure 6-1 for the scala.collection package.

If you want an immutable collection that has efficient indexing, your default choice would generally be Vector. An immutable IndexedSeq creates a Vector, as shown here:

```
scala> val x = scala.collection.immutable.IndexedSeq(1,2,3)
val x: IndexedSeq[Int] = Vector(1, 2, 3)
```

An immutable LinearSeq creates a List, as shown here:

```
scala> val x = scala.collection.immutable.LinearSeq(1,2,3)
val x: scala.collection.immutable.LinearSeq[Int] = List(1, 2, 3)
```

An immutable Seq creates a List, too, as shown here:

```
scala> val x = scala.collection.immutable.Seq(1,2,3)
val x: Seq[Int] = List(1, 2, 3)
```

A collection in the package scala.collection.immutable is guaranteed to be immutable for everyone. Such a collection will never change after it is created. This means that accessing the same collection value at different points in time will always yield a collection with the same elements.

Immutable Set

Figure 6-3 illustrates the Set in the scala.collection.immutable package. The top part of the hierarchy looks the same as that shown in Figure 6-1 for the scala.collection package.

The difference between root collections (scala.collection) and immutable collections (scala.collection.immutable) is that clients of an immutable collection have a guarantee that nobody can mutate the collection as illustrated in the following code snippets.

Using an immutable set:

```
scala> val m = scala.collection.immutable.Set(1,2,3)
val m: Set[Int] = Set(1, 2, 3)
```

An immutable SortedSet creates a TreeSet:

```
scala> val m = scala.collection.immutable.SortedSet(1,2,3)
val m: scala.collection.immutable.SortedSet[Int] = TreeSet(1, 2, 3)
```

Using an immutable BitSet:

```
scala> val m = scala.collection.immutable.BitSet(1,2,3)
val m: scala.collection.immutable.BitSet = BitSet(1, 2, 3)
```

Immutable Map

Figure 6-4 illustrates the Map in the scala.collection.immutable package. The top part of the hierarchy looks the same as that shown in Figure 6-1 for the scala.collection package.

There are base mutable and immutable Map classes. Map is the base map, with both mutable and immutable implementations. In the following code snippets, you will see different ways to declare a Map in an immutable way.

Using an immutable Map without requiring an import:

```
scala> val m = Map(1 -> "a", 2 -> "b") bval m: Map[Int,String] = Map(1 ->
a, 2 -> b)
```

Using an immutable Map with the prefix:

```
scala> val m = scala.collection.immutable.Map(1 -> "a", 2 -> "b")
val m: Map[Int,String] = Map(1 -> a, 2 -> b)
```

Using an immutable SortedMap:

```
scala> val m = scala.collection.immutable.SortedMap(1 -> "a", 2 -> "b")
val m: scala.collection.immutable.SortedMap[Int,String] = Map(1 ->
a, 2 -> b)
```

The scala.collection.mutable package

As the name implies, this package includes collections that are mutable. The scala.collection.mutable package is the most extensive of the three packages. It is worth scanning through the API to look at the various types in this package and to see how they are used. By default, Scala always picks immutable collections. For instance, if you just write Set without any prefix or without having imported Set from somewhere, you get an immutable Set, and if you write iterable you get an immutable iterable collection, because these are the default bindings imported from the Scala package. To get the mutable default versions, you need to write explicitly `collection.mutable.Set` or `collection.mutable.Iterable`.

Note   A useful convention if you want to use both mutable and immutable versions of collections is to import just the `package collection.mutable`.

`import scala.collection.mutable`

Then a word like Set without a prefix still refers to an immutable collection, whereas `mutable.Set` refers to the mutable counterpart.

Now let's look at mutable Seqs, Sets, and Maps. It is worth noting that we will go through only partial implementations. The `scala.collection.mutable` package is extensive, and it is worth going through the Scala docs for a detailed treatment.

Figures 6-5, 6-6, and 6-7 illustrate the objects that contain the `scala.collection.mutable` package.

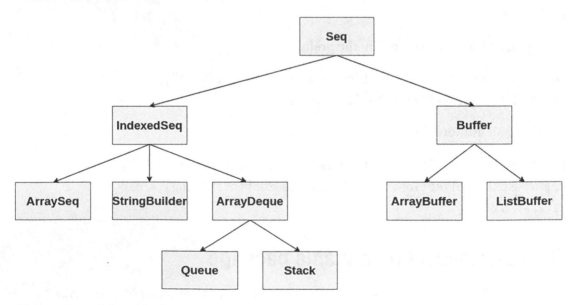

Figure 6-5. *Mutable Seq*

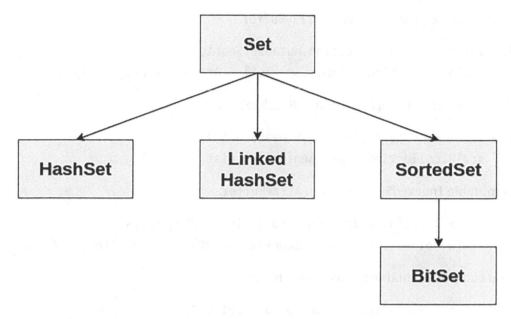

Figure 6-6. *Mutable Set*

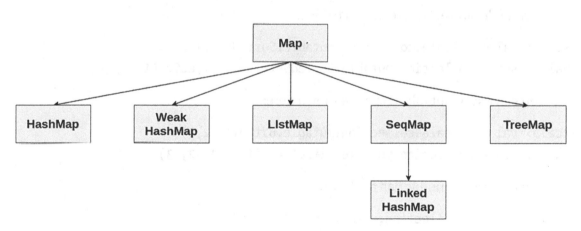

Figure 6-7. *Mutable Map*

As you can see, one of the main differences from the scala.collection package in Figure 6-1 is the Buffer type. Let's look at that now.

The Buffer type is implicitly mutable. There is no immutable Buffer. There are several subtypes of Buffer in the Scala libraries. The two most significant ones are ArrayBuffer and ListBuffer. You can create a buffer as shown here:

```
scala> val buffer = scala.collection.mutable.Buffer(1,2,3)
val buffer: scala.collection.mutable.Buffer[Int] = ArrayBuffer(1, 2, 3)
```

145

A mutable Seq is created as an ArrayBuffer.

```
scala> val x = scala.collection.mutable.Seq(1,2,3)
val x: scala.collection.mutable.Seq[Int] = ArrayBuffer(1, 2, 3)
```

A mutable LinearSeq is created as MutableList.

```
scala> val x = scala.collection.LinearSeq(1,2,3)
val x: scala.collection.LinearSeq[Int] = List(1, 2, 3)
```

A mutable IndexedSeq creates an ArrayBuffer.

```
scala> val x = scala.collection.mutable.IndexedSeq(1,2,3)
val x: scala.collection.mutable.IndexedSeq[Int] = ArrayBuffer(1, 2, 3)
```

You can use a mutable Set as shown here:

```
scala> val m = scala.collection.mutable.Set(1,2,3)
val m: scala.collection.mutable.Set[Int] = Set(1, 2, 3)
```

A mutable SortedSet creates a TreeSet.

```
scala> val m = scala.collection.mutable.SortedSet(1,2,3)
val m: scala.collection.mutable.SortedSet[Int] = TreeSet(1, 2, 3)
```

You can use a mutable BitSet as shown here:

```
scala> val m = scala.collection.mutable.BitSet(1,2,3)
val m: scala.collection.mutable.BitSet = BitSet(1, 2, 3)
```

You can use a mutable Map as shown here:

```
scala> val m = collection.mutable.Map(1 -> "a", 2 -> "b")
val m: scala.collection.mutable.Map[Int,String] = Map(2 -> b, 1 -> a)
```

The idea of this section was to give you an overview of the Scala collection hierarchy. You learned that there are three basic types named Seq, Set, and Map, which are then implemented in mutable and immutable packages. Now you will look at the immutable and mutable collection classes.

Using Immutable Collection Classes

Scala has a wide variety of collections classes. Collections are containers of things.
Those containers can be sequenced, linear sets of items as shown in the following code
snippets.

A List:

```scala
scala> val x = List(1,2,3,4)
val x: List[Int] = List(1, 2, 3, 4)
```

Filtering through a List:

```scala
scala> x.filter(a => a % 2 == 0)
val res14: List[Int] = List(2, 4)
scala> x
val res15: List[Int] = List(1, 2, 3, 4)
```

They may be indexed items where the index is a zero-based Int (such as an Array)
or any other type (such as a Map) as illustrated here.

Creating an Array:

```scala
scala> val a = Array(1,2,3)
val a: Array[Int] = Array(1, 2, 3)
scala> a(1)
val res16: Int = 2
```

Creating a Map:

```scala
scala> val m = Map("one" -> 1, "two" -> 2, "three" -> 3)
val m: Map[String,Int] = Map(one -> 1, two -> 2, three ->3)
scala> m("two")
val res17: Int = 2
```

The collections may have an arbitrary number of elements or be bounded to zero or
one element (such as an Option). Collections may be strict or lazy.

Lazy collections have elements that may not consume memory until they are
accessed (such as a Range). Let's create a Range.

```scala
scala> 0 to 10
val res1: scala.collection.immutable.Range.Inclusive = Range 0 to 10
```

The nifty thing about Ranges is that the actual elements in the Range are not instantiated until they are accessed. So you can create a Range for all positive integers but take only the first five elements. This code runs without consuming many gigabytes of RAM because only the elements that are needed are created.

Using Range as lazy collection:

```scala
scala> (1 to Integer.MAX_VALUE - 1).take(5)
val res2: Range = Range 1 to 5
```

Collections may be mutable (the contents of the reference can change) or immutable (the thing that the reference refers to is never changed). Note that immutable collections may contain mutable items.

Vector

You saw earlier that, by default, specifying that you want an IndexedSeq creates a Vector.

```scala
scala> val x = IndexedSeq(1,2,3)
val x: IndexedSeq[Int] = Vector(1, 2, 3)
```

Here's how to access the vector using an index:

```scala
scala> x(0)
res53: Int = 1
```

You can't modify a vector, so you add elements to an existing vector as you assign the result to a new variable.

```scala
scala> val a = Vector(1, 2, 3)
val a: Vector[Int] = Vector(1, 2, 3)
scala> val b = a ++ Vector(4, 5)
val b: Vector[Int] = Vector(1, 2, 3, 4, 5)
```

Use the updated method to replace one element in a vector while assigning the result to a new variable.

```scala
scala> val c = b.updated(0, "x")
val c: Vector[Matchable] = Vector(x, 2, 3, 4, 5)
```

You can also use all the usual filtering methods to get just the elements you want out of a vector.

```scala
scala> val a = Vector(1, 2, 3, 4, 5)
val a: Vector[Int] = Vector(1, 2, 3, 4, 5)
scala> val b = a.take(2)
val b: Vector[Int] = Vector(1, 2)
scala> val c = a.filter(_ > 2)
val c: Vector[Int] = Vector(3, 4, 5)
```

In these examples, you create each variable as a val and assign the output to a new variable just to be clear, but you can also declare your variable as a var and reassign the result back to the same variable.

```scala
scala> var a = Vector(1, 2, 3)
var a: Vector[Int] = Vector(1, 2, 3)
scala> a = a ++ Vector(4, 5)
var a: Vector[Int] = Vector(1, 2, 3, 4, 5)
```

You may have seen that mixing a mutable variable (var) with an immutable collection causes surprising behavior. For instance, when you create an immutable Vector as a var, it appears you can somehow add new elements to it.

```scala
scala> var int = Vector(1)
var int: Vector[Int] = Vector(1)
scala> int = int :+ 2
var int: Vector[Int] = Vector(1, 2)
scala> int = int :+ 3
var int: Vector[Int] = Vector(1, 2, 3)
scala> int.foreach(println)
1
2
3
```

Although it looks like you're mutating an immutable collection, what's really happening is that the int variable points to a new collection each time you use the :+. The int variable (var) is mutable so it's actually being reassigned to a new collection during each step. However, the elements in an immutable collection like Vector cannot be changed. If you want to change the elements in a mutable collection, use ArrayBuffer.

List[T]

Scala's List[T] is a linked list of type T. That means it's a sequential list of any type, including Java's primitives (Int, Float, Double, Boolean, Char) because Scala takes care of boxing (turning primitives into objects) for you. You can build a list using the same syntax you used to build an array with initial values, as shown here:

```scala
scala> List(1,2,3)
val res0: List[Int] = List(1, 2, 3)
```

Like the Array type, the List type is parametric and Scala will figure out the best type if you use this syntax. There is no syntax for making an uninitialized List. That is because lists are immutable. Once you have created a list, the values in it cannot be changed. Changing it would require making a new List. However, there is another way to put Lists together when you do not initially know all the values that will be stored in them. You can efficiently build Lists one element at a time if you add elements to the front of the List. To add elements to a List, you use the cons operator, ::. Internally, a List is made up of a cons cell (the scala.:: class [yes, that's two colons]) with a tail that refers to another cons cell or the Nil object. It's easy to create a List:

```scala
scala> 1 :: 2 :: 3 :: Nil
val res20: List[Int] = List(1, 2, 3)
```

This code creates three cons cells, each with an Int in it. Anything that looks like an operator with a : (colon), like the first character, is evaluated right to left. Thus, the previous code is evaluated just like the following:

```scala
scala> new ::(1, new ::(2, new ::(3, Nil)))
val res21: ::[Int] = List(1, 2, 3)
```

:: takes a "head" which is a single element and a "tail" which is another List. The expression on the left of the :: is the head, and the expression on the right is the tail. To create a List using ::, you must always put a List on the right side. That means that the right-most element must be a List, and in this case, you're using an empty List, Nil.

You can also create a List using the List object's apply method (which is defined as defapply[T](param: T*):List[T], which translates to "the apply method of type T takes zero or more parameters of type T and returns a List of type T").

```scala
scala> List(1,2,3)
val res22: List[Int] = List(1, 2, 3)
```

The type inferencer is pretty good at figuring out the type of the List, but sometimes you need to help it along.

```scala
scala> List(1, 44.5f, 8d)
val res27: List[AnyVal] = List(1, 44.5, 8.0)
scala> List[Number](1, 44.5, 8d)
val res28: List[java.lang.Number] = List(1, 44.5, 8.0)
```

If you want to prepend an item to the head of the List, you can use ::, which actually creates a new cons cell with the old list as the tail.

```scala
scala> val x = List(1,2,3)
scala> 99 :: x
val res0: List[Int] = List(99, 1, 2, 3)
```

Note that the List referred to by the variable x is unchanged, but a new List is created with a new head and the old tail. This is a very fast, constant-time, O(1), operation.

You can also merge two Lists to form a new List. This operation is O(n) where n is the number of elements in the first List:

```scala
scala> val x = List(1,2,3)
scala> val y = List(99, 98, 97)
scala> x ::: y
val res3: List[Int] = List(1, 2, 3, 99, 98, 97)
```

Getting Functional

The power of List and other collections in Scala comes when you mix functions with the collection operators. Let's say you want to find all the odd numbers in a List. It's easy.

```scala
scala> List(1,2,3).filter(x => x % 2 == 1)
val res4: List[Int] = List(1, 3)
```

The filter method iterates over the collection and applies the function (in this case, an anonymous function) to each of the elements. If the function returns true, the element is included in the resulting collection. If the function returns false, the element is not included in the resulting collection. The resulting collection is the same type of collection that filter was invoked on. If you invoke filters on a List[Int], you get a

List[Int]. If you invoke filters on an Array[String], you get an Array[String] back. In this case, you've written a function that performs mod 2 on the parameter and tests to see whether the result is 1, which indicates that the parameter is odd.

You can also write a method called isOdd and pass the isOdd method as a parameter (Scala will promote the method to a function).

```
scala> def isOdd(x: Int) = x % 2 == 1
isOdd: (Int)Boolean
scala> List(1,2,3,4,5).filter(isOdd)
val res6: List[Int] = List(1, 3, 5)
```

filter works with any collections that contain any type, like so:

```
scala> "99 Red Balloons".toList.filter(Character.isDigit)
val res9: List[Char] = List(9, 9)
```

In this case, you're converting a String to a List[Char] using the toList method and filtering the numbers. The Scala compiler promotes the isDigit static method on Character to a function, thus demonstrating interoperability with Java and that Scala methods are not magic.

Another useful method for picking the right elements out of a List is takeWhile, which returns all the elements until it encounters an element that causes the function to return false. For example, let's get all the characters up to the first space in a String:

```
scala> "Elwood eats mice".takeWhile(c => c != ' ')
val res16: String = Elwood
```

Transformation

The map method in List (and Seq) transforms each element of a collection based on a function. For example, say you have a List[String] and want to convert it to all lowercase.

```
scala> List("A", "Cat").map(s => s.toLowerCase)
val res29: List[java.lang.String] = List(a, cat)
```

You can shorten the function so the code reads

```
scala> List("A", "Cat").map(_.toLowerCase)
val res30: List[java.lang.String] = List(a, cat)
```

The number of elements in the returned collection is the same as the number of elements in the original collection, but the types may be different. If the function passed into map returns a different type, then the resulting collection is a collection of the type returned from the function. For example, you can take a List[String] and calculate the length of each String, which will result in a List[Int]:

```
scala> List("A", "Cat").map(_.length)
val res31: List[Int] = List(1, 3)
```

map provides a very powerful and uniform way to transform data from one type to another. You can transform your Strings to lowercase, to a List of their length, and you can extract data from a collection of complex objects. For example, if you have a database query that returns records of type Person defined as having a first method that returns a String containing the person's first name, you can create a List of the first names of the people in the List.

```
scala> trait Person {def first: String}
// defined trait Person
scala> val d = new Person {def first = "David" }
scala> val e = new Person {def first = "Elwood"}
scala> val a = new Person {def first = "Archer"}
scala> List(a, d, e).map(_.first)
val res35: List[String] = List(Archer, David, Elwood)
```

Or, if you're writing a web app, you can create an <li> (an HTML list element) containing the first name of each Person in your List.

```
scala> List(a,d,e).map(n =>"<li>" + {n.first} + "</li>")
val res21: List[String] = List(<li>Archer</li>, <li>David</li>,
<li>Elwood</li>)
```

You can combine the operations. Let's update the Person trait:

```
trait Person:
    def first: String
    def valid: Boolean
```

Now you can write code to find all the valid `Person` records and return the first names.

def validPeople(in: List[Person])=

```
in.filter(_.valid).map(_.first)
```

Reduxio

Scala has other abstractions for common collections operations. `reduceLeft` allows you to perform an operation on adjacent elements of the collection where the result of the first operation is fed into the next operation. For example, if you want to find the biggest number in a `List[Int]`:

```
scala> List(8, 6, 22, 2).reduceLeft(_ max _)
val res50: Int = 22
```

In this case, `reduceLeft` takes 8 and 6, and feeds them into your function, which returns the maximum value of the two numbers: 8. Next, `reduceLeft` feeds 8 (the output of the last iteration) and 22 into the function, resulting in 22. Next, reduceLeft feeds 22 and 2 into the function, resulting in 22. Because there are no more elements, `reduceLeft` returns 22.

You can use `reduceLeft` to find the longest word.

```
scala> List("moose", "cow", "A", "Cat").
       reduceLeft((a, b) => if a.length > b.length then a else b)
val res41: java.lang.String = moose
```

Because Scala's `if` expression works like Java's ternary operator, the `if` in the previous code returns a if it's longer than b. You can also find the shortest word.

```
scala> List("moose", "cow", "A", "Cat").
       reduceLeft((a, b) => if a.length < b.length then a else b)
val res42: java.lang.String = A
```

`reduceLeft` throws an exception on a Nil (empty) List. This is correct behavior as there is no way to apply the function on the members of the List as a Nil List has no elements.

foldLeft is similar to reduceLeft, but it starts with a seed value. The return type of the function and the return type of foldLeft must be the same type as the seed. The first example is summing up List[Int]:

```
scala> List(1,2,3,4).foldLeft(0) (_ + _)
val res43: Int = 10
```

In this case, the seed value is 0. Its type is Int. foldLeft feeds the seed and the first element of the List, 1, into the function, which returns 1. Next, foldLeft feeds 1 (the result of the previous iteration) and 2 (the next element) into the function, resulting in 3. The process continues, and the sum of the List[Int] is generated: 10. You can generate the product of the List the same way.

```
scala> List(1,2,3,4).foldLeft(1) (_ * _)
val res44: Int = 24
```

But because the return type of foldLeft is the type of the seed, not the type of the List, you can figure out the total length of a List[String].

```
scala> List("b", "a", "elwood", "archer").foldLeft(0)(_ + _.length)
val res51: Int = 14
```

Sometimes you need to work with more than one collection at a time. For example, say you want to generate the List of products of the numbers from 1 to 3.

```
scala> val n = (1 to 3).toList
val n: List[Int] = List(1, 2, 3)
scala> n.map(i => n.map(j => i * j))
val res53: List[List[Int]] = List(List(1, 2, 3), List(2, 4, 6),
List(3, 6, 9))
```

You have nested map invocations, and this results in a List[List[Int]]. In some cases, this may be what you want. In other cases, you want the results in a single List[Int]. In order to nest the map operations but flatten the results of nested operations, you use the flatMap method.

```
scala> n.flatMap(i => n.map(j => i * j))
val res58: List[Int] = List(1, 2, 3, 2, 4, 6, 3, 6, 9)
```

Look Ma, No Loops

So far, you've written a bunch of code that manipulates collections without explicit looping. By passing functions (that is, logic) to methods that control the looping, you let the library writers define the looping, and you define the logic in your app. However, syntactically, nested map, flatMap, and filter can get ugly. For example, if you want to find the product of the odd numbers from 1 to 10 times the even numbers from 1 to 10, you could write the following:

```scala
scala> def isOdd(in: Int) = in % 2 == 1
scala> def isEven(in: Int) = !isOdd(in)
scala> val n = (1 to 10).toList
scala> n.filter(isEven).flatMap(i => n.filter(isOdd).map(j => i * j))
val res60: List[Int] = List(2, 6, 10, 14, 18, ... 10, 30, 50, 70, 90)
```

Scala provides the for comprehension, which offers a syntactically pleasing nesting of map, flatMap, and filter. You can convert the nested statements from the previous example into a syntactically pleasing statement.

```scala
scala> for {i <- n if isEven(i); j <- n if isOdd(j)} yield i * j
val res59: List[Int] = List(2, 6, 10, 14, 18, ... 10, 30, 50, 70, 90)
```

The for comprehension is not a looping construct but is a syntactic construct that the compiler reduces to map, flatMap, and filter. In fact, the lines

```scala
n.filter(isEven).flatMap(i => n.filter(isOdd).map(j => i * j))
```

and

```scala
n.filter(isEven).flatMap(i => n.filter(isOdd).map(j => i * j))
```

are generated as a result in the same bytecode. The for comprehension can be used with any class, including user-generated classes, that implements map, flatMap, filter, and foreach. This means you can create your own classes that work with the for comprehension.

Lists also work well with Scala's pattern matching and recursive programming. You'll be exploring pattern matching in depth in Chapter 5. For this example, pattern matching is a lot like Java's switch statement, but it can be used to compare things that are more complex than Ints, and Scala's pattern matching allows you to match some elements and extract, or capture, others into variables.

The pattern-matching syntax is the same as the List construction syntax. For example, if you are matching against List[Int], case 1 :: Nil => will match List(1). case 1 :: 2 :: Nil => will match List(1,2). case 1 :: rest => will match any List that starts with 1 and will put the tail of the List into the variable rest.

The following example converts a List[Char] of Roman numerals to their Arabic numeral equivalent. The code matches the List to a series of patterns. Based on the matched pattern, a value is returned. The patterns are matched in order of appearance. However, the compiler may optimize the patterns by eliminating duplicate tests[2]. The code to convert from Roman numerals to Ints is here:

```scala
def roman(in: List[Char]): Int =
    in match
        case 'I' :: 'V' :: rest => 4 + roman(rest)
        case 'I' :: 'X' :: rest => 9 + roman(rest)
        case 'I' :: rest => 1 + roman(rest)
        case 'V' :: rest => 5 + roman(rest)
        case 'X' :: 'L' :: rest => 40 + roman(rest)
        case 'X' :: 'C' :: rest => 90 + roman(rest)
        case 'X' :: rest => 10 + roman(rest)
        case 'L' :: rest => 50 + roman(rest)
        case 'C' :: 'D' :: rest => 400 + roman(rest)
        case 'C' :: 'M' :: rest => 900 + roman(rest)
        case 'C' :: rest => 100 + roman(rest)
        case 'D' :: rest => 500 + roman(rest)
        case 'M' :: rest => 1000 + roman(rest)
        case _ => 0
```

case 'I' :: 'V' :: rest => 4 + roman(rest) tests the first two characters, and if they are IV, the method returns 4 plus the Roman numeral conversion of the rest of the List[Char]. If the test falls through to case _ => 0, there are no more Roman numerals, 0 is returned, and there's no more recursion, so no more calls back into the roman() method. Without explicit looping or length testing or explicit branching logic, you've written a concise, readable method.

---

[2] You can see exactly how Scala turns patterns into code by typing scalac -print FileName.scala. This will cause the Scala compiler to emit desugared code that looks strangely like Java code.

Scala's List and other sequential collections provide powerful ways to define business logic in a concise, maintainable way.

Range

Ranges are often used to populate data structures and to iterate over for loops. Ranges provide a lot of power with just a few methods, as shown in these examples:

```
scala> 1 to 10
val res0: scala.collection.immutable.Range.Inclusive = Range(1, 2, 3, 4, 5,
6, 7, 8, 9, 10)
scala> 1 until 10
val res1: Range = Range 1 until 10
scala> 1 to 10 by 2
val res2: Range = inexact Range 1 to 10 by 2
scala> 'a' to 'c'
val res3: collection.immutable.NumericRange.Inclusive[Char] =
NumericRange a to c
```

You can use Ranges to create and populate sequences:

```
scala> val x = (1 to 10).toList
val x: List[Int] = List(1, 2, 3, 4, 5, 6, 7, 8, 9, 10)
```

In the next section, you're going to explore tuples, which are fixed-length collections where each element can be a different type.

Stream or LazyList

A Stream/LazyList is like a List, except that its elements are computed lazily, in a manner similar to how a view creates a lazy version of a collection. Because Stream/LazyList elements are computed lazily, a Stream/LazyList can be long...infinitely long. Like a view, only the elements that are accessed are computed. Other than this behavior, a Stream/LazyList behaves similar to a List.

Just like a List can be constructed with ::, a Stream can be constructed with the #::
method, using Stream.empty at the end of the expression instead of Nil.

```
scala> val stream = 1 #:: 2 #:: 3 #:: Stream.empty
val stream: scala.collection.immutable.Stream[Int] = Stream(1, ?)
```

Take into consideration that the previous block of code is only valid in the version of
Scala 2.12.0 or down. If you want that block of code to work in the latest version of Scala,
you need to do the following:

```
scala> 1 #:: 2 #:: 3 #:: LazyList.empty
val res16: LazyList[Int] = LazyList(<not computed>)
```

The REPL output shows that the stream begins with the number 1 but uses a ?
to denote the end of the stream. This is because the end of the stream hasn't been
evaluated yet.

For example, given a LazyList like

```
scala> val lazyList = LazyList.range(1, 10000)
val lazyList: LazyList[Int] = LazyList(<not computed>)
```

you can attempt to access the head and tail of the LazyList. The head is returned
immediately:

```
scala> lazyList.head
val res18: Int = 1
```

but the tail isn't evaluated yet:

```
scala> lazyList.tail
val res17: LazyList[Int] = LazyList(<not computed>)
```

The <not computed> is the way a lazy collection shows that the end of the collection
hasn't been evaluated yet.

Tuples

Have you ever written a method that returns two or three values? Let's write a method that takes a List[Double] and returns the count, the sum, and the sum of squares returned in a three-element Tuple, a Tuple3[Int, Double, Double]:

```
scala> def sumSq(in: List[Double]): (Int, Double, Double) =
     |      in.foldLeft((0, 0d, 0d))((t, v) => (t._1 + 1, t._2 + v,
         t._3 + v * v))
def sumSq(in: List[Double]): (Int, Double, Double)
```

The sumSq method takes a List[Double] as input and returns a Tuple3[Int, Double, Double]. The compiler desugars (Int, Double, Double) into Tuple3[Int, Double, Double]. The compiler will treat a collection of elements in parentheses as a Tuple. You seed the foldLeft with (0, 0d, 0d), which the compiler translates to a Tuple3[Int, Double, Double]. The function takes two parameters: t and v. t is a Tuple3, and v is a Double. The function returns a new Tuple3 by adding 1 to the first element of the Tuple, adding v to the second element of the Tuple, and adding the square of v to the third element of the Tuple. Using Scala's pattern matching, you can make the code a little more readable:

```
scala> def sumSq(in: List[Double]) : (Int, Double, Double) =
     |      in.foldLeft((0, 0d, 0d)){
     |      case ((cnt, sum, sq), v) => (cnt + 1, sum + v, sq + v * v)}
def sumSq(in: List[Double]): (Int, Double, Double)
```

You can create Tuples using a variety of syntax. The following example shows how to declare a Tuple in Scala 2.12 or down, in case you open a project that contains old code:

```
scala> Tuple2(1,2) == Pair(1,2) // Only valid in Scala 2.12 or down
scala> Pair(1,2) == (1,2)
scala> (1,2) == 1 -> 2
```

The last example, 1 -> 2, is a particularly helpful and syntactically pleasing way to pass pairs around. Pairs appear in code very frequently, including name/value pairs for creating Maps.

Map[K, V]

A Map is a collection of key/value pairs. Any value can be retrieved based on its key. Keys are unique in the Map, but the values need not be unique. In Java, Hashtable and HashMap are common Map classes. The default Scala Map class is immutable. This means that you can pass an instance of Map to another thread, and that thread can access the Map without synchronizing. The performance of Scala's immutable Map is indistinguishable from the performance of Java's HashMap.

You create a Map like so:

```
scala> var p = Map(1 -> "David", 9 -> "Elwood")
var p: Map[Int,String] = Map(1 -> David, 9 -> Elwood)
```

You create a new Map by passing a set of Pair[Int, String] to the Map object's apply method. Note the use of a var p rather than a val p. This is because the Map is immutable, so when you alter the contents on the Map, you must assign the new Map back to p.

You can add an element to the Map.

```
scala> p + (8 -> "Archer")
val res20: Map[Int, String] = Map(1 -> David, 9 -> Elwood, 8 -> Archer)
```

But you haven't changed the immutable Map.

```
scala> p
val res21: Map[Int, String] = Map(1 -> David, 9 -> Elwood)
```

In order to update p, you must assign the new Map back to p.

```
scala> p = p + (8 -> "Archer")
p: Map[Int, String] = Map(1 -> David, 9 -> Elwood, 8 -> Archer)
```

or

```
scala> p += (8 -> "Archer")
```

And you can see that p is updated.

```
scala> p
res7: Map[Int,String] = Map(1 -> David, 9 -> Elwood, 8 -> Archer)
```

You can get elements out of the Map.

```
scala> p(9)
res12: String = Elwood
```

What happens when you ask for an element that doesn't exist?

```
scala> p(88)
java.util.NoSuchElementException: key not found: 88
```

This is mighty inconvenient. If you try to get an element that's not in the Map, you get an exception. That's kind of jarring. So far, you haven't seen much in Scala that results in exceptions being thrown, but it makes logical sense. If you request something that doesn't exist, that's an exceptional situation. Java's Map classes handle this situation by returning null, which has two drawbacks. First, you have to null-test the result of every Map access. Second, it means you can't store a null in a Map. Scala has a kinder and gentler mechanism for dealing with this situation. The get() method of Map returns an Option (Some or None) that contains the result:

```
scala> p.get(88)
val res10: Option[String] = None
scala> p.get(9)
val res11: Option[String] = Some(Elwood)
```

You can return a default value if the key is not found.

```
scala> p.getOrElse(99, "Nobody")
val res55: String = Nobody
scala> p.getOrElse(1, "Nobody")
val res56: String = David
```

You can also use flatMap with Options to find all the values with keys between 1 and 5.

```
scala> 1 to 5 flatMap(p.get)
val res28: IndexedSeq[String] = Vector(David)
```

In this case, you create a range of numbers from 1 to 5. You flatMap this collection, passing in a function, p.get. "Wait," you say, "p.get isn't a function, it's a method, but I didn't include the parameter." Scala is very cool, because if it's expecting a function with parameters of a particular type and you pass a method that takes those parameters, Scala will promote the method with its missing parameters to a function, as you saw in Chapter 2 with the explanation about functions versus methods. You'll explore `Options` in the next subsection.

Let's continue exploring `Map`. You can remove elements from your `Map`.

```
scala> p -= 9
scala> p
res20: Map[Int,String] = Map(1 -> David, 8 -> Archer)
```

You can test the `Map` to see whether it contains a particular key.

```
scala> p.contains(1)
res21: Boolean = true
```

You can use `reduceLeft` on the collection of values to find the largest String.

```
scala> p.values.reduceLeft((a, b) => if a > b then a else b)
res23: java.lang.String = David
```

You can test whether any of the values contains the letter "z."

```
scala> p.values.exists(_.contains("z"))
res28: Boolean = false
```

You can also add a bunch of elements to a `Map` using the `++` method.

```
scala> p ++= List(5 -> "Cat", 6 -> "Dog")
scala> p
val res39: Map[Int,String] = Map(1 -> David, 8 -> Archer, 5 -> Cat,
6 -> Dog)
```

And you can remove a bunch of keys with the `-` method.

```
scala> p --= List(8, 6)
scala> p
val res40: Map[Int, String] = Map(1 -> David, 5 -> Cat)
```

Maps are Scala collections and have collection manipulation methods. This means you can use methods including `map`, `filter`, and `foldLeft`. One of the tricky parts of using Java's immutable collections is iterating over the collection and simultaneously removing elements. In my code, I have to create an accumulator for the keys I'm going to remove, loop over the collection, find all the keys to remove, and then iterate over the collection of keys to remove and remove them from the collection. Not only that, but I frequently forget how brittle Hashtable is and inevitably forget this sequence and get some nasty runtime errors. In Scala, it's much easier. There's a simpler way to remove unwanted elements from a Map.

```
def removeInvalid(in: Map[Int, Person]) =
    in.filter(kv => kv._2.valid)
```

Pretty cool, huh? Map has a filter method that works just like List's filter method. The kv variable is a pair representing the key/value pair. The filter method tests each key/value pair by calling the function and constructing a new Map that contains only the elements that passed the filter test.

Mutable Collections

The List, Set, and Map immutable collections we are familiar with cannot be changed after they have been created. They can, however, be transformed into new collections. For example, you can create an immutable map and then transform it by removing one mapping and adding another.

```
scala> val immutableMap = Map(1 -> "a", 2 -> "b", 3 -> "c")
val immutableMap: Map[Int,String] = Map(1 -> a, 2 -> b, 3 -> c)
scala> val newMap = immutableMap - 1 + (4 -> "d")
val newMap: Map[Int,String] = Map(2 -> b, 3 -> c, 4 -> d)
```

Removing "a" and adding "d" gives you a different collection, while the original collection of immutableMap remains the same.

```
scala> println(newMap)
Map(2 -> b, 3 -> c, 4 -> d)
scala> println(immutableMap)
Map(1 -> a, 2 -> b, 3 -> c)
```

What you end up with is a completely new collection stored in newMap. The original collection, immutableMap, remains untouched.

However, there are times when you do want mutable data, such as when creating a mutable data structure that is only used within a function.

You can create mutable collections directly from immutable collections. The List, Map, and Set immutable collections can all be converted to the mutable collection. mutable.Buffer type with the toBuffer method. Here is an example of converting an immutable map to a mutable one and then changing it back:

```
scala> val m = Map(1->"a", 2 -> "b")
val m: Map[Int,String] = Map(1 -> a, 2 -> b)
scala> val b = m.toBuffer
val b: scala.collection.mutable.Buffer[(Int, String)] =
ArrayBuffer((1,a), (2,b))
```

The map, containing key-value pairs, is now a sequence of tuples. You can now add a new entry.

```
scala> b += (3 ->"c")
val res35: scala.collection.mutable.Buffer[(Int, String)] =
ArrayBuffer((1,a), (2,b), (3,c))
```

After adding a new entry, you can change the buffer to map again.

```
scala> val newMap = b.toMap
val newMap: Map[Int,String] = Map(1 -> a, 2 -> b, 3 -> c)
```

The buffer methods toList and toSet can be used in addition to toMap to convert a buffer to an immutable collection. The most straightforward way to modify collections is with a mutable collection type. You will look at some mutable collection classes in the following sections.

Mutable ArrayBuffer

The ArraryBuffer is a collection that contains elements of the same type where you can change the size of the structure without changing the values.

Creating an ArrayBuffer:

```
scala> import scala.collection.mutable.ArrayBuffer
scala> val ints = ArrayBuffer[Int]()
val ints: scala.collection.mutable.ArrayBuffer[Int] = ArrayBuffer()
```

Adding elements to the ArrayBuffer:

```
scala> ints ++= 1
val res0: scala.collection.mutable.ArrayBuffer[Int] = ArrayBuffer(1)
```

Adding multiple elements to the ArrayBuffer:

```
scala> ints ++= List(2,3,4)
val res1: scala.collection.mutable.ArrayBuffer[Int] = ArrayBuffer(1,
2, 3, 4)
```

Removing elements to the ArrayBuffer:

```
scala> ints -= 1
val res0: scala.collection.mutable.ArrayBuffer[Int] = ArrayBuffer(2,3,4)
```

Mutable Queue

A queue is a first-in, first-out (FIFO) data structure. Scala offers both an immutable queue and mutable queue. You can create an empty, mutable queue of any data type. This code shows a mutable queue for int:

```
scala> import scala.collection.mutable.Queue
scala> var ints = Queue[Int]()
var ints: scala.collection.mutable.Queue[Int] = Queue()
```

Note   While the collection.immutable package is automatically added to the current namespace in Scala, the collection.mutable package is not. When creating mutable collections, make sure to include the full package name for the type.

Once you have a mutable queue, you can add elements to it using +=, ++=, and enqueue, as shown in these examples.

Adding elements to the queue:

```
scala> ints ++= 1
val res36: scala.collection.mutable.Queue[Int] = Queue(1)
```

Adding multiple elements to the queue:

```scala
scala> ints += (2, 3) //This is deprecated in Scala 2.13.0
res47: scala.collection.mutable.Queue[Int] = Queue(1, 2, 3)
```

Using enqueue:

```scala
scala> ints.enqueue(4)
val res49: scala.collection.mutable.Queue[Int] = Queue(1, 2, 3, 4)
```

Because a queue is a FIFO, you typically remove elements from the head of the queue, one element at a time, using dequeue.

```scala
scala> ints.dequeue
res50: Int = 1
scala> ints
res51: scala.collection.mutable.Queue[Int] = Queue(2, 3, 4)
```

A Queue is a collection class that extends from Iterable and Traversable, so it has all the usual collection methods, including foreach, map, and so on.

Mutable Stack

A stack is a last-in, first-out (LIFO) data structure. Scala has both immutable and mutable versions of a stack. The following examples demonstrate how to use the mutable Stack class.

Creating an empty, mutable stack of the int data type:

```scala
scala> import scala.collection.mutable.Stack
scala> var ints = Stack[Int]()
val ints: scala.collection.mutable.Stack[Int] = Stack()
```

You can also populate a stack with initial elements when you create it.

```scala
scala> val ints = Stack(1, 2, 3)
val ints: scala.collection.mutable.Stack[Int] = Stack(1, 2, 3)
```

You can now push elements onto the stack with push.

```scala
scala> ints.push(4)
val res41: ints.type = Stack(4, 1, 2, 3)
```

Creating a stack:

```
scala> ints.push(5, 6 ,7)
val res42: ints.type = Stack(7, 6, 5, 4, 1, 2, 3)
```

To take elements off the stack, pop them off the top of the stack.

```
scala> val lastele = ints.pop
val lastele: Int = 7
```

With this, we complete the discussion of mutable collections and this chapter. The Scala collections framework is broad, rather than deep, and deserves a book of its own. Nevertheless, this chapter showed you how to use a variety of Scala's collection types.

Performance of the Collections

Not all the types of collections have the same performance in their different methods. You need to consider some aspects before choosing one instead of another. The description of each entry exists in Table 6-6. Tables 6-7 and 6-8 describe the performance of each method.

Table 6-6. *Nomenclature to Describe Performance*

Entry	Explanation
C	The operation takes (fast) constant time.
eC	The operation takes effectively constant time, but this might depend on some assumptions such as maximum length of a vector or distribution of hash keys.
aC	The operation takes amortized constant time. Some invocations of the operation might take longer, but if many operations are performed on average, only a constant time per operation is taken.
Log	The operation takes time proportional to the logarithm of the collection size.
L	The operation is linear; that is, it takes time proportional to the collection size.
-	The operation is not supported.

Table 6-7. *Performance of the Sequence*

Collection	Type	Head	Tail	Apply	Update	Prepend	Append	Insert
List	Immutable	C	C	L	L	C	L	-
LazyList	Immutable	C	C	L	L	C	L	-
ArraySeq	Immutable	C	L	C	L	L	L	-
Vector	Immutable	eC	eC	eC	eC	eC	eC	-
Queue	Immutable	aC	aC	L	L	L	C	-
Range	Immutable	C	C	C	-	-	-	-
String	Immutable	C	L	C	L	L	L	-
ArrayBuffer	Mutable	C	L	C	C	L	aC	L
ListBuffer	Mutable	C	L	L	L	C	C	L
StringBuilder	Mutable	C	L	C	C	L	aC	L
Queue	Mutable	C	L	L	L	C	C	L
ArraySeq	Mutable	C	L	C	C	-	-	-
Stack	Mutable	C	L	L	L	C	L	L
Array	Mutable	C	L	C	C	-	-	-
ArrayDeque	Mutable	C	L	C	C	aC	aC	L

Table 6-8. *Performance of Set and Map*

Collection	Type	Lookup	Add	Remove	Min
HashSet/HashMap	Immutable	eC	eC	eC	L
TreeSet/TreeMap	Immutable	Log	Log	Log	Log
BitSet	Immutable	C	L	L	eC
VectorMap	Immutable	eC	eC	aC	L
ListMap	Immutable	L	L	L	L
HashSet/HashMap	Mutable	eC	eC	eC	L
WeakHashMap	Mutable	eC	eC	eC	L
BitSet	Mutable	C	aC	C	eC
TreeSet	Mutable	Log	Log	Log	Log

Summary

This chapter gave you a tour of the Scala collections framework and showed you three main packages of the framework. This chapter delved deeply into how to use Lists. You saw many ways to work with Lists. You explored basic operations like head and tail, the higher-order operations like map, and the utility methods in the List object. Lists are just one kind of collection that Scala supports, however. This chapter provided an overview of the Scala collections library and the most important classes and traits in it. With this foundation, you should be able to work effectively with Scala collections and know where to look in Scaladoc when you need more information.

Table 6-9 summarizes most of the common collections and the meaning of each of them.

Table 6-9. *Which Collections Are Mutable or Immutable*

Collection	Immutable	Mutable	Description
ArrayBuffer		✓	An indexed sequence of mutable elements
LazyList	✓		An immutable LinkedList where the elements are computed only if they're needed
List	✓		A sequence of immutable elements
ListBuffer		✓	An indexed sequence of elements in a List
Map	✓	✓	A collection that contains key/value pairs
Set	✓	✓	A collection that does not contain duplicates
Vector	✓		A sequence of immutable elements

You'll turn your attention to the internals of Scala traits in the next chapter.

CHAPTER 7

Traits and Enums

In this chapter, you will learn two of the most useful features of Scala. These features exist in other languages that use the JVM, like Java or Kotlin—not with the same name but with the same concept behind the scenes.

One of them is traits. Traits function as interfaces in the Java universe and help you construct reusable parts of a program and deal with the tribulations of multiple inheritances, sidestepping the disadvantages of single inheritance by means of mixing compositions.

The second concept is enumerations (enums), which help you encapsulate in one place all possible values of a specific type. For example, a level of logging could have five possible values: INFO, WARN, DEBUG, ERROR, and FATAL. Also, enums provide a way to create methods with the idea of interacting with the values.

One thing to mention: These features are not entirely new in the latest version of Scala. Both exist in the previous version with a lot of differences. The most relevant case is enums, which is like a new way to do things with the idea of simplifying the use for the developers.

Traits

A *trait* provides code reusability in Scala by encapsulating the method and state, and then offering the possibility of mixing them into classes, thus allowing code reuse. In this way, a class can be mixed in with a myriad of traits, unlike inheritance where each class is allowed to inherit from just one superclass. Moreover, other than using the keyword `trait`, a trait definition resembles a class definition, as shown here:

```
scala> trait Gliding:
     |     def java () =
     |         println("gliding")
// defined trait Gliding
```

© David Pollak, Vishal Layka, and Andres Sacco 2022
D. Pollak et al., *Beginning Scala 3*, https://doi.org/10.1007/978-1-4842-7422-4_7

This trait named Gliding does not declare a superclass, so like a class, it has the default superclass of AnyRef. The Gliding trait is a simple example but adequate way to show how traits work.

The following are some of the things you can do with a trait:

- Have concrete abstract fields or methods

- Create a constructor that receives certain parameters

- Combine or extend different traits

- Restrict or limit which classes can use it

You can think of a trait as similar to an interface in Java where you can define a certain default behavior. In Java 8 or previous versions, this is not possible to do, and one class can extend from multiple interfaces to have multiple inheritances.

Table 7-1 shows the same block of code in the different languages that use the JVM.

Table 7-1. *Different Ways to Express the Idea of a Trait*

Language	Example
| Java | ```java
interface Gliding {
    default void gliding() {
        System.out.println("gliding");
    }
}
``` |
| Kotlin | ```kotlin
internal interface Gliding {
    fun gliding() {
        println("gliding")
    }
}
``` |
| Scala | ```scala
trait Gliding:
    def gliding () =
        println("gliding")
``` |
```

Everything looks fine but how can you use this trait in a class and invoke one of the methods? This is how:

```scala
scala> class ConcreteClass extends Gliding
// defined class ConcreteClass
scala> val instance = ConcreteClass()
val instance: ConcreteClass = ConcreteClass@78e043e4
scala> instance.gliding()
gliding
```

Using Traits as Mixins

With single inheritance, a class can inherit methods and fields from only one class. Multiple inheritances enable the class to inherit methods and fields from more than one class. However, multiple inheritances can be problematic as the order of inheriting classes may affect the behavior of the subclass inadvertently.

The mixin composition is a better approach for solving the problems of multiple inheritances, sidestepping the drawbacks of single inheritance. In Java, a class can implement any arbitrary number of interfaces toward multiple abstractions. Unlike Java, Scala provides a mechanism for defining and using reusable code in interfaces, which is valid for all classes implementing the interface. You have abstract classes for defining and using such reusable code, but a class can extend only one abstract class, eliminating the possibility of multiple inheritances.

The term *mixin* is used for such reusable code that could be independently maintained. You can use traits in a way similar to the way in which Java interfaces are used. When you add implementation to traits, they become mixins. You can create a trait that inherits from a class, as well as a class that extends a trait. Once a trait is defined, it can be mixed into a class using the extends keyword. This code shows a class that mixes in the Gliding trait using extends:

```scala
scala> class Glider extends Gliding:
|     override def toString = "glider"
// defined class Glider
```

You can use the extends keyword to mix in a trait; in that case, you implicitly inherit the trait's superclass. In the following code, the class Glider mixes in Gliding. You can use the methods inherited from a trait as follows:

```
scala> val glider = Glider()
val glider: Glider = glider
scala> glider.gliding()
gliding
```

A trait also defines a type. Here's an example in which Gliding is used as a type:

```
scala> val g: Glider = glider
g: Glider = glider
scala> g.gliding()
gliding
```

In the example shown earlier, the type of g is a Glider trait, and so g could be initialized with any object whose class mixes in Glider.

In the following code, class Glider inherits an implementation of gliding from trait Glider. The class Glider could override gliding as illustrated above.

```
scala> class Glider extends Gliding:
     |      override def toString = "glider"
     |      override def gliding() = println("race for now " + toString)
// defined class Glider
```

Because Glider overrides Gliding's implementation of gliding, you get a new behavior when you call it.

```
scala> glider.gliding()
race for now glider
```

Fundamentally, traits are akin to Java interfaces. As with interfaces, you can just declare the methods in your trait that you want your extending classes to implement, as shown here:

```
trait TraitA:
    def methodA(): Unit
    def methodAWithParam(param :String): Unit
    def methodWithReturnType: String
```

This code shows a trait that declares methods that don't take any argument. The methods without an argument can be declared with a def keyword followed by the method name, as illustrated in the first method, def methodA. If a method requires parameters, you can list them as usual.

One trait can extend another trait, as shown here:

```
trait TraitB extends TraitA:
    def methodB(): Unit
```

When a class extends a trait, use the extends and with keywords based on whether the class extends one trait or several traits. When a class extends one trait, use the extends keyword.

```
class ClassA extends TraitA:
    // code
```

If a class extends more than one trait, use extends for the first trait and with to mix in the other traits.

```
class ClassA extends TraitA with TraitB:
    // code
```

If a class extends a class and a trait, always use extends before the class name, and use with before the trait's name.

```
class ClassA extends ClassB with TraitA with TraitB:
    // code
```

A class extending the trait must implement all the abstract methods of the trait, unless the class extending the trait is itself abstract.

```
class ClassA extends TraitA:
    def methodA(): Unit = print("methodA")
    def methodAWithParam(param :String): Unit = print(param)
    def methodWithReturnType: String = "something"
```

Here ClassA is not declared abstract and therefore it implements all abstract methods of trait TraitA.

Note   A trait can be comprised of both abstract and concrete methods.

However, if a class extends a trait but does not implement the abstract methods defined in the trait, the class extending the trait must be declared abstract.

```
abstract class ClassA extends TraitA:
    def methodA(): Unit { // code... }
    def methodAWithParam(param :String): Unit{ // code... }
```

Here ClassA does not implement the methodWithReturnType method of TraitA. The subclass of a trait can choose, if it prefers, to override the trait's method.

The following code illustrates a Vehicle trait that provides an implementation for the drive method:

```
trait Vehicle:
    def drive() = println("Driving")
    def race(): String
```

In the following code, drive is a concrete method and race is an abstract method. The Car class here does not override the drive method of Vehicle trait.

```
class Car extends Vehicle:
    def race(): String = "Racing the car"
```

The Boat class in the following code overrides the drive method of the Vehicle trait:

```
class Boat extends Vehicle:
    override def drive() = println("float")
    def race() = "Racing boat."
```

Note   Although Scala has abstract classes, it's recommended to use traits instead of abstract classes to implement base behavior because a class can extend only one abstract class, but it can implement multiple traits. If you want the base behavior to be inherited in Java code, use an abstract class.

You can also use fields in your traits. The fields of a trait can be declared as either var or val and can be concrete by defining the field with an initial value or abstract by not assigning an initial value. The following code illustrates a trait named CarTrait with an abstract field door and a concrete field seat:

```
trait CarTrait:
    var door: Int
    var seat = 4
```

The next code illustrates a Car class that extends the CarTrait. As you can see, you don't need to use the override keyword to override var fields door and seat.

```
class Car extends CarTrait:
    var door = 4
    seat = 5
```

However, you need to use the override keyword in a subclass of a trait to override a val field.

```
trait CarTrait:
    val door: Int
class Car extends CarTrait:
    override val door = 5
```

In the class Car that extends the CarTrait trait, you need to define the values for the abstract fields. Otherwise, you need to define the class as abstract.

As you can see, traits can declare fields and maintain state. The syntaxes of the class definition and the trait definition are exactly the same, except that a class definition can have the parameters passed to the primary constructor of a class but a trait definition cannot have such parameters.

```
class Car(door: Int )
trait Car (door: Int) // does not compile - Car is already defined as
                             class Car
```

In the next section, you will explore using traits for modeling complex class hierarchies that you cannot model in Java.

Traits and Class Hierarchies

One of the big challenges with developing a class hierarchy when you are constrained by single inheritance is figuring out what things should be base classes and where things should go in the class hierarchy. If you're modeling living things, how do you model things with legs when that can include any animal? Should there be LeggedAnimals and

LeglessAnimals? But then, how do you deal with Mammals and Reptiles? Maybe you can make HasLegs an interface, but then you can give a Plant a leg. Scala to the rescue.

You've already seen that traits can implement methods. Additionally, traits can have rules about what kind of classes and other traits they can be mixed into. Further, you can declare method parameters that are a consolidation of types, such as:

```
def foo(bar: Baz with Blarg with FruitBat)
```

Only instances of classes that extend Baz, Blarg, and FruitBat may be passed into this method.

```
abstract class LivingThing
abstract class Plant extends LivingThing
abstract class Fungus extends LivingThing
abstract class Animal extends LivingThing
```

Good so far. A LivingThing must be a plant, fungus, or animal. But, what about legs? Who can have legs?

```
trait HasLegs extends Animal:
  def walk() = println("Walking")
```

The HasLegs trait extends Animal. But Animal is a class, so what does it mean for a trait to extend a class? It means that the compiler will only let you mix HasLegs into something that subclasses from Animal. Thus, you've defined that only animals have legs, but any type of animal can have legs. It's the same for HasWings.

```
trait HasWings extends Animal:
  def flap() = println("Flap Flap")
```

But only things with wings can fly. This is a different notation. You define the rules of the self type with this: HasWings =>. The compiler flags an error if this trait is not mixed into a class that also extends HasWings. So, you can use self types to define the rules for what classes a given trait can be mixed into.[1]

```
trait Flies:
  this: HasWings => def fly()  = println("I'm flying")
```

---

[1] Self types can also be used to discover at compile time what class a trait has been mixed into. See http://www.scala-lang.org/node/124.

And Birds have wings and legs:

```
abstract class Bird extends Animal with HasWings with HasLegs
```

One little comment before you continue: You can use the keyword with or the comma to concatenate more than one trait. They work in the same way.

```
abstract class Bird extends Animal, HasWings, HasLegs
```

Let's define a couple of different Birds:

```
class Robin extends Bird with Flies
class Ostrich extends Bird
```

All mammals have a bodyTemperature.

```
abstract class Mammal extends Animal:
  def bodyTemperature: Double
```

Some animals know their name, and if they do, they respond to their name.

```
trait KnowsName extends Animal:
  def name: String
```

So, in the following code, a Dog is a Mammal that has legs and knows (responds to) its name.

```
class Dog(val name: String) extends Mammal with HasLegs with KnowsName:
  def bodyTemperature: Double = 99.3
```

Some cats and children are known as mammals that know their names but sometimes ignore their names.

```
trait IgnoresName:
  this: KnowsName => def ignoreName(when: String): Boolean

  def currentName(when: String): Option[String] =
    if ignoreName(when) then None else Some(name)
```

Now you can define a Cat class that has legs, knows its name, and ignores its name except at dinner time.

```
class Cat(val name: String) extends Mammal with HasLegs with KnowsName with
IgnoresName:
  def ignoreName(when: String) =
      when match
        case "Dinner" => false
        case _ => true

  def bodyTemperature: Double = 99.5
```

Some Animals can be Athletes, and Runners are Athletes with legs:

```
trait Athlete extends Animal
```

Here is a Runner trait:

```
trait Runner:
  this: Athlete with HasLegs => def run() = println("I'm running")
```

A Person is a Mammal with legs and knows its name:

```
class Person(val name: String) extends Mammal with HasLegs with KnowsName:
  def bodyTemperature: Double = 98.6
```

A Biker is a Person but may only be added to an Athlete:

```
trait Biker extends Person:
  this: Athlete=> def ride() = println("I'm riding my bike")
```

And finally, let's define some Genders.

```
trait Gender
trait Male extends Gender
trait Female extends Gender
```

You've defined a complex hierarchy of classes and traits. Let's see what you can do with these classes. First, let's try to create a Dog that's also a Biker:

```
scala> val bikerDog = new Dog("biker") with Athlete with Biker
-- Error:
```

```
1 |val bikerDog = new Dog("biker") with Athlete with Biker
  |                     ^^^^^
  |                             illegal trait inheritance: superclass
  |                             Dog does not derive from trait Biker's
  |                             superclass Person
```

Cool, the compiler enforced your rule about Bikers needing to be Persons. Let's create some valid LivingThings. Please note that you can combine different traits as part of the object creation. So, archer is an instance of a class that is a subclass of Dog that implements Athlete, Runner, and Male. The Scala compiler automatically creates this new, anonymous class for you.

```
scala> val archer = new Dog("archer") with Athlete with Runner with Male
archer: Dog with Athlete with Runner with Male = $anon$1@18bbc98

scala> val dpp = new Person("David") with Athlete with Biker with Male
dpp: Person with Athlete with Biker with Male = $anon$1@7b5617

scala> val john = new Person("John") with Athlete with Runner with Male
john: Person with Athlete with Runner with Male = $anon$1@cd927d

scala> val annette = new Person("Annette") with Athlete with Runner
with Female
annette: Person with Athlete with Runner with Female = $anon$1@1ec41c0
```

You've got a bunch of Animals. Let's see what you can do with them.

```
scala> def goBiking(b: Biker) = println(b.name + " is biking")
goBiking: (Biker)Unit
scala> goBiking(dpp)
David is biking
```

What happens if you try to send Annette on a bike ride?

```
scala> goBiking(annette)
-- Error:
1 |goBiking(annette)
  |         ^^^^^^^
  |         Found:    (annette : Person & Athlete & (Runner & Female))
  |         Required: Biker
```

This makes sense. The method requires a Biker, and Annette is not a Biker. However, just as you can compose a class out of traits, you can require that a class implement more than one trait in order to be the parameter to a method.

```scala
scala> def charityRun(r: Person with Runner) = r.run()
charityRun: (Person with Runner)Unit
```

The charityRun method can only be called with a parameter that is a subclass of Person and also implements the Runner trait.

```scala
scala> charityRun(annette)
I'm running
```

What if you try to call the method with a Runner that is not a Person?

```scala
 scala> charityRun(archer)
<console> :7: error: type mismatch;
found     : Dog with Athlete with Runner with Male
required  : Person with Runner
       charityRun(archer)
```

You can define the parameter in terms of traits. The womensRun method may only be called with a parameter that's both a Runner and a Female.

```scala
scala> def womensRun(r: Runner with Female) = r.run()
womensRun: (Runner with Female)Unit
scala> womensRun(annette)
I'm running
scala> val madeline = new Cat("Madeline") with Athlete with Runner
with Female
madeline: Cat with Athlete with Runner with Female = $anon$1@11dde0c
scala> womensRun(madeline)
I'm running
```

In this way, you've modeled complex relationships. You've modeled things in a way that you cannot do with Java. Scala's compositional rules are very powerful tools for defining complex class hierarchies and for specifying the rules for composing classes as well as the rules for passing parameters into methods. In this way, you can make sure that the charityRun method can only be called with valid parameters rather than testing for parameter correctness at runtime and throwing an exception if the parameter is not correct. This increased modeling flexibility combined with enhanced type safety gives the architect another tool to help developers write correct code.

Conflicts of Method Names

Everything looks great using traits, but what happens if you extend from two different traits that contain the same method? To see this problem with one example, let's create two traits:

```
scala> trait TraitOne:
     |     def text = "One"
// defined trait TraitOne
scala> trait TraitTwo:
     |     def text = "Two"
// defined trait TraitTwo
```

Now, create a class that extends from both traits and sees what happens.

```
scala> class Concrete extends TraitOne with TraitTwo
1 |class Concrete extends TraitOne with TraitTwo
  |       ^
  |     class Concrete inherits conflicting members:
  |       method text in trait TraitOne of type => String  and
  |       method text in trait TraitTwo of type => String
  |     (Note: this can be resolved by declaring an override in class
  |     Concrete.)
```

The error that appears in the console tries to explain that the compiler can't decide which implementation of the method to use. There are ways to solve this problem. One of them is to override the method and define the behavior.

```
scala> class Concrete extends TraitOne with TraitTwo:
     |     override def text = "Class"
// defined class Concrete
```

This solution compiles, but you lose the behavior of the methods that exist in both traits. To solve this problem, you can create new methods that call the methods of the traits using super.

```
scala> class Concrete extends TraitOne with TraitTwo:
     |      override def text = "Class"
     |      def textOne = super[TraitOne].text
     |      def textTwo = super[TraitTwo].text
// defined class Concrete
```

Now see what happens when you create an instance of the Concrete class.

```
scala> val con = Concrete()
val con: Concrete = Concrete@269bf0ac
scala> con.text
val res0: String = Class
scala> con.textOne
val res1: String = One
scala> con.textTwo
val res2: String = Two
```

One last comment: This problem only occurs when the methods of both traits have the same name, parameters, and return. If some of them are different, the problem won't appear because the compiler detects that they are different methods.

Limiting the Use of a Trait

Sometimes when you create a certain trait, you want it to only be used in a specific situation. To solve this problem, there are two different approaches: one limits access to the class/trait that extends from another one, and the other option is where the class/trait has a specific method.

Limiting Access by Class

The idea of this type of limitation is that only the class/trait that contains certain traits can use it. Let's see this concept with a concrete example.

```
scala> trait Engine:
     |     val enable = true
// defined trait Engine

scala> trait Vehicle:
     |     this: Engine => def drive = println("driving")
// defined trait Vehicle
```

In the example, all classes/traits that extend from this trait need to extend to Engine. If not, an exception appears.

```
scala> class Car extends Vehicle
1 |class Car extends Vehicle
  |       ^
  |       illegal inheritance: self type Car of class Car does not conform
  |       to self type Engine
  |       of parent trait Vehicle
```

If you modify the previous definition of the class Car and extend from Vehicle and Engine, everything works fine.

```
scala> class Car extends Vehicle, Engine
// defined class Car
```

This type of limitation appears in the examples in the section "Using Traits as Mixins."

Limiting Access by Method

Let's see the way to limit the use to only classes/traits that have a particular method. First, create a trait with the definition of the method.

```
scala> trait Vehicle:
     |     this: {def drive(): Unit} => println("drive")
```

Now create a class named Car that does not contain the method drive to see what happens.

```
scala> class Car extends Vehicle:
     |        def notDrive(): Unit = println("drive")
1 |class Car extends Vehicle:
     |        ^
     |        illegal inheritance: self type Car of class Car does not conform
     |        to self type Object{drive(): Unit}
     |        of parent trait Vehicle
```

If you define the method with the same structure that appears in the trait, everything works.

```
scala> class Car extends Vehicle:
     |        def drive(): Unit = println("drive")
// defined class Car
```

Type Parameters or Type Members

Traits offers a way to write code that you can use in any generic type or with certain types that cover one condition. A practical example of this is to imagine that you want to print the status of all components. The following example shows how you can do it:

```
scala> class Component:
     |        override def toString = "enable"
     |
     | trait Status[A]:
     |     def status(a: A): Unit = println(a.toString)
     |
     | class Screen extends Status[Component]
```

In the example, the Screen class defines which types support the status to print the status. Let's see what happens when you invoke the method:

```
scala> val screen = Screen()
val screen: Screen = Screen@61dd1c3d
scala> val component = Component()
```

```
val component: Component = enable
scala> screen.status(component)
enable
```

Passing Parameters on Traits

Scala 3 lets you pass parameters in the constructor like an abstract class, so you can pass parameters from the concrete class to a trait.

```
scala> trait Vehicle(val model: String):
     |       override def toString = s"model: $model"
     |
     | class Car(override val model:String) extends Vehicle(model):
     |       override def toString = "car's " + super.toString()
// defined trait Vehicle
// defined class Car
```

Now if you create an instance of the class Car with any value, you can use the value that saves it in the constructor of the trait from the class.

```
scala> val car = Car("C4")
scala> println(car.toString())
car's model: C4
```

Enumerations

Enumerations (enums) are not a new feature in Scala 3. In fact, they exist in Scala 2 but they are not simple to use, so many developers do not use them a lot. This was one of the main reasons why Martin Odersky and Scala's team decided to refactor the entire feature to give it a new face.

So what is an enumeration? An enumeration is a way to group a set of contents that have the same relationship. An example of the use of enumeration is information that has certain defined values in a person like gender or marital status.

```
enum Genre:
    case MALE, FEMALE, NO_BINARY

enum MaritalStatus:
    case SINGLE, MARRIED, DIVORCED
```

The way to define an enumeration is simple. You only need to use the keyword enum. To specify the possible values, you need to use the keyword case.

Now is time to use this constant in a simple way. Let's create a class named Person that has two parameters in the constructor.

```
scala> val anna = Person(Genre.FEMALE, MaritalStatus.SINGLE) ass
Person(genre: Genre, maritalStatus: MaritalStatus):
    override def toString() = s"Genre: $genre - Marital status:
    $maritalStatus"
```

The next step is to create an instance of the class, passing the values, and to print the result.

```
scala> val anna = Person(Genre.FEMALE, MaritalStatus.SINGLE)
val anna: Person = Genre: FEMALE - Marital status: SINGLE
scala> println(anna.toString())
Genre: FEMALE - Marital status: SINGLE
```

Having all possible values in one place is great but what happens if you don't want to persist the entire String in the database? To solve this problem, enums let you pass variables that represent one value. Let's change the Gender enum to show each possible value.

```
enum Genre(val code: Int):
    case MALE extends Genre(1)
    case FEMALE extends Genre(2)
    case NO_BINARY extends Genre(3)
```

If you want to know the code of one of the values of the enum, you only need to call the field code.

```
scala> println(Genre.MALE.code)
1
```

Enums give you by default a set of methods or operations to interact with the values. They are shown in Table 7-2.

Table 7-2. *Enumeration Operations*

Method	Description	Example
ordinal	A unique integer associated with each possible value that appears	`scala> println(Genre.MALE.ordinal)` `0`

values	To obtain as an Array all possible values	`scala> Genre.values`
		`val res0: Array[Genre] =`
		`Array(MALE, FEMALE, NO_BINARY)`

fromOrdinal	Obtains the value in the enum from an ordinal position	`scala> Genre.fromOrdinal(2)` `val res1: Genre = NO_BINARY`
valueOf	Obtains the value in the enum from a string	`scala> Genre.valueOf("MALE")` `val res2: Genre = MALE`

Note that enums in Scala are not the same as in Java. It is the same situation that happens with collections, so to obtain great performance, try to not use it.

The way to use an enum from Java is to extend and parametrize with the type.

```
scala> enum Genre extends Enum[Genre]:
     |     case MALE, FEMALE, NO_BINARY
// defined class Genre
```

As you can see, enumerations can help reduce duplicate code or keep all possible values of something in one place. Try to use them only when you have a finite and small number of values.

Algebraic Data Types in Enums

ADT (algebraic data types) is a classification where you can define a set of values enumerating all the values that it contains. Enums support the use of ADTs and add specific methods. Let's see this concept with a simple example.

```scala
scala> enum Options[+T]:
     |    case Some(x: T)
     |    case None
// defined class Options
```

As you can see, `Options` is a parametrized enum with two simple cases. The way to use it is simple, as with any common enum.

```scala
scala> Options.Some(1)
val res6: Options[Int] = Some(1)
```

```scala
scala> Options.None
val res7: Options[Nothing] = None
```

You can create a custom method to interact with the different values, as you do with a common enumeration.

```scala
scala> enum Options[+T]:
     |       case Some(x: T)
     |       case None
     |
     |       def isDefined: Boolean = this match
     |         case None => false
     |         case _      => true
     |
// defined class Options
```

The way to invoke the method in the enumeration is simple. You just call the method of a particular value.

```scala
scala> Options.None.isDefined
val res8: Boolean = false
```

Union and Intersection Types

These are new features that appear in Scala 3 to combine different things.

Union types let you receive, return, or interact in some way with different types. Let's see this concept with a practical example. Create a method that returns two possible types depending on one parameter.

```scala
scala> class Car
     | class Boat
scala> def createVehicle(vehicleType: Int): Car | Boat =
     |     vehicleType match
     |         case 1 => Car()
     |         case _ => Boat()
def createVehicle(vehicleType: Int): Car | Boat
```

Note that the order of classes in the union type does not have a particular constraint. You can invert the order and the code will perform the same way.

```scala
scala> def createVehicle(vehicleType: Int): Boat | Car =
     |     vehicleType match
     |         case 1 => Car()
     |         case _ => Boat()
def createVehicle(vehicleType: Int): Boat | Car
```

When you invoke the method and pass the parameters, you get the concrete instance of one particular class.

```scala
scala> val vehicle = createVehicle(1)
val vehicle: Car | Boat = Car@11ce721f
```

Union types are ideal when you need to return or pass more than one type, but when more types are added to the code, the complexity grows.

Intersection types are not so different from union types. The idea behind the intersection type is to combine the functionality of two or more different types.

```scala
scala> trait Printable:
     |     def print() =
     |         println("print")
     |
```

```
| trait Status:
|     def isEnable() =
|         println("isEnable")
|
| class Component extends Printable, Status
|
| def checkComponent(x: Printable & Status) =
|     x.print()
|     x.isEnable()
// defined trait Printable
// defined trait Status
// defined class Component
def checkComponent(x: Printable & Status): Unit
```

In the example, checkComponent needs to receive something that contains both traits to use the methods inside. This approach is a good way to not directly specify one concrete class or another trait. It says, "Send me something that contains both traits."

Now let's see what happens when you create an instance of the class Component.

```
scala> val component = Component()
scala> checkComponent(component)
print
isEnable
```

As you can see, everything works well, but if you send something that does not cover both traits, an exception will appear.

```
scala> class Button extends Printable
scala> val button = Button()
scala> checkComponent(button)
1 |checkComponent(button)
  |               ^^^^^^
  |              Found:    (button : Button)
  |              Required: Printable & Status
```

Summary

This chapter shows how traits work and how to use them. You saw how a trait encapsulates method and field definitions, which can then be reused by mixing them into classes. You saw that traits are similar to multiple inheritances, but they avoid some of the difficulties of multiple inheritances.

In this chapter, you explored the advantages of enumerations in Scala to reduce the complexity when you have several values connected in some way. Also, you learned different ways to combine methods or parameters in the code using union and intersection types.

CHAPTER 8

Scala Type System

The two fundamental design considerations of a programming language are static versus dynamic typing and strong versus weak typing. Types in a programming language are checked at compile time and can be inferred by a compiler. Scala is a strong and statically typed language with a unified type system.

In static typing, a variable is bound to a particular type. In dynamic typing, the type is bound to the value instead of the variable. Scala and Java are statically typed languages, whereas JavaScript, Python, Groovy, and Ruby are dynamically typed languages.

If a type is static and strongly typed, every variable must have a definite type. If a type is dynamic and strongly typed, every value must have a definite type. However, in the case of weak typing, a definite type is not defined. Scala, Java, and Ruby are principally strongly typed languages. Some languages, such as C and Perl, are weakly typed.

Scala is the best of both worlds, in that it feels like a dynamically typed language, because of type inference, and at the same time, it gives you all the benefits of static typing in terms of an advanced object model and an advanced type system.

This chapter explores ideas such as which type parameters should be covariant, contravariant, or invariant under subtyping, using `implicit` judiciously, and so forth.

Unified Type System

Scala has a unified type system, enclosed by the type `Any` at the top of the hierarchy and the type `Nothing` at the bottom of the hierarchy, as illustrated in Figure 8-1. All Scala types inherit from `Any`. The subtypes of `Any` are `AnyVal` (value types, such as Int and Boolean) and `AnyRef` (reference types, as in Java). As you can see in Figure 8-1, the primitive types of Java are enclosed under `AnyVal` and, unlike Java, you can define your own `AnyVal`. And also unlike Java, Scala does not have wrapper types, such as Integer, to be distinguished from primitive types, such as int.

© David Pollak, Vishal Layka, and Andres Sacco 2022
D. Pollak et al., *Beginning Scala 3*, https://doi.org/10.1007/978-1-4842-7422-4_8

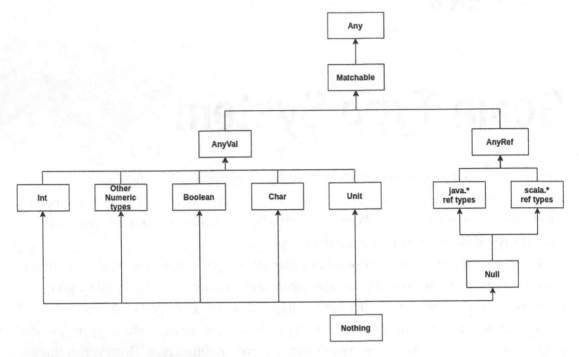

Figure 8-1. *Unified object model*

As you can see in Figure 8-1, Any is a supertype of both AnyRef and AnyVal. AnyRef corresponds to java.lang.Object and is the supertype of all objects. AnyVal, on the other hand, represents the value, such as int and other JVM primitives. Because of this hierarchy, it becomes possible to define methods that take Any, thus being compatible with both scala.Int instances as well as java.lang.String, as shown here:

```
scala> import scala.collection.mutable.ListBuffer
import scala.collection.mutable.ListBuffer
scala> val list = ListBuffer[Any]()
list: scala.collection.mutable.ListBuffer[Any] = ListBuffer()
scala> val x= 2
x: Int = 2
scala> list += x
res12: list.type = ListBuffer(2)
scala> class Book
defined class Book
scala> list += new Book()
res13: list.type = ListBuffer(2, Book@15e8485)
```

You can limit a method to only be able to work on Value types, as seen here:

```
def test(int: AnyVal) = ()
test(5)
test(5.12)
test(new Object)
```

In this code, test(5) takes an Int that extends AnyVal, and test(5.12) takes a Double that also extends AnyVal. Test(new Object) takes an Object that extends AnyRef. Refer to Figure 8-1. Test(new Object) fails to compile.

```
scala> def test(int: AnyVal) = ()
test: (int: AnyVal)Unit
scala> test(5)
scala> test(5.12)
scala> test(new Object)
<console>:9: error: type mismatch;
-- Error:
1 |test(new Object)
  |     ^^^^^^^^^^
  |the result of an implicit conversion must be more specific than AnyVal
```

The idea is that this method will only take Value classes, be it Int or your own Value type. This implies that Java code is not as type-safe as Scala code. You're probably thinking, "But Java is a statically typed language. Doesn't it give me all the safety that Scala does?" The answer is no. Take a look at the following code and spot the problem:

```
public class Bad {
    public static void main(String[] argv) {
        Object[] a = argv;
        a[0] = new Object();
    }
}
```

This is legal Java code, and here's what happens when you run the code:

```
> java Bad Hello
Exception in thread "main" java.lang.ArrayStoreException: java.lang.Object
at Bad.main(Bad.java:4)
```

Java allows you to assign a `String[]` to `Object[]` because a `String` is a subclass of `Object`, so if the array was read-only, the assignment would make sense. However, the array can be modified. The modification demonstrated shows one of Java's "type-unsafety" features. We'll discuss why this happened and the complex topic of invariant, covariant, and contravariant types later in this chapter. Let's start looking at how Scala makes the architect's job easier and also makes the coder's job easier.

Type Parameterization

Scala's parameterized types are similar to generics in Java. If you are familiar with Java or C#, you might already have some understanding of parameterized types. Scala's parametrized types provide the same features as Java generics, but with extended functionalities.

Note   Classes and traits that take type parameters are called generic; the types they generate are called parameterized types.

One straightforward syntactical difference is that Scala uses square brackets ([...]), while Java uses angle brackets (<...>). For example, a list of strings would be declared as shown here:

```
val list : List[String] = List("A", "B", "C")
```

Scala allows angle brackets to be used in the method name. So, to avoid ambiguities, Scala uses square brackets for parameterized types.

Types in Scala are used to define classes, abstract classes, traits, objects, and functions. Type parameterization lets you make them generic. As an example, `Sets` can be defined as generic in the following manner: `Set[T]`. However, unlike Java which allows raw types, in Scala you are required to specify type parameters. That is to say, `Set[T]` is a trait but not a type because it takes a type parameter.

As a result, you cannot create variables of type `Set`.

```
scala> def test(s: Set) ={}
-- Error:
1 |def test(s: Set) ={}
  |            ^^^
  |            Missing type parameter for Set
```

Instead, trait Set enables you to specify parameterized types, such as Set[String], Set[Int], or Set[AnyRef].

```scala
scala> def test(s: Set[AnyRef]) = {}
def test(s: Set[AnyRef]): Unit
```

For example, trait Set defines a generic set where the specific sets are Set[Int] and Set[String] and so forth. Thus, Set is a trait and Set[String] is a type. The Set is a generic trait.

Note   In Scala, List, Set, and so on can also be referred to as type constructors because they are used to create specific types. You can construct a type by specifying a type parameter. For example, List is the type constructor for List[String] and List[String] is a type. While Java allows raw types, Scala requires that you specify type parameters and does not allow you to use just a List in the place of a type, as it's expecting a real type—not a type constructor.

In light of inheritance, type parameters raise an important question regarding whether Set[String] should be considered a subtype of Set[AnyRef]. That is, if S is a subtype of type T, then should Set[S] be considered a subtype of Set[T]? Next, you will learn a generic type concept that defines the inheritance relation and answers the aforementioned question.

Variance

Variance defines inheritance relationships of parameterized types, which brings to light whether a Set[String], for example, is a subtype of Set[AnyRef]. A declaration like class Set[+A] means that Set is parameterized by a type A. The + is called a variance annotation.

Variance is an important and challenging concept. It defines the rules by which parameterized types can be passed as parameters. In the beginning of the chapter, we showed how passing a String[] (Java notation) to a method expecting an Object[] can cause problems. Java allows you to pass an array of something to a method expecting an array of something's superclass. This is called covariance. On the surface, this makes a lot of sense. If you can pass a String to a method expecting an Object, why can't you pass an Array[String] (Scala notation) to a method expecting an Array[Object]? Because Array is mutable; it can be written to in addition to being read from, so a method that takes an Array[Object] may modify the Array by inserting something that cannot be inserted into an Array[String].

Defining the type variance for type parameters allows you to control how parameterized types can be passed to methods. The variance comes in three flavors: invariant, covariant, and contravariant. Type parameters can be individually marked as covariant or contravariant and are by default invariant. Variance in Scala is defined by using + and - signs in front of type parameters.

Covariant Parameter Types

Covariant parameter types are designated with a + before the type parameter. A covariant type is useful for read-only containers. Scala's List is defined as List[+T], which means that it's covariant on type T. List is covariant because if you pass a List[String] to a method that expects a List[Any], then every element of the List satisfies the requirement that is an Any and you cannot change the contents of the List. Figure 8-2 gives a very clear picture of covariance, such as if S extends T, then Class[S] extends Class[T].

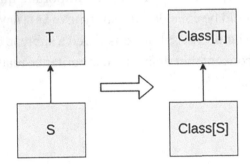

Figure 8-2. *Covariance in Scala*

Tip   Covariance: If S extends T then Class[S] extends Class[T].

Let's define an immutable class, Getable. Once an instance of Getable is created, it cannot change, so you can mark its type, T, as covariant.

```
scala> class Getable[+T](val data: T)
defined class Getable
```

Let's define a method that takes a Getable[Any].

```scala
scala> def get(in: Getable[Any]) =
     |        println("It's "+in.data)
def get(in: Getable[Any]): Unit
```

You define an instance of Getable[String] here:

```scala
scala> val gs = Getable("String")
gs: Getable[java.lang.String] = Getable@10a69f0
```

You can call get with gs.

```scala
scala> get(gs)
It's String
```

Let's try the same example but pass a Getable[java.lang.Double] into something that expects a Getable[Number].

```scala
scala> def getNum(in: Getable[Number]) = in.data.intValue
getNum: (Getable[java.lang.Number])Int
scala> def gd = Getable(java.lang.Double.valueOf(33.3))
gd: Getable[java.lang.Double]
scala> getNum(gd)
res7: Int = 33
```

Yes, the covariance works the way you expect it to. You can make read-only classes covariant. This means that contravariance is good for write-only classes.

Contravariant Parameter Types

So, if covariance allows you to pass List[String] to a method that expects List[Any], what good is contravariance? Contravariance indicates if S extends T, then Class[T] extends Class[S], as illustrated in Figure 8-3.

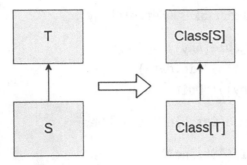

Figure 8-3. *Contravariance in Scala*

Tip   Contravariance: If S extends T, then `Class[T]` extends `Class[S]`.

Let's first look at a write-only class, `Putable`.

```
scala> class Putable[-T]:
     |     def put(in: T) =
     |         println("Putting "+in)
     |
// defined class Putable
```

Next, let's define a method that takes a `Putable[String]`.

```
scala> def writeOnly(in: Putable[String])=
     |     in.put("Hello")
def writeOnly(in: Putable[String]): Unit
```

And let's declare an instance of `Putable[AnyRef]`.

```
scala> val p = Putable[AnyRef]
val p: Putable[AnyRef] = Putable@fb79241
```

And what happens if you try to call `writeOnly`?

```
scala> writeOnly(p)
Putting Hello
```

Okay, so you can call a method that expects a `Putable[String]` with a `Putable[AnyRef]` because you are guaranteed to call the put method with a `String`, which is a subclass of `AnyRef`. Standing alone, this is not particularly valuable, but if you have a class that does something with input that results in output, the value of contravariance becomes obvious.

The inputs to a transformation are contravariant. Calling something that expects at least any `AnyRef` with a `String` is legal and valid. But the return value can be covariant because you expect to get back a number, so if you get an `Integer`, a subclass of `Numbers`, you're okay. Let's see how it works. You define DS with a contravariant `In` type and a covariant `Out` type.

```scala
scala> trait DS[-In, +Out]:
     |      def apply(i: In): Out
     |
// defined trait DS
```

Let's create an instance that will convert Any into an Int.

```scala
scala>  val t1 = new DS[Any, Int]{def apply(i: Any) = i.toString.toInt}
val t1: DS[Any, Int] = anon$1@430aae8e
```

After that, create a method that invoke apply method on the trait:

```scala
scala> def check(in: DS[String, Any]) = in("333")
def check(in: DS[String, Any]): Any
```

And you call to check with t1.

```scala
scala> check(t1)
res14: Any = 333
```

Invariant Parameter Types

In Scala, `Array[T]` is invariant. This means that you can only pass an `Array[String]` to `foo(a: Array[String])` and that you can only pass an `Array[Object]` to `bar(a: Array[Object])`. Figure 8-4 gives a clear picture of invariant parameter types.

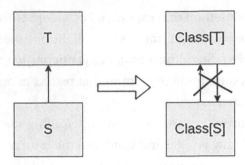

Figure 8-4. *Invariance in Scala*

This ensures that what is read from or written to the array is something of the correct type. So, for anything that's mutable, the type parameter should be invariant. You do this by doing nothing with the type parameter. So, let's define an invariant class.

```scala
class Holder[T](var data: T)
```

The class holds data of type T. Let's write a method.

```scala
scala> def add(in: Holder[Int])= in.data = in.data + 1
def add(in: Holder[Int]): Unit
scala> val h = Holder(0)
val h: Holder[Int] = Holder(0)
scala> add(h)
scala> h.data
val res1: Int = 1
```

Because the add method expects an Int to come out of Holder and puts an Int back into Holder, the type of Holder must be invariant. This does not mean that invariant containers lose their ability to hold subclasses of their declared type. Holder[Number] can contain a Double, and an Array[Object] can contain String, Integer, and so on. Let's put a Double into Holder[Number]:

```scala
scala> val nh = Holder[Number](33.3d)
val nh: Holder[Number] = Holder(33.3)
```

Now define a method that rounds the number.

```scala
scala> def round(in: Holder[Number]) =
     |      in.data = in.data.intValue
def round(in: Holder[Number]): Unit
```

Call the round method and let's see what you get out the other side.

```scala
scala> round(nh)
scala> nh.data
res16: java.lang.Number = 33
```

You put in a Number and got back a Number. What's the underlying class for Number?

```scala
scala> nh.data.getClass
res17: java.lang.Class[_] = class java.lang.Integer
```

An Integer is a subclass of Number, so you can put an Integer or a Double into Holder[Number]. You reserve the ability to use class hierarchies with invariant type parameters. Let's finally see what happens when you try to pass a Holder[Double] into round.

```scala
scala>  val dh = Holder(33.3d)
val dh: Holder[Double] = Holder(33.3)

scala> round(dh)
-- Error:
1 |round(dh)
  |      ^^
  |      Found:    (dh : Holder[Double])
  |      Required: Holder[Number]
```

So, invariant type parameters protect you when you have mutable data structures such as arrays.

Rules of Variance

So, you've successfully defined and used an invariant type. The invariant type was mutable, so it both returned and was called with a particular type. You created a covariant type that was an immutable holder of a value. Finally, you created a transformer that had contravariant input and covariant output. Wait, that sounds like a function. That's right, Scala's FunctionN traits have contravariant parameters and covariant results. This leads us to the simple rules of variance:

- Mutable containers should be invariant.

- Immutable containers should be covariant.

- Inputs to transformations should be contravariant, and outputs from transformations should be covariant.

Type Bounds

When defining a parameterized type, bounds allow you to place restrictions on type parameters. Thus, a bounded type is restricted to a specific type or its derived type.

Upper Type Bounds

An upper bound type is restricted to a specific type or one of its derived types. Scala provides the upper bound relation operator (<:), which you can use to specify an upper bound for a type.

The type parameter A <: AnyRef means any type A that is a subtype of AnyRef. The <: operator signifies that the type to the left of the <: operator must be a subtype of the type to the right of the <: operator. Moreover, the type on the left of the <: operator could be the same type as the right of the <: operator.

The type parameter A <: AnyRef means that the type to the left of the <: operator must be derived from the type to the right of the <: operator or the type to the left of the <: operator could be the same type as the right of the <: operator. In other words, the upper type bounds (and, as we will explain in the next section, lower type bounds) restrict the allowed types that can be used for a type parameter when instantiating a type from a parameterized type, as illustrated in the following code.

Trait Test:
```scala
def test[A <: AnyRef]: Unit
```

In the code above, the upper type bound says that any type used for parameter A must be a subtype of AnyRef.

The upper type bound is different from type variance in that type variance determines how actual types of the type are related, for example how the actual types List[AnyRef] and List[String] of the type List are related. Let's explore this with examples.

Define an Employee class hierarchy.

```scala
scala> class Employee (val name: String)
defined class Employee
scala> class Internal (name: String) extends Employee(name)
defined class Internal
scala> class FreeLancer(name: String) extends Employee(name)
defined class FreeLancer
scala> class Customer (name: String)
defined class Customer
```

Now define a function that takes a parameter with an upper bound.

```scala
scala> def employeeName [A <: Employee](emp: A) = println(emp.name)
def employeeName[A <: Employee](emp: A): Unit
```

Now test the employeeName.

```scala
scala> employeeName (Internal("Paul"))
Paul
```

Now test with FreeLancer.

```scala
scala> employeeName (FreeLancer("John"))
John
```

Now test with the Customer class.

```scala
scala> employeeName(Customer("Peter"))
-- Error:
1 |employeeName(Customer("Peter"))
  |             ^^^^^^^^^^^^^^^^^
```

```
|           Found:    Customer
|           Required: Employee
|
|           The following import might make progress towards fixing the
|           problem:
|
|               import collection.Searching.search
```

As you can see, because of the upper bound restriction, this code does not compile, as the Customer class is not a subtype of Employee.

Lower Type Bounds

A lower bound type is restricted to a specific type of its supertype. The type selected must be equal to or a supertype of the lower bound restriction. The following defines a lower type bound:

```
class A{
    type B >: List[Int]
    def someMethod(a : B) = a
}
```

You define type B inside class A to have a lower bound of List[Int]. You instantiate a variable st as a subtype of A as shown here:

```
scala> val st = A { type B = Traversable[Int] }
val st: A{B = Iterable[Int]} = anon$1@3ef3f661
```

You can call some method with a Set class. This is because Set, even if not a supertype of the List class, is a subtype of Traversable.

Extension Methods

Scala 2 lets you add new methods to some types using the keyword implicit, but in Scala 3, this feature has had modifications and now requires using two different keywords like using/given.

The following sections explain both approaches of the same feature. This is important because you may see Scala 2 code in some projects.

Scala 2 Implicit Class

Using types, especially when type inferencing makes them invisible, is simple and doesn't take a lot of thought away from the task at hand. Well-defined types and type interactions will stay out of the library consumer's way but will guard against program errors.

You've seen a little bit of stuff so far that looks like magic. The String class seems to have grown methods:

```scala
scala> "Hello".toList
res0: List[Char] = List(H, e, l, l, o)
```

You may be wondering how a Java class that is final could have additional methods on it. Well, Scala has a feature called an implicit conversion. If you have an instance of a particular type, and you need another type, and there's an implicit conversion in scope, Scala will call the implicit method to perform the conversion. For example, some date-related methods take Long and some take java.util.Date. It's useful to have conversions between the two. Let's create a method that calculates the number of days based on a Long containing a millisecond count.

```scala
scala> def millisToDays(in: Long): Int = (in / (1000L * 3600L * 24L)).toInt
```

You can calculate the number of days by passing a Long to the method.

```scala
scala> millisToDays(5949440999L)
res3: Int = 68
```

Let's try to pass a Date to the method.

```scala
scala> import java.util.Date
import java.util.Date
scala> millisToDays(Date().getTime())
val res2: Int = 18931
```

But sometimes it's valuable to convert between one type and another. We are used to the conversion in some contexts: Int ➤ Long, Int ➤ Double, and so on. Let's define a method that will automatically be called when you need the conversion.

```scala
scala> import scala.language.implicitConversions
scala> implicit def dateToLong(d: Date):Long = d.getTime
def dateToLong(d: java.util.Date): Long
```

And this allows you to call millisToDays with a Date instance.

```scala
scala> millisToDays(Date())
val res3: Int = 18931
```

You may think that implicit conversions are dangerous and reduce type safety. In some cases, this is true. You should be very careful with them, and their use should be an explicit design choice. However, sometimes implicit conversions (e.g., Int ➤ Long) are very valuable, such as when you have a method that takes a parameter that must be a Long.

```scala
scala> def m2[T <: Long](in: T): Int = (in / (1000L * 3600L * 24L)).toInt
def m2[T <: Long](in: T): Int
scala> m2(33.toLong)
res8: Int = 0
```

What is the scope of implicit? The Scala compiler considers an implicit in the current scope if

- The implicit is defined in the current class or in a superclass.

- The implicit is defined in a traitor super trait or is mixed into the current class or a superclass.

- The implicit is defined on the companion object of the current target class.

- The implicit is available on an object that has been imported into the current scope.

When designing libraries, be careful about defining implicits and make sure they are in as narrow a scope as is reasonable. When consuming libraries, make sure the implicits defined in the objects are narrow enough and are not going to cause problems such as getting stuff from every Option.

Implicit conversions are powerful tools and potentially very dangerous. We mean wicked dangerous. Back in the day, we put the following implicit into a library:

```
implicit def oToT[T](in: Option[T]): T = in.get
```

This was convenient, very convenient. We no longer had to test `Options`. We just passed them around, and they were converted from an `Option` to their underlying type. And when we removed the implicit, we had 150 code changes to make. That was 150 latent defects. Using implicits to convert to a class that has a particular method is a good reason. There's very little likelihood of damage.

```
scala> implicit def oToT[T](in: Option[T]): T = in.get
def oToT[T](in: Option[T]): T
```

Until Scala 2.10, implicit conversion was handled by implicit `def` methods that took the original instance and returned a new instance of the desired type. Implicit methods have been supplanted by implicit classes, which provide a safer and more limited scope for converting existing instances.

Scala 2.10 introduced a new feature called implicit classes. An implicit class is a class marked with the `implicit` keyword. This keyword makes the class's primary constructor available for implicit conversions when the class is in scope.

To create an implicit class, simply place the `implicit` keyword in front of an appropriate class. Here's an example:

```
scala> object Helper:
     |     implicit class Greeting(val x: Int):
     |         def greet = "Hello " + x
     |
// defined object Helper
```

To use this class, just import it into the scope and call the greet method.

```
scala> import Helper._
scala> println(3.greet)
Hello 3
```

For an implicit class to work, its name must be in scope and unambiguous, like any other implicit value or conversion.

Implicit classes have the following restrictions:

- They must be defined inside another trait/class/object.

```
object Helpers:
    implicit class RichInt(x: Int) // OK!

implicit class RichDouble(x: Double) // WRONG!
```

- They may only take one non-implicit argument in their constructor.

```
implicit class RichDate(date: java.util.Date) // OK!
implicit class Indexer[T](collecton: Seq[T], index: Int)
// WRONG!
implicit class Indexer[T](collection: Seq[T])(implicit
index: Index) // OK!
```

While it's possible to create an implicit class with more than one non-implicit argument, such classes aren't used during implicit lookup.

- There may not be any method, member, or object in scope with the same name as the implicit class. This means an implicit class cannot be a case class.

```
object Bar
implicit class Bar(x: Int) // WRONG!
val x = 5
implicit class x(y: Int) // WRONG!
implicit case class Baz(x: Int) // WRONG!
```

Scala 3 Given/Using Clauses

As you read at the beginning of this section, the feature of implicit introduces some changes in Scala 3 which differ from the previous version. In the following sections, you will see some of them.

Implicit Conversions

This feature reduces the complexity, but it does not disappear completely. Let's see an example that takes a Double and converts it into a new type.

```
scala> import scala.language.implicitConversions
     |
     | case class Euros(amount: Double):
     |     override def toString = f"$$$amount%.2f"
     |
     | given Conversion[Double,Euros] = d => Euros(d)
// defined case class Euros
lazy val given_Conversion_Double_Euros: Conversion[Double, Euros]
scala> given_Conversion_Double_Euros(3)
val res7: Euros = $3.00
```

Take into consideration that you can create more than one implicit conversion using given. One last thing: You can continue using the mechanism of `implicit` at least in version 3.0.1 but consider migrating these functionalities to the new version of the feature because Scala will deprecate some functionalities that are not supported in the latest version.

There are some considerations when using this feature:

- You can't chain the use of given to transform into something intermediate. You can only convert from one type to another one.

- You can only use the conversion declared in the same scope.

Givens and Imports

As you read in the previous section, one of the restrictions of the use of given sentences is the need to be in the same scope. Scala 3 offers a way to import and include in the same scope.

```
object A:
    val name = "o"
    def hello(s: String) = s"$s, hello from $name"
    class A1
    class A2
```

```
class A3
given a1: A1 = A1()
given a2: A2 = A2()
given a3: A3 = A3()
```

Let's see some possible ways to import the given sentences:

```
import A.{given _} // Imports ONLY the givens
import A.{given a1} // Imports explicitly a1
import A.{given _, _} // Imports everything in A
import A._ // Imports everything EXCEPT the givens
import A.*       // Imports everything EXCEPT the givens
import A.given   // Imports ONLY the givens
```

Using this type of import, you can declare in an explicit way which things you need to use in your classes or objects.

Using Clauses

In Scala, it is not necessary to explicitly pass parameters to a method. In previous version of Scala, this functionality is connected directly with `implicit`, but in Scala 3.x.x, the same functionality has a new keyword named `using`.

To explain this concept well, let's create some types of order.

```
trait Ord[T]:
  def compare(x: T, y: T): Int
  extension (x: T) def < (y: T) = compare(x, y) < 0
  extension (x: T) def > (y: T) = compare(x, y) > 0

given intOrd: Ord[Int] with
  def compare(x: Int, y: Int) =
    if x < y then -1 else if x > y then +1 else 0

given listOrd[T](using ord: Ord[T]): Ord[List[T]] with

  def compare(xs: List[T], ys: List[T]): Int = (xs, ys) match
    case (Nil, Nil) => 0
    case (Nil, _) => -1
    case (_, Nil) => +1
```

```
  case (x :: xs1, y :: ys1) =>
    val fst = ord.compare(x, y)
    if fst != 0 then fst else compare(xs1, ys1)
```

Now create a method that receives numbers and, depending on the type of order, obtains the maximum value.

```
def max[T](x: T, y: T)(using ord: Ord[T]): T =
  if ord.compare(x, y) < 0 then y else x
```

As you can see, your method receives two parameters of the same type and does not use a specific type of Ord, which you can define when you invoke another part of the code.

```
scala> max(1, 9)(using intOrd)
val res8: Int = 9
scala> max(List(2,5, 1), List(1,2,3))(using listOrd)
val res11: List[Int] = List(2, 5, 1)
```

Summary

In this chapter, you learned Scala's rules about variance, type bounds, and given/using classes.

CHAPTER 9

Scala and Java Interoperability

This chapter describes how Scala is translated to Java and the use of Java annotations in the Scala framework. The goal of this chapter is to show you how easily you can integrate Scala with Java. You'll also learn how Scala annotations help in integration, such as when generating JavaBean-style getters and setters.

Scala at a Glance

One of the main design goals of Scala is to run on a JVM and provide interoperability with Java. The need for Scala and Java interoperability arises when you want to use existing Java libraries or frameworks. Scala code is often used in tandem with large Java programs and frameworks. Even though integration with Java is easy for the most part, we encourage you to use pure Scala as much as possible. When you are working with a Java library or framework, first try to find something equivalent in Scala. Use Java if there's no equivalent Scala library available.

Scala is compiled to Java bytecodes, and you can use tools like Java class file disassembler `javap` to disassemble bytecodes generated by the Scala compiler. By running on a JVM you can take advantage of all the frameworks and tools built into other JVM languages. In most cases, Scala features are translated into Java features so that Scala can easily integrate with Java. However, some Scala features don't directly map to Java, and in such a case, you have to learn how to handle features that are available in Java but not in Scala. The features that are available in Java but not in Scala are static members and checked exceptions. An example of a Scala feature that is not available in Java is traits. If you are using Java from Scala, you have to deal with mutability, exceptions, and nulls that are interdicted in the Scala world. Because Scala works seamlessly with Java, most of the time you can combine the languages without worrying too much.

Note that the Long Term Support (LTS) version of Java at the time of writing is 11, which means new features could appear in new versions of Java which are compatible in some way with Scala.

Translating Java Classes to Scala Classes

The interoperability between Scala classes and Java classes makes it straightforward to replace or extend an existing Java class with a Scala class. The following code shows a class declaration in Java.

```
public class Book {}
```

Here is the Scala code:

```
class Book
```

As you learned in Chapter 3, you don't need braces when there's no content and everything is public in Scala by default.

Now define a Java class with a constructor that binds instance variables with accessors.

```
public class Book {
  private final int isbn;
  private final String title;

  public Book(int isbn, String title) {
    this.isbn = isbn;
    this.title = title;
  }

  public int getIsbn() {
    return isbn;
  }

  public String getTitle() {
    return title;
  }
}
```

As you can see, the constructor binds the instance variables `isbn` and `title` with accessors `getIsbn` and `getTitle`. Let's see the Scala equivalent.

```
class Book(val isbn: Int, val title: String)
```

In version 14 or up in Java, records make an appearance, which reduce a lot this code, making it similar to the code in Scala. The only thing you need to consider is that the record can't be extended in any way.

```
public record Book (int isbn, String title) {}
```

As you can see in the Scala code above, adding `val` makes the constructor arguments bind to a field of the same name. The following code shows the Java class `NonFiction` with a constructor that calls the superclass:

```
public class NonFiction extends Book {
  public NonFiction(int isbn, String title) {
    super(isbn, title);
  }
}
```

Here is the Scala equivalent:

```
class NonFiction (isbn: Int, title: String) extends Book(isbn, title)
```

As you can see, the primary constructor goes in the declaration. What about the multiple constructors? You will see them in the section that follows. Let's compare the mutable and immutable instance variables in Java and Scala. This code illustrates the mutable instance variable in Java:

```
public class Book {
  private String title = "Beginning Scala";

  public String getTitle() {
    return title;
  }

  public void setTitle(String t) {
title = t;
  }
}
```

This code illustrates the Scala equivalent:

```
class Book:
  var  title = "Beginning Scala"
```

As you can see, just writing var in the class body defines a mutable field. Now let's see the immutable instance variables in Java and Scala. This code illustrates an immutable instance variable in Java:

```
public class Book {
  private final int isbn = 999;

  public int getIsbn() {
    return isbn;
  }
}
```

This code illustrates the Scala equivalent:

```
class Book:
  val isbn = 999
```

As you may have noticed, isbn is also the name of an accessor method.

Translating Java Imports into Scala Imports

Imports in both languages are similar; they only change some parts of the syntax. Scala introduces a feature that lets you only import specific classes of one package using braces, like other popular languages like Kotlin.

Java imports from different packages:

```
import com.modA.ClassA;
import com.modB.ClassB1;
import com.modB.ClassB2;
import com.modC.*;
```

The Scala equivalent:

```
import com.modA.ClassA;
import com.modB.{ClassB1, ClassB2} // You can stack multiple imports from
                                    the same package in braces.
import com.modC._ // Underscore in Scala imports is equivalent of * in
                  Java imports.
```

Translating Multiple Constructors

Let's now see how to translate multiple constructors while refactoring a Java class to a Scala class. For instance, take the Book Java class shown here:

```java
public class Book {
    private Integer isbn;
    private String title;

    public Book(Integer isbn) {
        this.isbn = isbn;
    }

    public Book(Integer isbn, String title) {
        this.isbn = isbn;
        this.title = title;
    }

    public Integer getIsbn() {
        return isbn;
    }

    public void setIsbn(Integer isbn) {
        this.isbn = isbn;
    }

    public String getTitle() {
        return title;
    }
```

```
    public void setTitle(String title) {
        this.title = title;
    }
}
```

As you can see, the Book Java class has two constructors, one that takes ISBN as the parameter and the other that takes ISBN and title as the parameters. The Book Java class also has getters and setters for title and ISBN. Now let's refactor the Book Java class into a Scala class with class parameters and create an instance.

```
class Book ( var isbn: Int, var title: String)
```

You can try this code in the REPL:

```
scala> class Book (var isbn: Int, var title: String)
defined class Book
scala> val book = new Book(999, "Beginning Scala") book: Book =
Book@10ddb0e
```

However, a constructor that takes only a single parameter, title, does not exist in the Scala definition. For example, if you create the Book instance with a constructor that takes a single title parameter, you will get an error in the REPL:

```
scala> new Book("Beginning Java")
1 |new Book("Beginning Java")
  |         ^^^^^^^^^^^^^^^^^
  |         Found:    ("Beginning Java" : String)
  |         Required: Int
```

To complete your refactoring of the Java class, you need an extra constructor.

```
class Book (var isbn: Int, var title: String):
    def this(title: String) = this(0, title)
```

Is this code comprehensible to you? As you may recall, any auxiliary constructor must immediately call another this(...) constructor and call the primary constructor to make sure all the parameters are initialized. You learned about auxiliary constructors in Chapter 3.

Now you can try the code in the REPL.

```
scala> class Book (var isbn: Int, var title: String):
     |      def this(title: String) = this(0, title)
defined class Book
scala> val book1 = new Book(999, "Beginning Scala")
book1: Book = Book@132c5fd
scala> val book2 = new Book("Beginning Java")
book2: Book = Book@3e4e8a
```

This time, you created an instance with the auxiliary constructor.

Now access title and ISBN in the REPL.

```
scala> book1.title
res38: String = Beginning Scala
scala> book2.title
res39: String = Beginning Java
scala> book1.isbn
res40: Int = 9999
```

You can also set title as following:

```
scala> book2.title = "Beginning Groovy"
book2.title: String = Beginning Groovy
scala> book2.title
res42: String = Beginning Groovy
```

So you can get and set title and ISBN. But if you compare the code with the extra constructor with the Java code showing the Book class at the beginning of this section, you will see that you did not add the corresponding getters and setters. But you can still get and set ISBN and title because of the generated getters and setters that follow the Scala convention. When you compile the code with the extra constructor with scalac and then disassemble it with javap, you'll see that no corresponding getter or setter methods are generated and the only getters and setters that are generated are the ones that follow the Scala convention as shown below:

```
$ scalac Book.scala
$ javap Book
```

Here is code compiled from Book.scala:

```
public class Book {
    public int isbn();
    public void isbn_$eq(int);
    public java.lang.String title();
    public void title_$eq(java.lang.String);
    public Book(int, java.lang.String);
    public Book(java.lang.String);
}
```

So the class definition generates getter and setters that follow Scala conventions but don't follow Java conventions. Generating getters and setters that follow Java conventions becomes important when you need to interact with a Java class or a library that accepts only classes that conform to the JavaBean specification. You will see this in the next section.

JavaBean Specification-Compliant Scala Classes

To ensure compatibility with Java frameworks, you may need Java-style getters and setters on the fields of your class to interact with a Java class or library that accepts only classes that conform to the JavaBean specification. To have Java-style getters and setters is to annotate the field with the scala.beans.BeanProperty, as shown in the following lines of code:

```
import scala.beans.BeanProperty
```

```
class Book(@BeanProperty var isbn:Int, @BeanProperty var title:String)
```

You can run this code in the REPL.

```
scala> import scala.beans.BeanProperty
import scala.beans.BeanProperty
scala> class Book(@BeanProperty var isbn:Int, @BeanProperty var
title:String)
defined class Book
```

You can see how the @BeanProperty annotation works by compiling the Book class and then disassembling it. First, it saves these contents to a file named Book.scala and then compiles the class.

```
$ scalac Book.scala
```

After it's compiled, it's disassembled with the javap command.

```
$ javap Book
```

This code shows the compiled Book class from Book.scala:

```
public class Book {
  public Book(int, java.lang.String);
  public int getIsbn();
  public void setIsbn(int);
  public java.lang.String getTitle();
  public void setTitle(java.lang.String);
  public int isbn();
  public void isbn_$eq(int);
  public java.lang.String title();
  public void title_$eq(java.lang.String);
}
```

As you can see from the disassembled code, the methods getTitle, setTitle, getIsbn, and setIsbn have all been generated because of the @BeanProperty annotation. Note that without these methods, your class will not follow the JavaBean specification.

Let's see code compiled from Book.scala without the @BeanProperty.

```
public class Book {
  public Book(int, java.lang.String);
  public int isbn();
  public void isbn_$eq(int);
  public java.lang.String title();
  public void title_$eq(java.lang.String);
}
```

> **Note** Use the @BeanProperty annotation on your fields, making sure you declare each field as a var. If you declare your fields as type val, the setter methods (setTitle, setIsbn) won't be generated.

You saw how to use the @BeanProperty annotation on class constructor parameters. In the same manner, you can also use the @BeanProperty annotation on fields in a Scala class.

Next, you will learn to use a Scala feature not available in Java, such as traits.

Java Interfaces and Scala Traits

A Java class can't extend a Scala trait that has implemented methods (see Chapter 7 for more detail about traits). To understand the problem, let's first look at a regular Java interface.

```
public interface Book {
  public boolean isBestSeller();
}
```

The Scala equivalent is as follows:

```
trait Book:
    def isBestSeller: Boolean
```

As you can see, isBestSeller is an abstract method. In Scala, methods are denoted with a def keyword. But isBestSeller in the Scala code is an abstract method. How do you represent the abstract method in Scala? In Scala, if there is no = assignment, then methods denoted with a def keyword or functions denoted with a val keyword are abstract. For example, let's look at a Java method that returns some value.

```
public String someMethod(int arg1, boolean arg2) {
  return "voila";
}
```

The Scala equivalent is shown here.

```
def someMethod(arg1: Int, arg2: Boolean): String = "voila"
```

As you can see, = denotes the implementation.

Now let's look at an abstract Java method.

```
abstract int doTheMath(int i);
```

Here is the Scala equivalent of an abstract Java method doStuff:

```
def doTheMath(i: Int): Int
```

Note   If there's no definition provided with =, then it's automatically abstract.

Now let's go back to the original problem. A Java class can't extend a Scala trait that has implemented methods. So if you are trying to use a Scala trait (that has implemented methods in it) from Java, you will run into a problem. To demonstrate the problem, first create a trait with a simple implemented method named add.

```
trait Computation:
    def add(a: Int, b: Int) = a + b
```

You've written a Scala trait with implemented methods and need to be able to use an add method from a Java application, shown here:

```
public class DoTheMath {
    public static void main(String[] args) {
        DoTheMath d = new DoTheMath();
        // do the math here
    }
}
```

The type Computation cannot be the superclass of Java class DoTheMath simply because a superclass in Java must be a class; that is, the Java class DoTheMath cannot use the extend keyword to extend Computation. Moreover, the Java class DoTheMath cannot implement the trait Computation because in Java you implement interfaces, and the trait Computation has an implemented behavior, so Computation is not a like a regular Java interface. To be able to use the implemented method add of a Scala trait Computation from the Java class DoTheMath, you must wrap the trait Computation in a Scala class. This code shows a Scala class that wraps the trait Computation:

```
class JavaInteroperableComputation implements Computation
```

Now the Java class DoTheMath can extend the Scala JavaInteroperableComputation class and access the add method.

```
public class DoTheMath extends JavaInteroperableComputation {
    public static void main(String[] args) {
        DoTheMath d = new DoTheMath();
        d.add(3,1);
    }
}
```

Note   Wrap your Scala traits with implemented behavior in the Scala class for its Java callers.

Java Static Members and Scala Objects

Java code often refers to the static keyword to implement a Singleton object, as shown here:

```
public class Book{
    private static Book book;
    private Book() {}
    public static synchronized Book getInstance() {
        if (book == null) {
book = new Book();
        }
        return book;
    }
}
```

There is no such thing as static in Scala. In Java, static does not belong to an object, can't be inherited, and doesn't participate in polymorphism, thus statics aren't object-oriented. Scala, on the other hand, is purely object-oriented. Scala does not support static, but instead provides the notion of an object in place of the class declaration. If you need to refactor the above Java code into Scala, simply use the object declaration instead of a class, as shown here:

```
object Book
```

Scala objects give you an extra advantage in that they can also extend interfaces and traits. Scala provides a special syntax that gives you a Singleton for free, without all the syntax involved in declaring it (see the Java code above). But what if you want to mix static and instance members? In Java, you can do this like so:

```java
public class Book {
    public String getCategory() {
        return "Non-Fiction";
    }

    public static Book createBook() {
        return new Book();
    }
}
```

In addition to the notion of an object, Scala provides the notion of a companion object, which consists of an object that cohabitates with a class of the same name in the same package and file. For more information about companion objects, see Chapter 3. The companion object enables storing of static methods, and from this, you have full access to the classes' members, including private ones. Scala allows you to declare both an object and a class of the same name, placing the static members in the object and the instance members in the class. The Scala equivalent of the Java code just above is the following:

```scala
class Book:
    def getCategory() = " Non-Fiction"

object Book:
    def createBook() = Book()
```

Handling Exceptions

You can define the Scala method shown here without declaring that it throws an exception:

```scala
class SomeClass:
    def aScalaMethod() =
        throw new Exception("Exception")
```

This method can then be called from Java as shown here:

```
public static void main(String[] args) {
    SomeClass s = new SomeClass();
    s.aScalaMethod();
}
```

However, when the Java developer calls aScalaMethod, the uncaught exception causes the Java method to fail:

```
[error] (run-main) java.lang.Exception: Exception!
java.lang.Exception: Exception!
at SomeClass.aScalaMethod
```

If you don't mark the aScalaMethod method with the @throws annotation, a Java developer can call it without using a try/catch block in their method or declaring that their method throws an exception.

For the Java callers of your Scala methods, add the @throws annotation to your Scala methods so they will know which methods can throw exceptions and what exceptions they throw. For example, this code shows how to add the @throws annotation to let callers know that the aScalaMethod method can throw an exception.

```
class SomeClass:
    @throws(classOf[Exception])
    def aScalaMethod() =
        throw new Exception("Exception")
```

Your annotated Scala method works just like a Java method that throws an exception. If you attempt to call aScalaMethod from a Java class without wrapping it in a try/catch block, or declaring that your Java method throws an exception, the compiler (or your IDE) will throw an error.

In your Java code, you write a try/catch block, as usual, to handle the exception.

```
SomeClass = new SomeClass();
try {
    s.aScalaMethod();
} catch (Exception e) {
    System.err.println("Caught the exception.");
    e.printStackTrace();
}
```

Java Optional and Scala Option

Java, like many other languages, introduces a mechanism to reduce problems associated with null values. The name of this mechanism is Optional. Scala has the same concept but with the name of Option.

Scala provides a converter to transform the response of a block of code in Java that uses Optional to Option because, as you read in the first chapters of this book, the types are not exactly the same in both languages (for example, in Java, you can use Integer or int, but in Scala, you can just use Int).

Declaring an Optional value in Java is like doing it in Scala. Here is the Java code:

```java
import java.util.Optional;

public class JBook {
    public Optional<Integer> calculatePrice() {
        return Optional.empty();
    }

    public Optional<String> getName() {
        return Optional.of("IT");
    }
}
```

Here is the Scala code:

```scala
class SBook:
  def calculatePrice(): Option[Integer] = None
  def getName(): Option[String] = Option("IT")
```

As you can see, the syntaxes are more or less the same. The next step is to use an Optional value in Scala and transform it to an Option value, which is the correct type to use.

Now let's see how you can use and transform from Optional to Option in Scala.

```scala
import java.util.Optional
import scala.jdk.javaapi.OptionConverters

val optionalPrice = Optional.of(1) //Optional(1)
val optionPrice = OptionConverters.toScala(optionalPrice) //Some(1)

val optionName = Some("Beginning Scala") //Some
val optionalName = OptionConverters.toJava(optionName)//Optional
```

As you can see, the way to transform made easy by using a special converter that exists in Scala. The inverse process is more or less the same. Let's modify this example to return Option instead of Optional.

```
import java.util.Optional;
import scala.jdk.javaapi.OptionConverters;

public class JBook {
    public Option<Integer> calculatePrice() {
        return OptionConverters.toScala(Optional.empty());
    }

    public Option<String> getName() {
        return OptionConverters.toScala(Optional.of("IT"));
    }
}
```

Use Java Collections in Scala

In Chapter 6, you read a lot about collections in Scala and how to improve the performance instead of the same collections of Java, but these reasons do not reduce the chance that you can use Java collections in Scala, or vice versa, to zero.

Scala provides a set of classes and methods that convert from one collection to another of different languages. The following code shows how to create a Seq in Scala and transform it into a Java object:

```
scala> import scala.jdk.javaapi.CollectionConverters
scala> val seq = Seq(1,2,3)
val seq: Seq[Int] = List(1, 2, 3)
scala> val list = CollectionConverters.asJava(seq)
val list: java.util.List[Int] = [1, 2, 3]
```

Now do it in an inverse way in Scala. This code shows how from a Java collection you can create a Scala collection. You create a ArrayLIst and transforming it to a Buffer.

```
scala> import scala.jdk.javaapi.CollectionConverters
scala> import java.util.List
scala> import java.util.ArrayList
```

```
scala> val javaObject = java.util.ArrayList(java.util.List.of(1,2,3))
scala> val scalaObject = CollectionConverters.asScala(javaObject)
val scalaObject: scala.collection.mutable.Buffer[Int] = Buffer(1, 2, 3)
```

You can use the same converter to do the same operations in your Java applications, but first, you need to understand the equivalence between the collections of Java and Scala. Table 9-1 shows you the correlations between the languages.

Table 9-1. *Correlations Between the Different Collections*

Scala	*Java*
scala.collection.Iterable	java.lang.Iterable
scala.collection.Iterator	java.util.Iterator
scala.collection.mutable.Buffer	java.util.List
scala.collection.mutable.Set	java.util.Set
scala.collection.mutable.Map	java.util.Map
scala.collection.concurrent.Map	java.util.concurrent.ConcurrentMap

Take into consideration that if you want to use Scala code in a Java project, you need to include one dependency that provides all the methods and the classes to use it. The following code shows the correct dependency to include (check the version noted and update it if necessary in your code).

```
<!-- https://mvnrepository.com/artifact/org.scala-lang/scala3-library -->
<dependency>
    <groupId>org.scala-lang</groupId>
    <artifactId>scala3-library_3</artifactId>
    <version>3.0.2</version>
</dependency>
```

Summary

This chapter showed how Scala is translated to Java, which is especially important if you call Scala code from Java. You learned that in most cases, Scala features are translated to Java features so that Scala can easily integrate with Java. You learned how to handle features that are available in Java but not in Scala, such as static members and checked exceptions, and how to use Scala features such as traits in Java code. You also learned how Scala annotations help in integration, such as by generating JavaBean-style get and set. Scala code is often used in tandem with large Java programs and frameworks.

CHAPTER 10

DSL and Parser Combinator

A domain-specific language (DSL) is a special-purpose language designed to express solutions to problems that belong to a particular problem domain. DSLs have an advantage over a general-purpose language such as Scala and Java. Unfortunately, these general-purpose languages have drawbacks. For example, if you want to execute a task on a database, then it is necessary to write a computer program to execute this task using a general-purpose language. However, a DSL could be used to perform several such tasks on a database. And this is why some experts regard SQL as a DSL. The scope of this chapter is to introduce you to the world of DSLs and how they interact with Scala.

Some well-known examples of DSLs include ErlangOTP[1], HTML, SQL, Verilog[2], Mathematica[3], YACC[4], Xpath[5], CSS[6], YAML[7], MATLAB[8], and ANT.

A Closer Look at DSLs

DSLs are focused on a domain or problem and can be of an external or internal type. An external DSL defines a new language with its custom grammar and parser combinator. An internal DSL defines a new language as well but within the syntactical boundaries

---

[1] www.erlang.org/faq/introduction.html

[2] www.verilog.com/

[3] www.wolfram.com/mathematica/

[4] http://dinosaur.compilertools.net/yacc/

[5] www.w3.org/TR/xpath/

[6] www.w3.org/Style/CSS/Overview.en.html

[7] http://en.wikipedia.org/wiki/YAML

[8] http://nl.mathworks.com/products/matlab/

© David Pollak, Vishal Layka, and Andres Sacco 2022
D. Pollak et al., *Beginning Scala 3*, https://doi.org/10.1007/978-1-4842-7422-4_10

of another language. No custom parser is necessary for internal DSLs. Instead, they are parsed just like any other code written in the language. Interest in DSLs has surged recently, driven in part by the Ruby[9] and Groovy[10] communities because they are very easy to implement in these languages. Ant[11], which uses XML, is an example of an external DSL. Gant[12], on the other hand, uses Groovy to solve the same problem and is an example of an internal DSL. Groovy with its metaprogramming[13] capabilities and flexible syntax is better suited to designing and implementing internal DSLs. As an illustration, using Groovy's optional parameters and MOP[14], you can turn this code that only a programmer can love

```
println this.class.getResourceAsStream('readme.txt').getText()
```

into

```
write 'readme.txt'.contents()
```

You do not have to be a Groovy programmer to notice that with the second option, even a non-programmer has a chance of understanding the intent of the code. As you'll see, Scala provides excellent support for the creation of internal and external DSLs.

A DSL is usually useful to simplify the interaction with a system by application to a small, particular domain. A DSL can be targeted to programmers by providing a simplified API to communicate with a system, or it may concern business users who might understand a domain well enough to create some scripts but are not programmers and could have difficulty dealing with a general-purpose programming language. You can think of a DSL like a program that you write once and introduce modifications over time for people who understand the idea or the problem that the DSL solves.

A DSL offers two ways for abstractions:

1. Limiting the vocabulary that you can use because it is related to the terms or words that are connected with the problem.

---

[9] www.ruby-lang.org/en/

[10] http://groovy.codehaus.org/

[11] http://ant.apache.org/

[12] http://gant.codehaus.org/

[13] http://en.wikipedia.org/wiki/Metaprogramming

[14] http://c2.com/cgi/wiki?MetaObjectProtocol

2. Offers the developers a certain level of abstractions about the structures or some little details about one particular language.

There are some cons to using DSLs:

- They are complex to create because the techniques to create them are not very simple and require some effort at the beginning.

- It's not simple to maintain where the domain changes.

- It's difficult to hide details of errors for the users.

Regarding the structure of a DSL, a DSL has three principles:

1. The artifacts that are connected in some way with the problem domain. A DSL needs to provide a level of abstraction of the artifacts but needs to provide the mechanism to connect the artifacts with the vocabulary.

2. The vocabulary is one of the most important things in a DSL because it establishes a way to understand the problem that the DSL is trying to solve.

3. A DSL script is the interface for the domain users and does not need to have complexity in the implementation.

An internal DSL is easy to create because it does not need anything in particular. You can write it using simple code. In contrast, external DSLs need to create grammar and parsers.

Internal DSLs

Internal DSLs are most often embedded in a host language with the addition of syntactic sugar through tricks and special constructs of the language. Many of these languages support a meta-object protocol that you can use to implement dynamic behaviors onto your DSL. Most of these languages are dynamically typed, such as Ruby and Groovy. Groovy was used as a host language for the DSL in the example at the beginning of the chapter. Statically typed languages, such as Scala, offer abstraction capabilities to model your DSL.

Some of the features of Scala that make it a host language for an internal DSL are

- Implicit conversions

- Scala's advanced type system

- Currying

- Infix and postfix operator notations

- Syntactic sugar

- Dynamic method invocation

- Flexible rules for names

For example, you can omit the parentheses and dot for any method that takes a single parameter, as shown:

```
map.get("key") is equivalent to map get "key"
```

In this section, you will learn how to build an internal DSL using Scala as a host language. Implicit conversion (see Chapter 8) gets you halfway to adding methods to a final class. The second half of the journey is that the Scala compiler looks at a possible implicit conversion from the type you have to a type with the method that you're invoking. The Scala compiler inserts code to call the implicit conversion and then calls the method on the resulting instance. The ability to add new methods to existing classes has a lot of value for making code more readable and expressive. More importantly, implicit conversions make it possible to define DSLs in Scala. As a library producer, you can create syntactically pleasing ways to express concepts in a type-safe way. Wouldn't it be nice to express a period as 3 days or 15 seconds? That would make code a lot more readable than (3L * 24L * 3600L * 1000L). Wouldn't it be great to set a timeout or a trigger within 2 hours? Let's define a library using implicit conversions and then break it down.

```
import java.util.Date
import scala.language.implicitConversions

object TimeHelpers:
  case class TimeSpanBuilder(val len: Long):
    def seconds = TimeSpan(TimeHelpers.seconds(len))
    def second = seconds
    def minutes = TimeSpan(TimeHelpers.minutes(len))
    def minute = minutes
```

```scala
    def hours = TimeSpan(TimeHelpers.hours(len))
    def hour = hours
    def days = TimeSpan(TimeHelpers.days(len))
    def day = days
    def weeks = TimeSpan(TimeHelpers.weeks(len))
    def week = weeks

  def seconds(in: Long): Long = in * 1000L
  def minutes(in: Long): Long = seconds(in) * 60L
  def hours(in: Long): Long = minutes(in) * 60L
  def days(in: Long): Long = hours(in) * 24L
  def weeks(in: Long): Long = days(in) * 7L

  given longToTimeSpanBuilder: Conversion[Long,TimeSpanBuilder] = in =>
TimeSpanBuilder(in)
  given intToTimeSpanBuilder: Conversion[Int,TimeSpanBuilder] = in =>
TimeSpanBuilder(in)

  def millis = System.currentTimeMillis

  case class TimeSpan(millis: Long) extends Ordered[TimeSpan]:
    def later = new Date(millis + TimeHelpers.millis)
    def ago = new Date(TimeHelpers.millis - millis)
    def +(in: TimeSpan) = TimeSpan(this.millis + in.millis)
    def -(in: TimeSpan) = TimeSpan(this.millis - in.millis)
    def compare(other: TimeSpan) = millis compare other.millis

  object TimeSpan:
    given tsToMillis: Conversion[TimeSpan, Long] = in => in.millis

  class DateMath(d: Date):
    def +(ts: TimeSpan) = Date(d.getTime + ts.millis)
    def -(ts: TimeSpan) = Date(d.getTime - ts.millis)

  given dateToDM: Conversion[Date, DateMath] = in => DateMath(in)
```

You import java.util.Date because you're going to make use of it.

```scala
import java.util.Date
```

You then define a class that takes a Long as a parameter and has a series of methods that convert the Long into a TimeSpanBuilder represented by the length.

```
case class TimeSpanBuilder(val len: Long):
    def seconds = TimeSpan(TimeHelpers.seconds(len))
    def second = seconds
    def minutes = TimeSpan(TimeHelpers.minutes(len))
    def minute = minutes
    def hours = TimeSpan(TimeHelpers.hours(len))
    def hour = hours
    def days = TimeSpan(TimeHelpers.days(len))
    def day = days
    def weeks = TimeSpan(TimeHelpers.weeks(len))
    def week = weeks
```

Then you define a bunch of helper methods (called from TimeSpanBuilder) that convert to the correct number of milliseconds.

```
def seconds(in: Long): Long = in * 1000L
def minutes(in: Long): Long = seconds(in) * 60L
def hours(in: Long): Long = minutes(in) * 60L
def days(in: Long): Long = hours(in) * 24L
def weeks(in: Long): Long = days(in) * 7L
```

Next, you define a bunch of implicit methods that convert from Int or Long into a TimeSpanBuilder. This allows the methods such as minutes or days in TimeSpanBuilder to appear to be part of Int and Long.

```
//Scala 3 format
given longToTimeSpanBuilder: Conversion[Long,TimeSpanBuilder] = in =>
TimeSpanBuilder(in)
given intToTimeSpanBuilder: Conversion[Int,TimeSpanBuilder] = in =>
TimeSpanBuilder(in)

//Scala 2 format
implicit def longToTimeSpanBuilder(in: Long): TimeSpanBuilder =
TimeSpanBuilder(in)
```

```
implicit def intToTimeSpanBuilder(in: Int): TimeSpanBuilder =
TimeSpanBuilder(in)
```

Then you define a helper method that gets the current time in milliseconds.

```
def millis = System.currentTimeMillis
```

You define the TimeSpan class that represents a period. You can do math with other Timespans or convert this TimeSpan into a Date by calling the later or ago methods. TimeSpan extends the Ordered trait so that you can compare and sort TimeSpans.

```
case class TimeSpan(millis: Long) extends Ordered[TimeSpan]:
  def later = new Date(millis + TimeHelpers.millis)
  def ago = new Date(TimeHelpers.millis - millis)
  def +(in: TimeSpan) = TimeSpan(this.millis + in.millis)
  def -(in: TimeSpan) = TimeSpan(this.millis - in.millis)
  def compare(other: TimeSpan) = millis compare other.millis
```

Next, you compare this TimeSpan to another to satisfy the requirements of the Ordered trait.

```
def compare(other: TimeSpan) = millis compare other.millis
```

Then you define a companion object that has an implicit method that will convert a Timespan into a Long. If there is an object with the same name as a class, that object is considered a companion object. If there are any implicit conversions defined in the companion object, they will be consulted if an instance of the class needs to be converted. You define an implicit conversion from TimeSpan to Long in the companion object. This results in TimeSpan instances being automatically converted to Long if the TimeSpan is assigned to a Long variable or passed as a parameter that requires a Long.

```
//Scala 3 format
object TimeSpan:
 given tsToMillis: Conversion[TimeSpan, Long] = in => in.millis

//Scala 2 format
object TimeSpan {
 implicit def tsToMillis(in: TimeSpan): Long = in.millis
}
```

You can define `TimeSpan` instances with simple syntaxes, such as 3 days. Periods can be converted to `Dates` with the `later` and `ago` methods. But it would be helpful to add addition and subtraction of `TimeSpans` to `Date` instances. That's pretty simple using implicit conversions. First, you define a `DateMath` class that has + and - methods that take a `TimeSpan` as a parameter.

```scala
class DateMath(d: Date):
  def +(ts: TimeSpan) = Date(d.getTime + ts.millis)
  def -(ts: TimeSpan) = Date(d.getTime - ts.millis)
```

Next you define the implicit conversion.

```scala
//Scala 3 format
given dateToDM: Conversion[Date, DateMath] = in => DateMath(in)
```

```scala
//Scala 2 format
implicit def dateToDM(d: Date) = new DateMath(d)
```

With the 50 or so lines of code written, let's see how it works.

```scala
scala> import TimeHelpers._
import TimeHelpers._
scala> 1.days
val res0: TimeHelpers.TimeSpan = TimeSpan(86400000)
scala> 5.days + 2.hours
val res1: TimeHelpers.TimeSpan = TimeSpan(439200000)
scala> (5.days + 2.hours).later
val res2: java.util.Date = Fri Nov 12 19:19:57 ART 2021
scala> import java.util.Date
import java.util.Date
scala> val lng: Long = 7.days + 2.hours + 4.minutes
lng: Long = 612240000
```

So, you've defined a nice DSL for periods, and it converts itself to `Long` when necessary. You saw how Scala's implicit conversions lead to very simple and concise DSLs. Choosing implicit conversions and designing domain-specific languages takes time, thought, and deliberation. Next is a brief introduction to external DSLs.

External DSLs

External DSLs build their language-processing infrastructure: the parsers, the lexers, and the processing logic. You need to define grammar (such as Backus–Naur Form[15] (BNF)). That is, you define all the rules that apply to parse a meaning or script successfully. Internal DSLs get this infrastructure free from the underlying host language, but you need to build them from scratch for external DSLs. In Scala, parser combinators are a notion close to the definition of BNF grammars and can provide very concise and elegant code when writing external DSLs. This module of parser combinators is not part of the Scala standard library but it's maintained for the community[16]. An external DSL has a separate infrastructure for lexical analysis, parsing, interpretation, compilation, and code generation. When you write a parser for an external DSL, you can use a parser generator tool such as Antlr[17]. Scala comes with a parser combinator library so you don't have to implement your own language infrastructure.

Summary

Scala's parser combinator library demonstrates the flexibility of Scala's syntax, the usefulness of implicit conversions, and the power of functional composition. The parser combinator is an excellent example of a domain-specific language. The domain is parsing text, and the syntax is nearly one-for-one with BNF. This library also gives you some idea of the kind of domain-specific languages you can create using Scala. There's nothing specific in the Scala compiler for the parser combinator library; it's just that: a library. On a practical level, using a single language, Scala, for defining your parser rather than using a tool like ANTLR means that you and your team use a single language for describing your system. This means that your brain thinks Scala. This means that you edit code in a single language and take advantage of the type safety of the language.

---

[15] http://en.wikipedia.org/wiki/Backus%E2%80%93Naur_Form

[16] https://index.scala-lang.org/scala/scala-parser-combinators/
scala-parser-combinators/1.1.1

[17] www.antlr.org/

CHAPTER 11

Simple Build Tool

During the different chapters of this book, you've mostly used the REPL to run the blocks of code and check the results. The command line is great because if you want to test something, it's not necessary to open an IDE or create a project. When you need to create something more complex, the REPL is the worst alternative, so there are other tools that you can use to compile and run your application.

As you know, software development includes many activities such as compiling the source code, executing different types of tests[1], and packaging the code into a file that can be deployed into different environments like development or production. Imagine compiling all the classes manually and later creating a package to deploy. This would take too much time, so you need to use a tool that does all this hard work for you!

Many tools handle all the activities related to the cycle of one application. Figure 11-1 shows a quick overview of the popular build tools in a timeline. Make[2] is atypical in this list, but it was included because it pioneered build automation. All the build tools except Make in Figure 11-1 are popular in the JVM landscape.

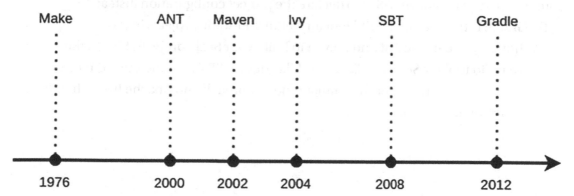

Figure 11-1. *Timeline of build tools*

---

[1] https://martinfowler.com/articles/microservice-testing/
[2] www.gnu.org/software/make/

© David Pollak, Vishal Layka, and Andres Sacco 2022
D. Pollak et al., *Beginning Scala 3*, https://doi.org/10.1007/978-1-4842-7422-4_11

As mentioned, Make pioneered build automation and allowed dependency management from the outset. Make remains widely used, especially in Unix.

Apache Ant[3] is similar to Make but is implemented in the Java language. Unlike Make, it uses XML to describe the build process and its dependencies. It necessitates the Java platform and befits building Java projects. Contrary to Ant, Maven[4] allows convention over configuration for the build procedure by providing sensible default behavior for projects.

Note   Convention over configuration (CoC) refers to, in general, a development approach centered on conventions. It enables developers to specify and configure only the unconventional aspects of the development.

Apache Ivy[5] is a dependency manager. It is a subproject of the Apache Ant project and helps to resolve project dependencies.

Note   Apache Ivy competes to a large extent with Apache Maven, which also manages dependencies. However, Maven is a complete build tool, whereas Ivy focuses purely on managing dependencies.

Gradle[6] builds upon Apache Ant and Apache Maven and uses a Groovy-based domain-specific language (DSL) to declare the project configuration instead of XML. Gradle is the standard build tool for Kotlin and some projects in Java.

Although you can use Ant and Maven to build your Scala projects, SBT[7] is the standard build tool for Scala applications. Like Maven, SBT uses the same directory structure and convention over the configuration approach and Apache Ivy for handling dependency management.

---

[3] http://ant.apache.org/
[4] http://maven.apache.org/
[5] http://ant.apache.org/ivy/
[6] https://gradle.org/
[7] www.scala-sbt.org/

In essence, the build automation automates all the steps in the build process with build tools like Ant, Maven, Ivy, Gradle, or SBT, and the best practice is to run the build continuously. This process is known as continuous integration. Several tools offer continuous integration, such as Hudson[8] and Jenkins[9].

Getting Started with SBT

In this section, you will see a brief overview of SBT and all the things you can do with this tool.

Why SBT?

As you read in the previous section, many tools help you build a project in different ways, but one of them, SBT, is the default standard in Scala. There are alternatives, like Mill[10], but it's not used very extensively in the community at the time of writing.

SBT has some interesting features that are important to mention:

- Depending on the size of the project, it does not require configuration (or just a little).

- It supports combined or mixed Scala/Java projects.

- It offers good integration with the most common IDEs like IntelliJ and VS Code.

- It has support with Coursier[11], which is a tool that manages dependencies in projects.

- It supports multiple subprojects.

- It has integration and support for the most common libraries for testing in Scala.

- You can run parallel tasks or in batch mode.

---

[8] http://hudson-ci.org
[9] http://jenkins-ci.org/
[10] https://github.com/com-lihaoyi/mill
[11] https://get-coursier.io/

Installing SBT

Chapter 1 covered installation instructions for different tools related to Scala and one of them was SBT.

Here are ways to install this tool depending on your operating system:

- For Mac OS/Linux, you can use brew, which is a tool to install/update different things.

    → `~ brew install sbt`

- For Windows platforms, you can download the MSI installer from the official page at `www.scala-sbt.org/download.html`.

After finishing the installation of the SBT, check if everything is installed in your system. To this, run the following command:

```
→ ~ sbt --version
sbt version in this project: 1.5.2
sbt script version: 1.5.2
```

Note that version 1.5.0 of SBT introduces support for Scala 3.0.0 so you need to install or update SBT to at least this version.

General Commands

SBT has many commands for executing different types of actions. To run any of these commands, you need to be in the root directory of your project. Table 11-1 lists some of the most important commands in SBT.

Table 11-1. *Commands in SBT*

Command	Description
about	Provides general information about the version of SBT and Scala on your machine
clean	Removes the files that are generated with SBT
compile	Compiles the different files that exist in the directories src/main/scala and src/main/java
console	Opens a REPL with the configurations of your project including all dependencies
help	Shows all commands that are available to run on SBT. Also, you can ask for one command and obtain the information about which parameters support it.
Test	Compiles and runs tests

The official documentation[12] on the SBT web site offers detailed information about all commands.

Creating a Hello World Project

Now that you know some of the common commands, it is time to create your first project to see SBT in action. You can create a project using the simple SBT commands or you can use the skeletons that exist on Giter8. Giter8 provides a skeleton for the most common applications (Spark, Akka, Play, Scala Native, and many more). If you want to know the available templates, please visit the official documentation[13].

To create a simple project that only has "hello world," you can use the template with the same name offered by Giter8. To do this, open a terminal and write the command sbt new with the name of the template.

```
$ sbt new scala/hello-world.g8
[info] welcome to sbt 1.5.5 (Homebrew Java 11.0.12)
[info] set current project to new (in build file:/tmp/sbt_8076aba/new/)
A template to demonstrate a minimal Scala application
name [Hello World template]: helloWorld
```

---

[12] www.scala-sbt.org/1.x/docs/Command-Line-Reference.html
[13] https://github.com/foundweekends/giter8/wiki/giter8-templates

251

After you execute this command, you'll see a directory named helloWorld on your machine with all the configurations and the Main class. If you open the file Main.scala that exists in src/main/scala, you will see something like this:

```
object Main extends App {
  println("Hello, World!")
}
```

If you want to run this application, you need to execute the command sbt run in the root directory and the result will appear in the same console.

```
$ sbt run
[info] welcome to sbt 1.5.5 (Homebrew Java 11.0.12)
[info] loading project definition from /home/helloworld/project
[info] loading settings for project helloworld from build.sbt ...
[info] set current project to hello-world (in build file:/home/helloworld/)
[info] running Main
Hello, World!
[success] Total time: 1 s, completed Sep 19, 2021, 11:32:55 PM
```

You can execute different commands in the interactive mode, which provides a command prompt with features such as tab completion and history.

```
$ sbt
[info] welcome to sbt 1.5.5 (Homebrew Java 11.0.12)
[info] loading project definition from /home/scala/helloworld/project
[info] loading settings for project helloworld from build.sbt ...
[info] set current project to hello-world (in build file:/home/scala/
helloworld/)
[info] sbt server started at local:///home/.sbt/1.0/server/
e383aa762cd5b7c5e9f6/sock
[info] started sbt server
sbt:hello-world>
```

Interactive mode remembers what you typed previously (history), even if you exit SBT and restart it. SBT lists all the history commands when you type ! at the SBT prompt, as shown here:

```
sbt:hello-world> !
History commands:
    !!      Execute the last command again
    !:      Show all previous commands
    !:n         Show the last n commands
    !n      Execute the command with index n, as shown by the !: command
    !-n     Execute the nth command before this one
    !string     Execute the most recent command starting with 'string'
    !?string     Execute the most recent command containing 'string'
```

SBT lets you dynamically change the version of Scala with a simple command on the command line of SBT.

```
sbt:hello-world> ++3.0.0!
[info] Forcing Scala version to 3.0.0 on all projects.
[info] Reapplying settings...
[info] set current project to hello-world (in build file:/home/scala/
helloworld/)
```

Project Structure

The structure of directories is very similar to Maven projects. If you check the tree of the root directory of the project that you created in the previous section, you will see something like this:

```
$ tree .
./
├── build.sbt
├── project
│   ├── build.properties
│   └── target
├── src
│   └── main
│       └── scala
│           └── Main.scala
└── target
    ├── global-logging
    └── task-temp-directory
```

If you want to add some Java classes, they will appear in a `java` directory in the `main` directory. Also, you can have folders with tests in Scala or Java and another one with the resources of the project, like so:

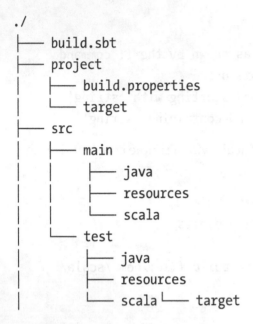

```
./
├── build.sbt
├── project
│   ├── build.properties
│   └── target
├── src
│   ├── main
│   │   ├── java
│   │   ├── resources
│   │   └── scala
│   └── test
│       ├── java
│       ├── resources
│       └── scala └── target
```

build.sbt

The `build.sbt` file contains the configuration of the project following the pattern of key/value, so to define the version of Scala you need to use `scala version := "3.0.0"`.

```
scalaVersion := "3.0.0" // 1
name := "hello-world" // 2
organization := "ch.epfl.scala" // 3

version := "1.0" // 4

libraryDependencies += "org.scala-lang.modules" %% "scala-parser-
combinators" % "1.1.2" // 5
```

Let's explain each of parts of `build.sbt`:

> 1: This setting is mandatory because it specifies which version of Scala is used in the project.

> 2: Refers to the name of the project. It's like the artifactId in Maven.

3: It's the way to group different projects of the same company or part of the company. You can think of this attribute like the groupId in Maven.

4: It's the version of the application.

5: This section contains all the dependencies that the project uses. You can define it as shown above or you can define it as a Seq of dependencies when you have more than one.

```
libraryDependencies ++= Seq(
"org.scala-lang.modules" %% "scala-parser-combinators" % "1.1.2"
)
```

If you want to change the name or the project or some of the attributes of the build.sbt, you can do it in the terminal using the command set.

```
sbt:hello-world> set name := "hello world"
[info] Defining name
[info] The new value will be used by Compile / compileEarly, Compile / doc
/ scalacOptions and 9 others.
[info] Run `last` for details.
[info] Reapplying settings...
[info] set current project to hello world (in build file:/home/scala/helloworld/)
```

After introducing the changes, you need to save using the command session save on the command line.

```
sbt:hello world> session save
[info] Reapplying settings...
[info] set current project to hello world (in build file:/home/scala/
helloworld/)
[warn] build source files have changed
[warn] modified files:
[warn]    /home/scala/helloworld/build.sbt
[warn] Apply these changes by running `reload`.
[warn] Automatically reload the build when source changes are detected by
setting `Global / onChangedBuildSource := ReloadOnSourceChanges`.
[warn] Disable this warning by setting `Global / onChangedBuildSource :=
IgnoreSourceChanges`.
```

Project Folder

This folder contains all the necessary things to run the project in SBT. The most relevant information of each directory or file is the following:

- `build.properties` contains all the information about the version of SBT.

  `sbt.version=1.5.5`

- `plugins.sbt` is optional and depends on if you have plugins enabled in SBT or not.

- `target` contains all the source code generated by SBT.

Src Folder

This directory has the same structure as the Maven repository, containing all the source code and the resources necessary to run the application. Some folders are optional and others are required. Here's a little explanation about the different folders:

- `main` **(required):** This folder contains all the sources and resources.

  - `scala` **(required):** Contains all the files separated or not in different packages with the code of the application.

  - `java` **(optional):** Contains all the files developed in Java. You can import Scala classes, as you saw in the previous chapters.

  - `resources` **(optional):** It has files in different formats that can be used in the application.

- `test` **(optional):** This folder contains all the tests of the application.

  - `scala` **(optional):** Contains all the tests of the Scala classes.

  - `java` **(optional):** Contains all the tests of the Java classes.

  - `resources` **(optional):** Has files in different formats that can be used in the application.

Build Definition

As mentioned, a build tool requires you to define the project configuration and dependencies in an artifact called a build definition.

In SBT, there are three types of build definitions:

- .sbt build definition

- .scala build definition

- Combination of .scala and .sbt build definitions

As you learned earlier, the base directory of your hello world project, the helloworld directory, is made up of the build definition .sbt file. In addition to the .sbt file, there may also be build definitions such as a .scala file located in the project/ subdirectory of the base directory.

In version 0.13.7 of SBT, you were required to separate the setting expression by blank lines. You could not write an .sbtfile as shown in the following example because it wouldn't compile because of the absence of blank lines:

```
name := "hello-world"
version := "1.0"
scalaVersion := "2.10.x"
```

This restriction does not exist from SBT 0.13.7 but we mentioned it because you may find yourself in situations where older versions of SBT are still being used with newer versions of Scala, and in such cases the build file without the blank lines won't compile.

In SBT, keys are defined for different purposes. A key can be grouped into one of the categories listed in Table 11-2.

Table 11-2. *Ways to Group Keys in SBT*

Key	Description
Setting key	When you define the key as a Setting key, the value of the key is computed on loading the project.
Task key	When you define the key as a Task key, the value of the key is recomputed each time it is executed.
Input key	When you define the key as an Input key, the value of the key takes command-line arguments as input.

The Setting keys provide build configuration. The keys such as `name`, `version`, and `scalaVersion` that you saw in the code above are Setting keys. You will look at two other useful types of setting keys, `libraryDependencies` and `resolvers` keys, in the following section.

The Task keys, as the name suggests, are geared toward tasks such as `clean`, `compile`, `test`, and so on.

Note   Because a Task key is computed on each execution, a Setting key cannot depend on a Task key. Trying to do so will throw an error.

The Input keys are the keys that have command-line arguments. An example of an input key is the `run` key. The `run` key is used to run a `main` class with command-line arguments. If no arguments are provided, a blank string is used. You execute without any arguments when you run the hello world project.

Note   Each key can have more than one value, but in different context called scopes. In a given scope, a key has only one value.

In the following section, you will learn about the Setting keys called `libraryDependencies` key and `resolvers` key.

LibraryDependencies and Resolvers

In previous sections, you read that a part in the `build.sbt` contains the list of the different libraries that use the project. The `libraryDependencies` key is used to declare managed dependencies and the `resolvers` key is used to provide additional resource URIs for automatically managed dependencies. As mentioned, SBT uses Coursier (previous versions of SBT use Apache Ivy) to implement managed dependencies. You should list your dependencies in the setting `libraryDependencies`. You can declare the dependencies as shown here:

```
libraryDependencies += groupID % artifactID % revision
```

In the code above, `groupId`, `artifactId`, and `revision` are strings. This way of declaring dependencies is similar to doing so in Maven, which is shown here:

```
<dependency>
    <groupId>org.scalatest</groupId>
    <artifactId>scalatest_3</artifactId>
    <version>3.2.9</version>
</dependency>
```

Now imagine that some of the dependencies are applicable in one particular scope of the application, such as the test dependency in the code above needs to be available only on test. The following code shows how you can restrict the use of one dependency to a particular scope:

```
libraryDependencies += groupID % artifactID % revision % configuration
```

This is the Maven version:

```
<dependency>
    <groupId>org.scalatest</groupId>
    <artifactId>scalatest_3</artifactId>
    <version>3.2.9</version>
    <scope>test</scope>
</dependency>
```

The operator += appends to the existing value. You can also use another operator, ++=, which appends the sequence of values to the existing value.

```
libraryDependencies ++= Seq(
  groupID % artifactID % revision,
  groupID % otherID % otherRevision
)
```

If you want to use the library dependency that is not in one of the default repositories, you need to add a resolver to help Coursier locate it. In order to provide the location of a repository, use the following syntax:

```
resolvers += name at location
```

Here name is the String name of the repository and `location` is the String location of the repository. The following shows how to add the additional repository:

```
resolvers += "Sonatype OSS Snapshots" at https://oss.sonatype.org/content/
repositories/snapshots
```

You add the sonatypeoss snapshots repository, which is located at the given URL.

One last thing to consider: Some libraries are compiled in Scala 2.13, so if you want to use them in Scala 3, you need to use `cross(CrossVersion.for3Use2_13)`. Take into consideration that the libraries need to be compiled at least with version 2.13 or up; if not, this approach will not work. This code shows how you can do it with one dependency:

```
libraryDependencies ++= Seq(
  ("org.querki" % "jquery-facade" % "2.0").cross(CrossVersion.for3Use2_13)
)
```

Plugins

A plugin is an artifact that extends the build definition, usually by adding new settings. In order to declare this plugin dependency, you need to pass the plugin's module ID to `addSbtPlugin` as shown below.

Next, you'll see how to use an assembly plugin using the hello world project you created earlier. You can obtain the SBT assembly plugin's module ID from the GitHub repository[14]. This plugin helps create the jar of the application.

First, create an `assembly.sbt` file for the plugin in the helloworld project directory: .

```
addSbtPlugin("com.eed3si9n" % "sbt-assembly" % "1.1.0")
```

Then enter the SBT console and type `assembly`. If everything works, you will see something like this:

```
sbt:hello world> assembly
[info] Strategy 'discard' was applied to a file (Run the task at debug
level to see details)
```

---

[14] https://github.com/sbt/sbt-assembly

```
[info] Strategy 'rename' was applied to 2 files (Run the task at debug
level to see details)
[success] Total time: 2 s, completed Sep 20, 2021, 4:43:04 PM
```

Now, package your code. To see the location of the jar file, you need to execute another command, which is show `assembly`.

```
sbt:hello world> show assembly
[info] Strategy 'discard' was applied to a file (Run the task at debug
level to see details)
[info] Assembly up to date: /home/scala/helloworld/target/
scala-3     .0.1     /hello world-assembly-1.0.jar
[info] /home/scala/helloworld/target/scala-3     .0.1     /hello world-
assembly-1.0.jar
[success] Total time: 0 s, completed Sep 20, 2021, 4:45:29 PM
```

One last thing: If you want to change the name of your assembly, you need to introduce the following line in your build.sbt:

```
assemblyJarName := "beginning-scala-1.0.jar"
```

One chapter is not enough to list all the features of SBT; it deserves a book of its own. For a detailed treatment on SBT, we recommend you go through the reference manual of SBT at www.scala-sbt.org/release/docs/. This chapter did provide a brief introduction to SBT, and now you know enough use it to build a web application in the next chapter.

Summary

In this chapter, you learned how to create a simple project with SBT and execute basic operations, such as compile, test, and run. You learned how to configure library dependencies and how to configure a dependency when it is not in a default repository. In the next chapter, you will learn how to create web applications in Scala.

Creating Web Applications

During this book, you have read about all the features that Scala offers for doing different things using structures, classes, and other elements, but as of yet you don't know how to combine these things in one place. As you can imagine, developers don't run different blocks of code using the REPL or the IDE. You need to combine them into one or more applications that do something like expose a set of endpoints in a REST application or a set of web pages of an e-commerce site.

In languages like Java, most developers use frameworks[1] like Spring Boot, JSF, and Vaadin, which offer more or less the same set of features to create an application. Scala offers a different set of frameworks to create applications. The only exception is Vaadin, which has a particular version for Java and another one for Scala. In this particular case, the best approach is not to try to use the frameworks that exist on Java because not use all the potential of Scala related to the performance and the compilation time.

In this chapter, you will learn more about the previous versions of architectures for creating applications and the new model, which encourages the creation of multiple applications, each with one specific proposal.

Architecture Types

A lot of things have changed since the second version of this book was written. At that time, most applications were big boxes that contained a lot of functionalities using the same block of libraries and sharing the block of code. Nowadays most of those applications are known as monoliths (Figure 12-1), which, for different motives related to the architecture and the velocity of introducing changes, are now discouraged.

---

[1] https://res.cloudinary.com/snyk/image/upload/v1623860216/reports/jvm-ecosystem-report-2021.pdf

© David Pollak, Vishal Layka, and Andres Sacco 2022
D. Pollak et al., *Beginning Scala 3*, https://doi.org/10.1007/978-1-4842-7422-4_12

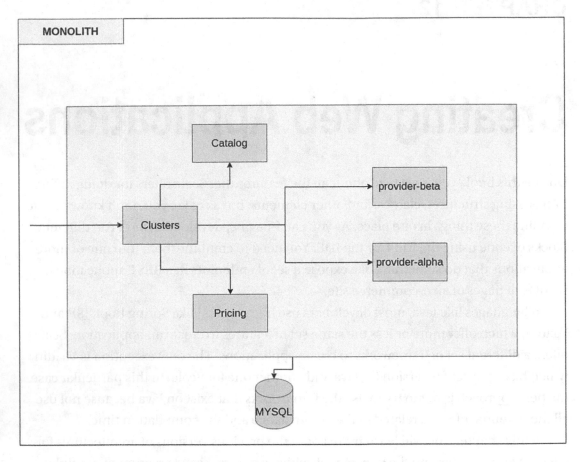

Figure 12-1. *One big application that contains all the logic*

Let's imagine a travel platform that offers different options of flights where you can obtain information from different providers and add some percentage of markup, with these functionalities all in the same place. Figure 12-2 presents some of the benefits and drawbacks of this approach.

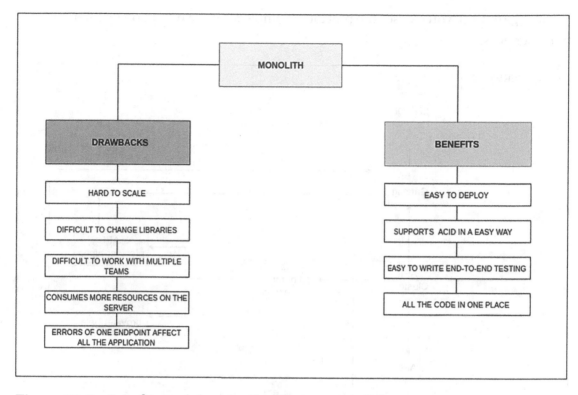

Figure 12-2. *Benefits and drawbacks of using monoliths*

This type of application contained everything including the web pages and all the logic of one system. This architecture is not connected exclusively with Scala; this situation happened in many other languages like Java with the use of JSF/Vaadin/ZK.

Nowadays most developers know about microservices and the benefits of using them, but in 2014 when Martin Fowler[2] wrote articles about this topic, some people looked at it as an utopian idea that had a lot of cons compared with the monolithic solution. This view changed some years ago for different reasons. One of them is connected directly with the emergence of containers, because they reduce the problems and complexity of deploying an application in different environments using different languages. Docker is one of the most known and extended implementations of containers.

---

[2] https://martinfowler.com/articles/microservices.html

In Figure 12-3, you can see the previous example after the migration to different microservices.

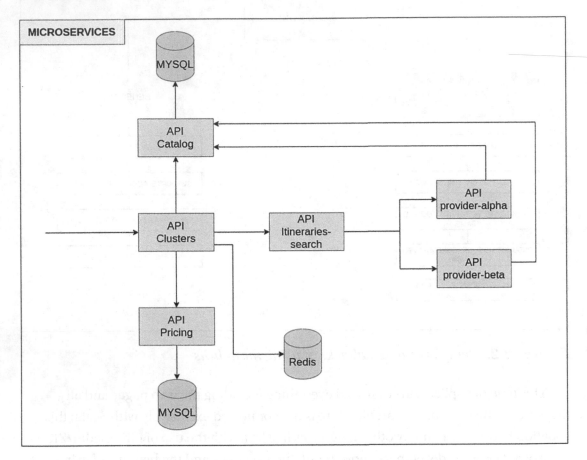

Figure 12-3. *A monolithic application split into microservices*

It's not in the scope of this book to explain everything about microservices, but Figure 12-4 shows a summary of the benefits and drawbacks.

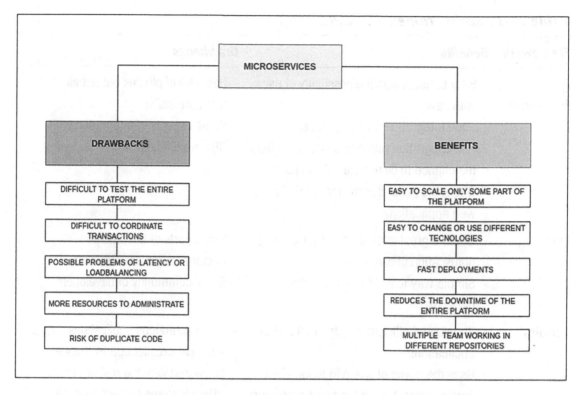

Figure 12-4. *Benefits and drawbacks of using microservices*

Now let's see some concrete examples of frameworks for creating these applications using Scala. Table 12-1 shows most of the common frameworks. There are many more frameworks, but some of them are not updated or do not cover the latest version of Scala 3.

Table 12-1. *Scala Frameworks and Libraries*

Framework	Benefits	Drawbacks
Play Framework[3]	- Easy to use, offers the possibility of use with Java - Good integration with most IDEs. - Has integration with databases and offers the chance to do remote calls in parallel - Offers the possibility to create REST API or web applications	- Has a lot of plugins but not all of them are stable - Some aspects of integration with SBT are difficult.
Lift[4]	- Offers a great level of security, including obfuscation of queries - Simple way to write queries to the database	- Some parts of the official documentation are outdated. - Small community of developers
Scalatra[5]	- Simple and efficient way to create REST applications - Uses the power of the JVM to increase performance- One of the first frameworks to create applications so many people know it	- For synchronous applications it does not have excellent performance compared with the rest of the list. - Offers features to create a basic service, but not one with a lot of complex features
Akka HTTP[6]	- Has a big number of developers and it's a well-documented framework - Has good integration with Akka by default	- It's a little slower than other frameworks.
Slick[7]	- Offers a query compiler and an easy way to connect with databases	- Has support with multiple databases but in the case of MySQL it has bad performance- Not a big community of developers

---

[3] www.playframework.com/
[4] http://liftweb.net/
[5] https://github.com/scalatra/scalatra#readme
[6] https://doc.akka.io/docs/akka-http/current/
[7] https://scala-slick.org/

In the following section, you will create one application that exposes HTML and another one that exposes a REST API. To create both applications, you will use Play Framework because it is one of the frameworks that most developers know, not just in Scala. Some Java applications use this framework, too.

Table 12-2 contains more detail about the Play Framework and the key features that you will use in the following sections.

Table 12-2. *Key Features of Play Framework*

Feature	Description
Asynchronous I/O	Service of long requests asynchronously using JBoss Netty[8] as its web server
Built-in web server	JBoss Netty web server out of the box, but Play web applications can also be packaged to be distributed to Java EE application servers
Dependency management	SBT for dependency management
Hot reloading	In development mode, the code is verified for updates upon new requests, and modified files are automatically recompiled. In case of an error, the error is displayed in the browser directly, unlike in classic web applications where the errors are displayed in the console of the application server.
In-memory database	Support for embedded databases like H2 out of the box.
Native Scala support	Support for Scala natively. Complete interoperability with Java
ORM	Ebean[9] as the ORM replacement of JPA for accessing databases
Stateless	Fully RESTful and without the Java EE session per connection
Templating	Use of Scala for the template engine
WebSocket	Out of the box WebSocket implementation to enable a bi-directional connection between a client and the server

---

[8] http://netty.io/
[9] www.avaje.org/

Setting Up the Application

As you read in previous chapters, there are tools that help you create the basic structure of a new application. In the case of Scala, the most used of these tools is SBT, which has a big number of features and plugins to do certain operations.

Let's create a new application from one of the most used templates of Play Framework.

```
$ sbt new playframework/play-scala-seed.g8
[info] welcome to sbt 1.5.5 (Homebrew Java 11.0.12)
[info] set current project to new (in build file:/tmp/sbt_59871ba1/new/)

This template generates a Play Scala project

name [play-scala-seed]: hello-world-web
organization [com.example]: com.scala

Template applied in /home/hello-world-web
```

If you run the command tree to see the layout of the project, you will see something like the following:

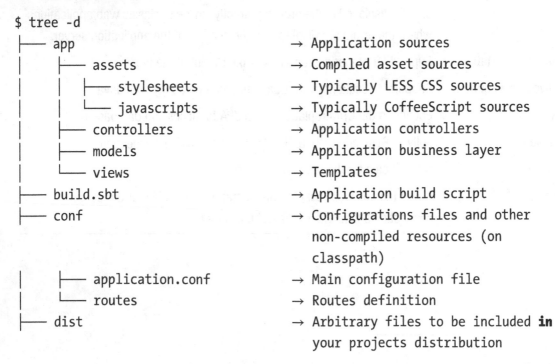

```
$ tree -d
├── app                        → Application sources
│   ├── assets                 → Compiled asset sources
│   │   ├── stylesheets        → Typically LESS CSS sources
│   │   └── javascripts        → Typically CoffeeScript sources
│   ├── controllers            → Application controllers
│   ├── models                 → Application business layer
│   └── views                  → Templates
├── build.sbt                  → Application build script
├── conf                       → Configurations files and other
│                                non-compiled resources (on
│                                classpath)
│   ├── application.conf        → Main configuration file
│   └── routes                 → Routes definition
├── dist                       → Arbitrary files to be included in
                                 your projects distribution
```

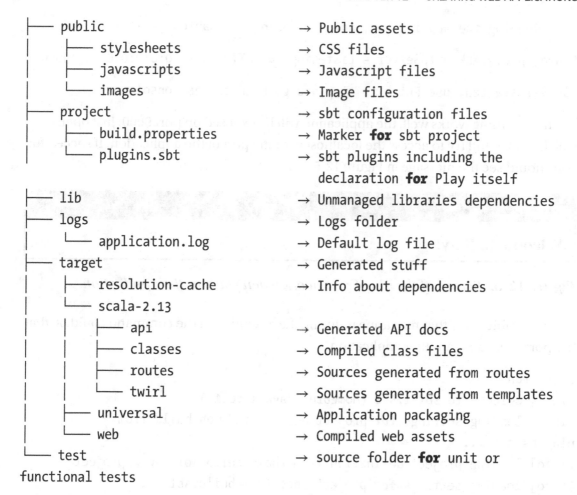

```
├── public                        → Public assets
│    ├── stylesheets              → CSS files
│    ├── javascripts              → Javascript files
│    └── images                   → Image files
├── project                       → sbt configuration files
│    ├── build.properties         → Marker for sbt project
│    └── plugins.sbt              → sbt plugins including the
│                                   declaration for Play itself
├── lib                           → Unmanaged libraries dependencies
├── logs                          → Logs folder
│    └── application.log          → Default log file
├── target                        → Generated stuff
│    ├── resolution-cache         → Info about dependencies
│    └── scala-2.13
│    │    ├── api                 → Generated API docs
│    │    ├── classes             → Compiled class files
│    │    ├── routes              → Sources generated from routes
│    │    └── twirl               → Sources generated from templates
│    ├── universal                → Application packaging
│    └── web                      → Compiled web assets
└── test                          → source folder for unit or
functional tests
```

After the execution of this command is finished, you have a project with the default structure of one project. Now, let's see if the project runs well.

```
$ cd hello-world-web
$ sbt run
[info] welcome to sbt 1.5.2 (Homebrew Java 11.0.12)
[info] loading settings for project hello-world-web-build from
plugins.sbt ...
[info] loading project definition from /home/hello-world-web/project
[info] loading settings for project root from build.sbt ...
[info] set current project to hello-world-web (in build file:/home/hello-
world-web/)
```

```
--- (Running the application, auto-reloading is enabled) ---

[info] p.c.s.AkkaHttpServer - Listening for HTTP on /0:0:0:0:0:0:0:0:9000

(Server started, use Enter to stop and go back to the console...)
```

If everything works well, the application will be exposed on port 9000. Just open a web browser and try to access the localhost with the port of the application. If successful, you should see the message in Figure 12-5.

Figure 12-5. *Screen of the Play Framework when you run the application*

A possible error that may appear during the execution of the command could be that the port is used for another application.

```
$ sbt run
[info] welcome to sbt 1.5.2 (Homebrew Java 11.0.12)
[info] loading settings for project hello-world-web-build from
plugins.sbt ...
[info] loading project definition from /home/hello-world-web/project
[info] loading settings for project root from build.sbt ...
[info] set current project to hello-world-web (in build file:/home/hello-
world-web/)

--- (Running the application, auto-reloading is enabled) ---

[error] a.i.TcpListener - Bind failed for TCP channel on endpoint
[/0.0.0.0:9000]
java.net.BindException: [/0.0.0.0:9000] Address already in use
    at java.base/sun.nio.ch.Net.bind0(Native Method)
    at java.base/sun.nio.ch.Net.bind(Net.java:455)
```

To solve this problem, you can run the command indicating that you want to use another port without changing anything in your application.

```
$ sbt "run 9090"
```

Last but not least in this introduction to creating applications, imagine that you need to debug your application using a particular port. With Play, it's a simple command to indicate the port.

```
$ sbt -jvm-debug 9999
Listening for transport dt_socket at address: 9999
```

Application Flow

Now it's time to understand how the flow of a Play Framework application works, from a request originated from a browser to a tool to generate the response, which could be HTML or JSON in the case of the REST API. Look at Figure 12-6 to understand the different layers in the application.

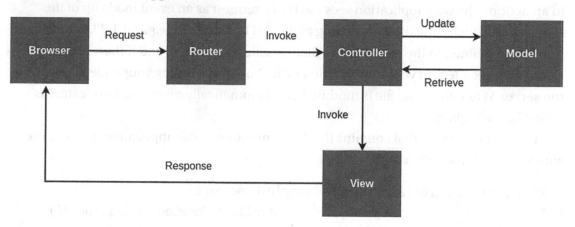

Figure 12-6. *MVC in Play Framework*

The request flow in the MVC architecture illustrated in Figure 12-6 constitutes following:

- The router intermediates the HTTP request and determines the action defined in the controller to process this request.

- The controller listens for HTTP requests, extracts appropriate data from the requests, and applies changes to the model. Also, the controller renders a template file to generate the view.

- The result of the action method is finally sent as an HTTP response.

Router

The router is the main entry point of the web application through the conf/routes file, which defines the routes required by the application. Each route comprises an HTTP method and a URI pattern. A call to an action method is associated with the URI. Conf/routes is the configuration file used by the built-in component called Router that translates each incoming HTTP request to an action call.

Note   The HTTP method can be any of the valid methods supported by HTTP (GET, POST, PUT, DELETE, and HEAD).

The router is responsible for mediating and translating an incoming HTTP request to an action. The web application sees the HTTP request as an event made up of the request path, including the query string and the HTTP method (e.g., GET, POST, etc.). Routes are defined in the conf/routes file. This file is compiled, and if there are any errors, you see them in your browser directly without recompiling your code or restarting the server. When the route file is modified, it is automatically reloaded. This feature is called hot reloading.

If you open the file that contains the different routes of the application, you will see something like the following:

```
# An example controller showing a sample home page
GET     /                           controllers.HomeController.index()

# Map static resources from the /public folder to the /assets URL path
GET     /assets/*file               controllers.Assets.versioned
                                    (path="/public", file: Asset)
```

As you can see, the declaration of a route is simple. You need to indicate the HTTP method with the route and which controller takes the request to generate the response.

Now, if you write a URL that is not defined in the routes file, you will see an exception like in Figure 12-7 in the browser or the tool that you use to consume the REST API like Postman[10] or Insomnia[11].

---

[10] www.postman.com/

[11] https://insomnia.rest/

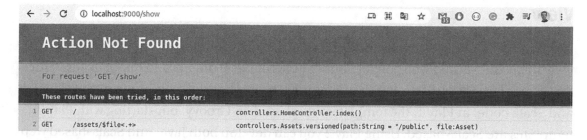

Figure 12-7. An exception that shows Play Framework can't access the route

Controller

The controller responds to requests, processes them, and invokes changes on the model. A controller in Play Framework is an object in Scala that extends the Controller type. This Controller type is provided in the `play.api.mvc` package. A Controller in Play Framework comprises a function called an action to process the request parameters and produces a result to be sent to the client. Controllers are, by default, defined in the `controllers` package under the source root, the app folder. A `Controller` in Java is a class and comprises a public, static method called an action.

Note   A controller is a type that extends a Controller provided in the `play.api.mvc` package.

Model

The model is the domain-specific representation of the information (in the form of data structures and operations) on which the application operates. The most commonly used object for such representation is the JavaBean. However, the JavaBean leads to plenty of boilerplate code. Play Framework reduces this boilerplate code by generating the getters and setters for you by means of byte-code enhancement. The model objects might contain persistence artifacts, such as JPA annotations if they need to be saved into persistent storage.

View

In a Java EE–based web application, the view is usually developed using JSP. That is, the view in JavaEE–based web applications consists of JSP elements and template text. Since Play is not Java EE–centric, the view comprises a template that contains a mix of HTML and Scala code. In Play 1, the templates were based on Groovy, but starting with Play 2, templates are Scala-based. Using Play 2 you can develop both Java- and Scala-based web applications and the templates are exactly the same.

Note   In Play 1, the templates were based on Groovy, but starting from Play 2, templates are Scala-based.

If you create a REST API, the view component does not exist in your application because the controller will generate the response in a JSON format.

Rest Application

You have created an application that contains a default route and HTML, but most microservices or applications delegate all the things related to the front end to other technologies like React, Angular, Vue, and NodeJS, so in this chapter you will create an API.

Defining the Endpoints

To begin building an API, you will create an object that represents the model. You will create the classic ToDoList, which has a model like this class:

```
case class TodoListItem(id: Long, description: String, isItDone: Boolean)
```

Next, you define the model that you use in the different endpoints. And it's time to create your first endpoint, which obtains the information of one TodoListItem. The following code shows the new route that you need to add in the routes file:

```
GET   /todo/:id      controllers.TodoListController.getById(id: Long)
```

Now it is time to create a controller, which contains the method to obtain the information of one element in particular. To do this, create a class named TodoListController in the folder controller with the code that follows:

```scala
package controllers

import javax.inject._
import models.{TodoListItem}
import play.api.libs.json._
import play.api.mvc.{Action, AnyContent, BaseController,
ControllerComponents}
import scala.collection.mutable

@Singleton
class TodoListController @Inject()(val controllerComponents:
ControllerComponents) extends BaseController {
  // Create a list of elements to simulate the information
  private val todoList = new mutable.ListBuffer[TodoListItem]()
  todoList += TodoListItem(1, "Beginning Scala", true)

  implicit val todoListJson = Json.format[TodoListItem]

  def getById(itemId: Long) = Action {
    val foundItem = todoList.find(_.id == itemId)
    foundItem match {
      case Some(item) => Ok(Json.toJson(item))
      case None => NotFound
    }
  }
}
```

You now have the controller and the logic, which if the element exists, returns the information, but if doesn't exist, it returns an HTTP Status 404. To check if everything works, just open your browser or your preferred tool for doing requests and type http://localhost:9000/todo/1.

```
{
    "id": 1,
    "description": "Beginning Scala",
    "isItDone": true
}
```

If you introduce an element that does not exist, you will see something like Figure 12-8.

This localhost page can't be found

No webpage was found for the web address: **http://localhost:9000/todo/23**

HTTP ERROR 404

Reload

Figure 12-8. Result of a request for a non-existent element

The actions in the controllers can return several types of results, one per each HTTP Status. Table 12-3 shows a brief summary of the most used methods; you can find the entire list on the official site of Play Framework[12].

---

[12] www.playframework.com/documentation/2.8.x/api/scala/play/api/mvc/Results.html

Table 12-3. *Commonly Used Results*

Result	Description
BadRequest	Generates a 400 BAD_REQUEST result
InternalServerError	Generates a 500 INTERNAL_SERVER_ERROR result
NotFound	Generates a 404 NOT_FOUND result
Ok	Generates a 200 OK result
Redirect	Generates a simple redirect result

Layers in the Application

As you can imagine, it is not a good practice to have all the logic in the controllers because there is no way to share the same logic across different endpoints. If you use Spring Boot in any of your Java applications, there are some concepts about the distribution of different layers of the logic.

The way to define a structure of layers depends on many things and there is no standard way to define all the layers. For example, Figure 12-9 shows a possible approach to defining layers in a Spring Boot application where most of the layers you can use in your Play Framework application.

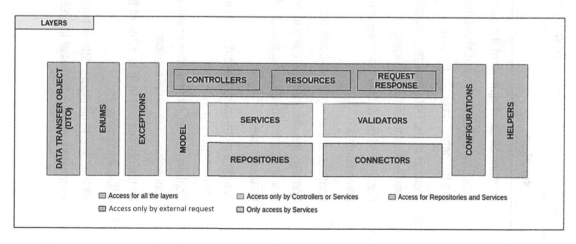

Figure 12-9. *Distribution of layers in a Spring Boot application*

Table 12-4 lists a little information about what is contained in each layer.

Table 12-4. Details About Each Layer in a Web Application

Layer	Description	Packages	Example
Controllers	Contains all the endpoints of the microservices	`*.controller`	UserController
Resources	Contains all documentation about the microservices, like the definition of the endpoints and Swagger	`*.controller.` documentation	UserResources
Request/Response	Location of the Data Transfer Object (DTO) that is used across the different layers	`*.dto.request,` `*.dto.response`	UserRequest, UserResponse
Services	Contains all the definitions of the services and the implementation	`*.service,` `*.service.impl`	IUserService, UserService
Validators	Contains all the logic to validate a request of a DTO	`*.validator`	UserValidator
Repositories	Contains the definition for using interfaces and in some cases contains the specification to do a particular query	`*.repository,` `*.repository.impl`	UserRepository
Connectors	Contains all the communications to external microservices or systems	`*.connector`	UserConnector
Connector Configuration	Contains all the configurations related with connectors to external services	`*.connector.` configuration	UserConnectorConfiguration
Helpers	All the classes that help in different things in the entire microservices	`*.helper`	UserHelper
Configuration	All the logic to configure different aspects of the microservices (e.g., format of the response, ports)	`*.configuration`	DatabaseConfiguration

Exceptions	Contains all the exceptions that each microservice can throw during the execution of a request	`*.exception`	`ApiException`
Model	Contains all the entities with access to the databases	`*.model`	User (no prefix/suffix)
Enums	All the enums used across the different layers	`*.enums`	No prefix/suffix
Data Transfer Object (DTO)	The DTO used across the different layers	`*.dto`	`UserDTO`

This is one possible approach. There are others, like hexagonal architecture[13] or onion architecture[14]. You need to analyze each possible approach, considering the tradeoffs of implementing each on your microservices.

To see all these concepts with a concrete example, let's create a TodoListService in the folder service that contains the logic of getting one item by id. The following code contains all the logic of this new service.

```
package service

import javax.inject._
import models.{TodoListItem}
import scala.collection.mutable

class TodoListService @Inject() () {

 private val todoList = new mutable.ListBuffer[TodoListItem]()
 todoList += TodoListItem(1, "Beginning Scala", true)

 def getById(itemId: Long) =
   todoList.find(_.id == itemId)
}
```

Now it's time to modify the old controller to call your new service. The following code contains the redefinition of the controller using the service:

```
package controllers

import javax.inject._
import models.{TodoListItem}
import play.api.libs.json._
import play.api.mvc.{Action, AnyContent, BaseController,
ControllerComponents}
import scala.collection.mutable
import service.{TodoListService}
```

---

[13] https://netflixtechblog.com/ready-for-changes-with-hexagonal-architecture-b315ec967749

[14] https://dev.to/barrymcauley/onion-architecture-3fgl

```scala
@Singleton
class TodoListController @Inject() (todoListService: TodoListService) (val
controllerComponents: ControllerComponents) extends BaseController {

  def getById(itemId: Long) = Action {
    val foundItem = todoListService.getById(itemId)
    foundItem match {
      case Some(item) => Ok(Json.toJson(foundItem))
      case None => NotFound
    }
  }
}
```

Custom Error Handler

When you develop an application, exceptions or errors are part of the process. Most exceptions do not look pretty or provide a lot of information about the cause of the error.

To clarify, the framework could throw an exception for any of these reasons:

- The application throws an exception in some part of the code.

- Something in the request is not correct, such as the request is invalid or the URL is not correct.

- It return an exception explicitly for some motive related to the business.

Play Framework provides a default error handler that shows you the exceptions, which is not the best approach for receiving HTML in the response. To reduce the size of the response and give some useful information to the consumers of the API, you can create a custom error handler[15] that implements the methods related to the errors of the clients and the server. The following code captures all the HTTP Status 4xx and 5xx errors and transforms an error into something more verbose:

---

[15]www.playframework.com/documentation/2.8.x/ScalaErrorHandling#Handling-errors

```scala
package exceptions

import play.api.http.HttpErrorHandler
import play.api.mvc._
import play.api.http.Status._
import play.api.mvc.Results._
import scala.concurrent._
import javax.inject.Singleton
import java.util.UUID
import play.api.libs.json.Json
import scala.util.control.NonFatal

@Singleton
class CustomErrorHandler extends HttpErrorHandler {
  // 4xx response
  override def onClientError(request: RequestHeader, statusCode: Int,
message: String): Future[Result] = {
    val id = UUID.randomUUID
    Future.successful(Status(statusCode)(Json.obj(
      "error" -> Json.obj(
        "id" -> id,
        "statusCode" -> statusCode.toString
      )
    )))
  }

  // 5xx response
  override def onServerError(request: RequestHeader, exception: Throwable):
Future[Result] = {
    exception match {
      case NonFatal(e) => {
        val id = UUID.randomUUID
        Future.successful(InternalServerError(Json.obj(
          "error" -> Json.obj(
            "id" -> id,
            "statusCode" -> INTERNAL_SERVER_ERROR.toString
          )
```

```
        )))
      }
    }
  }
}
```

After you define your custom error handler, nothing happens until you enable it in the `application.conf` file. To do this, you need to add the following line of code:

```
play.http.errorHandler = "exceptions.CustomErrorHandler"
```

Now do a request to a non-existent URL, such as `http://localhost:9000/todolist`. With the API with the error handler enabled, if everything works well, you will see an JSON response like this:

```
{
    "error": {
        "id": "f9e08428-2c53-4410-9e4c-d951185ab28e",
        "statusCode": "404"
    }
}
```

Summary

In this chapter, you learned how to create different types of applications, one that exposes HTML and another that exposes a set of endpoints, which is the standard nowadays to create microservices. You now know the different frameworks that exist to create each type of application, plus the pros and cons.

There are many frameworks, but in this chapter, you learned how to use Play Framework because it is one of the most used by Scala developers and some Java developers.

CHAPTER 13

Testing Your Code

Testing your code before launching it in production is a way to fix any error that you introduced when you developed a new feature. As you know, testing is a topic that has an incredible number of articles, talks, and discussions around different ways to write tests with the idea of reducing the complexity and increasing the coverage of your code.

Nowadays most developers spend a lot of time developing a new feature or solving a bug, plus writing different types of tests with the idea of reducing the risk of deploying in production a block of code with a problem. It is not the scope of this chapter to explain testing types, but Martin Fowler[1] has several articles that explain each type of testing with a lot of details.

Scala is no exception to these rules and for that reason there are many libraries that test the different blocks of code you saw in previous chapters. Two of these libraries which are connected in some way are ScalaTest[2] and ScalaMock[3]. You will see them in more detail in the following sections.

Testing with ScalaTest

This library helps you to test your code in Scala (Scala 2.x.x or up, Scala Native, Scala.js) but you can use it to test classes in Java. Also, this library has good integration with other tools like Junit, EasyMock, Mockito, ScalaMock, and ScalaCheck. If you use Java, this library does more or less the same as Junit with different assertions.

This library offers different styles of writing tests, and you can include methods after and before the execution of each test or the entire set of tests in one suite or class.

---

[1] https://martinfowler.com/testing/
[2] www.scalatest.org/
[3] https://scalamock.org/quick-start/

© David Pollak, Vishal Layka, and Andres Sacco 2022
D. Pollak et al., *Beginning Scala 3*, https://doi.org/10.1007/978-1-4842-7422-4_13

You can use this library in the REPL but the best way to use it is import in a project with SBT becasuse the resolution of where the dependency needs to be downloaded and the inclusion in the project is simple. To do this, open the `build.sbt` file of your project and include the dependency.

```
scalaVersion := "3.0.1"

name := "hello world"
organization := "ch.epfl.scala"
version := "1.0"

libraryDependencies += "org.scalatest" %% "scalatest" % "3.2.10" % "test"
```

Some considerations when you include this new dependency:

- Check for the latest version of the library because new versions appear many times a year to solve different bugs. You can check on MVNRepository.com[4] for this information.

- Include the dependency only in the scope of the test because if you do not indicate the correct scope of the dependency when SBT creates the package, it will include the dependency, which increments the final size. To include the dependency only in the scope of the test, you need to specify in the last part of the declaration `% "test"`, as in the code above.

When you create your project using SBT, the folder for the different tests may not exist. If you don't have the folder `src/test/scala`, create it.

After you include the dependency, you can run the test using the command `sbt test`, but you will see nothing in the console because you don't have any tests yet.

```
$ sbt test
[info] welcome to sbt 1.5.5 (Homebrew Java 11.0.12)
[info] loading settings for project helloworld-build from assembly.sbt ...
[info] loading project definition from /home/helloworld/project
[info] loading settings for project helloworld from build.sbt ...
[info] set current project to hello world (in build file:/home/helloworld/)
[success] Total time: 2 s, completed Oct 3, 2021, 3:18:03 PM
```

---

[4]https://mvnrepository.com/artifact/org.scalatest/scalatest

Writing Your First Test

The first thing that you need to write a test is a block of code to test. Use the following block of code:

```scala
class TemperatureCalculator {

 def fromCelsiusToFahrenheit(temperature: Float) =
   (temperature * 1.8) + 32
}
```

Now you can check if your logic is okay or not by creating an instance of the class and passing different values.

```scala
scala> val calculator = TemperatureCalculator()

scala> calculator.fromCelsiusToFahrenheit(0)
val res4: Double = 32.0
scala> calculator.fromCelsiusToFahrenheit(20)
val res5: Double = 68.0
```

It's time to translate these manual tests to something more automatic using ScalaTest. To do this, you need to create a class in the same package but in the directory src/test/scala with the name TemperatureCalculatorTest and the class needs to extend from AnyFlatSpec. The class name and the package name are only suggestions because languages like Java/Kotlin follow the same pattern, so you can consider this as a standard in the industry. The following code translates in a basic way the previous test that you did manually:

```scala
import org.scalatest.flatspec.AnyFlatSpec

class TemperatureCalculatorTests extends AnyFlatSpec {

 it should "return a temperature of 32.0 Fahrenheit when the Celsius
 is 0" in {
   val calculator = TemperatureCalculator()
   assert(calculator.fromCelsiusToFahrenheit(0) == 32.0)
 }
```

```
it should "return a temperature of 68 Fahrenheit when the Celsius is
20" in {
  val calculator = TemperatureCalculator()
  assert(calculator.fromCelsiusToFahrenheit(20) == 68)
 }
}
```

As you can see, the structure of the test is simple because each test starts with the words "it should" followed by a string with the description of what the test validates. Inside the declaration you invoke the different methods that you need in order to validate the logic and use the assert method to check if some condition is true or not.

If you run the command sbt test in the console, the result will be the following:

```
$ sbt test
[info] welcome to sbt 1.5.5 (Homebrew Java 11.0.12)
[info] loading settings for project helloworld-build from assembly.sbt ...
[info] compiling 1 Scala source to /home/scala/helloworld/target/
scala-3.0.1/test-classes ...
[info] TemperatureCalculatorTests:
[info] - should return a temperature of 32.0 Fahrenheit when the
Celsius is 0
[info] - should return a temperature of 68 Fahrenheit when the
Celsius is 20
[info] Run completed in 343 milliseconds.
[info] Total number of tests run: 2
[info] Suites: completed 1, aborted 0
[info] Tests: succeeded 2, failed 0, canceled 0, ignored 0, pending 0
[info] All tests passed.
[success] Total time: 6 s, completed Oct 3, 2021, 9:20:32 PM
```

You've created a new instance of the class TemperatureCalculator in each test, which does not make sense because the class is stateless. This means it is not saving anything; it's just receiving a parameter and returning the result without saving it anywhere. To solve this problem of duplicate code, there are several approaches. One is to instantiate the class outside the test. This approach is an option when you don't need to execute a block of code before running a test.

```scala
import org.scalatest.flatspec.AnyFlatSpec

class TemperatureCalculatorTests extends AnyFlatSpec {

  val calculator = TemperatureCalculator()

  it should "return a temperature of 32.0 Fahrenheit when the Celsius
  is 0" in {
    assert(calculator.fromCelsiusToFahrenheit(0) == 32.0)
  }
}
```

Ignoring the Execution of the Test

Everything looks fine with your test but from time to time you may need to ignore the execution of one of them or an entire class of tests for different motives. For that reason, ScalaTest provides a different mechanism for each situation. Let's start with the simplest situation: ignoring or disabling one of the tests.

To do this, you need to replace the words "it" or "in" with "ignore" in each test that you want to be ignored. The following code shows the previous test with the new keyword:

```scala
import org.scalatest.flatspec.AnyFlatSpec

class TemperatureCalculatorTests extends AnyFlatSpec {

  val calculator = TemperatureCalculator()

  ignore should "return a temperature of 32.0 Fahrenheit when the Celsius
  is 0" in {
    assert(calculator.fromCelsiusToFahrenheit(0) == 32.0)
  }

  it should "return a temperature of 68.0 Fahrenheit when the Celsius is
  20" in {
    assert(calculator.fromCelsiusToFahrenheit(20) == 68.0)
  }
}
```

When you run the command to check if the tests are successful, you will see the following result:

```
$ sbt test
[info] TemperatureCalculatorTests:
[info] - should return a temperature of 32.0 Fahrenheit when the Celsius is
0 !!! IGNORED !!!
[info] - should return a temperature of 68.0 Fahrenheit when the
Celsius is 20
[info] Run completed in 499 milliseconds.
[info] Total number of tests run: 1
[info] Suites: completed 1, aborted 0
[info] Tests: succeeded 1, failed 0, canceled 0, ignored 1, pending 0
[info] All tests passed.
[success] Total time: 7 s, completed Oct 3, 2021, 10:02:45 PM
```

Another case is when you need to ignore the entire class with all the tests. To do this, add the annotation @Ignore in the declaration of the class.

```
import org.scalatest.flatspec.AnyFlatSpec
import org.scalatest.Ignore

@Ignore
class TemperatureCalculatorTests extends AnyFlatSpec {
    val calculator = TemperatureCalculator()
    ......
}
```

Other Ways of Declaring the Test

As you know, there are many ways to write your test. One of them is using FlatSpec, which you saw in previous chapters, but there is another way which is relevant. The syntax in all cases is more or less the same but there are little differences. Let's see some of these ways to write tests using the previous code.

- Using FunSuite you don't have any keyword in the declaration. You just use the word test and inside declare a string that expresses the idea of the test. This approach is very familiar for Java and Junit developers, when you declare a method and include a @DisplayName that explains in detail the idea of the test.

```scala
import org.scalatest.funsuite.AnyFunSuite

class TemperatureCalculatorTests extends AnyFunSuite {

  val calculator = TemperatureCalculator()

  test("A calculate should return a temperature of 32.0 Fahrenheit when the
  Celsius is 0") {
    assert(calculator.fromCelsiusToFahrenheit(0) == 32.0)
  }

  test("A calculate should return a temperature of 68.0 Fahrenheit when the
  Celsius is 20") {
    assert(calculator.fromCelsiusToFahrenheit(20) == 68.0)
  }

}
```

As you can see in the code below, the output when you execute the test is more or less the same as with FlatSpec.

```
$ sbt test
[info] TemperatureCalculatorTests:
[info] - A calculate should return a temperature of 32.0 Fahrenheit when
the Celsius is 0
[info] - A calculate should return a temperature of 68 Fahrenheit when the
Celsius is 20
[info] Run completed in 315 milliseconds.
[info] Total number of tests run: 2
[info] Suites: completed 1, aborted 0
[info] Tests: succeeded 2, failed 0, canceled 0, ignored 0, pending 0
[info] All tests passed.
```

- Using FunSpec is a mix of the previous ways to write a test. You use the keyword describe to create a way to group the different types of tests that are connected in some way, but if you change a parameter, you get different results.

```
import org.scalatest.funspec.AnyFunSpec

class TemperatureCalculatorTests extends AnyFunSpec {

 val calculator = TemperatureCalculator()
 describe("A calculate ") {
   it("should return a temperature of 32.0 Fahrenheit when the Celsius
   is 0") {
     assert(calculator.fromCelsiusToFahrenheit(0) == 32.0)
   }
   it("should return a temperature of 68.0 Fahrenheit when the Celsius
   is 20") {
     assert(calculator.fromCelsiusToFahrenheit(20) == 68.0)
   }
 }
}
```

As you can see, the output when you execute the test is more or less the same as the FlatSpec but each line where you include in the describe keyword appears as a level.

```
$ sbt test
[info] TemperatureCalculatorTests:
[info] A calculate
[info] - should return a temperature of 32.0 Fahrenheit when the
Celsius is 0
[info] - should return a temperature of 68.0 Fahrenheit when the
Celsius is 20
[info] Run completed in 312 milliseconds.
[info] Total number of tests run: 2
[info] Suites: completed 1, aborted 0
[info] Tests: succeeded 2, failed 0, canceled 0, ignored 0, pending 0
[info] All tests passed.
```

One last comment about these styles of tests: All of them are included in the default library that you included in the first section of the chapter, but if you only want to include the dependency of one of these styles and exclude the rest, you can do it. The following code shows how to include only the dependency of scalatest-funsite.

```
libraryDependencies += "org.scalatest" %% "scalatest-funsuite" % "3.2.10"
% "test"
```

Using Matchers to Validate Results

ScalaTest uses matchers to validate if the results are correct or not. Matchers are a way to declare the conditions to validate in a more readability way for humans. It's similar to BDD.

Before using matchers, you need to include them in your test class. If you are not sure which matchers you will use, include all of them using _. Here is the entire package of matchers:

```
import org.scalatest.matchers.should.Matchers._
```

Now let's translate the previous validation with assert to matchers with the use of shouldBe.

```
import org.scalatest.flatspec.AnyFlatSpec
import org.scalatest.matchers.should.Matchers._

class TemperatureCalculatorTests extends AnyFlatSpec {

  val calculator = TemperatureCalculator()

  it should "return a temperature of 32.0 Fahrenheit when the Celsius
  is 0" in {
    val result = calculator.fromCelsiusToFahrenheit(0)

    result shouldBe 32.0
  }
}
```

As you can see, this way of validating if the result is correct or not is simple to understand. It's not a unique way to check the result; matchers offer different ways to do the same. The following code shows you different ways to do the same validation. The main difference is the complexity and the time to compile the conditions, but you can start following the spirit of Scala by using the method you consider the simplest.

```
result shouldBe 32.0
result should be (32.0)

result should equal (32.0)
result shouldEqual 32.0

result should === (32.0)
```

There are matchers to cover most common cases of validations. It's not just to check if the result is equal to a certain value. For example, the following code checks if one of the elements is in a List:

```
it should "list contain one of the elements" in {
 val result = List(1, 2, 3, 4, 5)

 result should contain oneOf (5, 7, 9)
}
```

Tagging Your Test

Imagine you have different classes or methods that are part of a big functionality and you want to check if everything related with that functionality still works fine after you introduce some modifications. You have options:

- Run all the tests and check if the test connected with the functionality is still working. The main constraint with this approach is you spend a lot of time remembering which classes or tests have some relationship to your modifications.

- Have a class that contains all the tests of the same functionality. This approach has a big problem in that you have tests from different classes in one file, so you can't know in a simple way which classes are tested.

- Use some way to group the different tests without modifying the structure that has a class of test per each class that exists in the code.

The last approach is the best way to solve the problem. ScalaTest lets you add tags to your tests and run only the test that has a particular tag. To do this, you need to create a custom tag and assign it to different tests. The following code shows how to define a custom tag. As a recommendation, create a package in the source of your test with the different tags that you will create because it is an easy way to identify all the tags that exist.

```scala
import org.scalatest.Tag

object CustomTag extends Tag("CustomTag")
```

After you define your custom tags, you need to mark which test uses the tag. To do this, use the keyword taggedAs(NameOfTag) in the definition of the test. This code shows how to mark one of the tests from the previous section with the CustomTag:

```scala
import org.scalatest.flatspec.AnyFlatSpec
import org.scalatest.matchers.should.Matchers._
import org.scalatest.Tag

object CustomTag extends Tag("CustomTag")

class TemperatureCalculatorTests extends AnyFlatSpec {

 val calculator = TemperatureCalculator()

 it should "return a temperature of 32.0 Fahrenheit when the Celsius is 0"
 taggedAs(CustomTag) in {
   val result = calculator.fromCelsiusToFahrenheit(0)

   result shouldBe 32.0
 }
 // Test without tags
 // ....
}
```

To run only the test that contains a specific tag, you only need to indicate to SBT with a simple command.

```
$ sbt "testOnly -- -n CustomTag"
[info] TemperatureCalculatorTests:
[info] - should return a temperature of 32.0 Fahrenheit when the
Celsius is 0
[info] Run completed in 366 milliseconds.
[info] Total number of tests run: 1
[info] Suites: completed 1, aborted 0
[info] Tests: succeeded 1, failed 0, canceled 0, ignored 0, pending 0
```

Before and After Methods

As you know, there are many cases where before and after the execution of a test case you need to prepare something. You may need to initialize variables with specific values or create a file. Frameworks like Junit in Java let you use methods after/before the execution of each test or the entire set of tests of the class.

To implement these features, just extend from BeforeAndAfter and create the before or after method.

```
import org.scalatest.flatspec.AnyFlatSpec
import org.scalatest._

class StringBuilderTests extends AnyFlatSpec with BeforeAndAfter {

  val builder = StringBuilder()

  before {
    builder.append("Scala 3")
  }
  after {
    builder.delete(0, builder.length)
  }

  it should "append to the default string" in {
    builder.append(" introduce a lot of features")
```

```scala
    assert(builder.toString === "Scala 3 introduce a lot of features")
  }
}
```

Summary

In this chapter, you learned how to create different tests to validate if the code that you created works well or not. This is crucial because it reduces the risk of deploying a block of code with bugs to production. Also, you need to consider the coverage of code that your tests check.

Scala Best Practices

Thanks for hanging in and reading all this way. You've covered a lot of ground. You've explored the Scala language and developed a collection of idioms for building applications using Scala. You know how Scala can be used by different team members in different ways. You've seen how Scala allows you to compose fine-grained pieces of code into complex systems that work well together.

But no technology is an island. No matter how good Scala is in the abstract, it's only valuable if it can help your organization produce better and more maintainable code, faster. The good news is that Scala compiles down to JVM bytecode and works great with existing Java libraries. If you're working at a Java shop, the cost of using Scala on some projects is minimal. You can test Scala with your existing Java test tools. You can store compiled Scala code in JAR and WAR files, so it looks and feels to the rest of your organization like what they're used to: Java bytecode. The operational characteristic of Scala code on web servers is indistinguishable from the operational characteristics of Java code.

Scala is not just a programming language; it is a new way of thinking and reasoning about programming. It will take you time to design code that fits into Scala paradigms and to discover and devise paradigms of your own. So, write that Java-style code in Scala and then apply the idioms and see how your code changes and how your thought patterns emerge. The first step is to recognize the functional style and the immediately obvious differences between imperative and functional styles.

General Best Practices

As you read in the different chapters of this book, Scala 3.x.x introduces a lot of modifications to reduce the complexity of the language and help developers understand the code in a simple way.

The following are some rules that apply to everything in the new version of Scala:

© David Pollak, Vishal Layka, and Andres Sacco 2022
D. Pollak et al., *Beginning Scala 3*, https://doi.org/10.1007/978-1-4842-7422-4_14

- Reduce the use of ;, (), and {}. As you remember, there is no constraint in using them in Scala 3, but it could be confusing when someone on your team does not include them in the code.

- Write simple functions that don't return an exception. Instead of an exception, return something like Option, Try, or Either.

- Use immutable fields using val. This practice reduces the risk of possible problems with concurrency.

- Don't allow null values in your variables. Use Option.

- Create a big number of unit tests in your application using ScalaTest[1]. You can use other frameworks like Junit[2] from Java[3] if you feel more comfortable with the format of writing test. Also, add some tools to know the coverage of your test. SonarQube[4] is a good choice.

- Check if the dependencies that you want to add in SBT[5] are compatible with the latest version of Scala 2.13.x or Scala 3.

The following sections explain these best practices in more detail.

Recognizing the Functional Style

Scala supports both functional and imperative styles of programming. If you come from an imperative background, that is, if you are a Java programmer, Scala also allows you to program in an imperative style, but it encourages a functional approach. The functional style of programming enables you to write concise and less error-prone code. However, programming in the functional style can prove to be a daunting task for a Java programmer. This section gives a few pointers for programming in the functional style. The first and foremost step is to recognize the difference between the imperative and functional styles in code.

---

[1] www.scalatest.org/

[2] https://junit.org/junit5/

[3] www.java.com/es/

[4] www.sonarqube.org/

[5] www.scala-sbt.org/

A quick way to distinguish between functional and imperative styles is that vars signify an imperative style and using vals is more akin to a functional approach. Therefore, transitioning from an imperative to a functional style means your program should be free of vars.

```scala
val strArray = Array("Vishal Layka", "David Pollak")
```

If you want to print the contents of the array shown above, and if you were a Java programmer before you moved to Scala, you might write the while loop akin to the while loop shown here:

```scala
def print(strArray: Array[String]): Unit =
    var i = 0
    while (i < strArray.length) {
        println(strArray (i))
        i += 1
    }
```

The above code uses a var and is therefore in the imperative style. When you run the code in the REPL, you get the following output:

```scala
scala> print(strArray)
Vishal Layka
David Pollak
```

You can transform this bit of code into a more functional style by first getting rid of the var, as shown here:

```scala
def print(strArray: Array[String]): Unit = {
    strArray.foreach(println)
}
```

As you can see, the refactored functional code is much clearer, more concise, and less error-prone than the original imperative code above. This last example is more functional but not purely functional.

Writing Pure Functions

So far, you refactored the print method above, which was in imperative style, to the example that followed, which is functional but not purely functional, because it causes side effects. For example, it prints the output to the output stream. The functional equivalent will be a more defining method that manipulates the passed args for printing. For example, it formats it, but does not print it and returns the formatted string for printing, as shown here:

```scala
def formatArgs(strArray: Array[String]) = strArray.mkString(":")
```

Note   If a function's result type is Unit, the function has side effects.

Now the function is purely functional; that is, it causes no side effects affected by var. The mkString method is defined on collections that are meant to return a string that result from calling toString on each element. You can call mkString on any iterable collection.

The overridden toString method is used to return the string representation of an object, as shown here:

```scala
val x = List("x", "y", "z")
println(x.mkString(" : "))
```

You get the following output:

```scala
scala> val x = List("x", "y", "z")
x: List[String] = List(x, y, z)
scala> println(x.mkString(" : "))
x : y : z
```

The function with no side effects doesn't print anything, like the print method in the more functional example did. You can pass the result of formatArgs to println to print the output shown here:

```scala
println(formatArgs(strArray))
```

You can run this in the REPL:

```scala
scala> val strArray = Array("Vishal Layka", "David Pollak")
```

```
strArray: Array[String] = Array(Vishal Layka, David Pollak)
scala> def formatArgs(strArray: Array[String]) = strArray.mkString(":")
formatArgs: (strArray: Array[String])String
scala> println(formatArgs(strArray))
Vishal Layka:David Pollak
```

That said, the essential useful feature of a program is to cause side effects; otherwise, it has no real application. Creating methods that do not cause side effects encourages you to minimize the code that would cause side effects, thus leading you to design robust programs.

Writing pure functions is not simple in the beginning because this concept is not popular or is impossible to do in other languages that use JVM. Some advice: Start writing pure functions simply to understand the concept. After that, generalize this concept in all the functions you can.

Leveraging Type Inferencing

Scala is a statically typed language. In a statically typed language, the values and the variables have types. Also, Scala is a type-inferred language, which means you do not have to write the boilerplate code because the boilerplate code is inferred by Scala. This type inference is a feature of a dynamic type language. In this manner, Scala merges the best of the two worlds.

Note   In a dynamic typed system, unlike static typing, only values have types; variables do not have types.

Let's create an array of Maps to illustrate how type inferencing works.

```
val books = Array(
    Map("title" -> "Beginning Scala", "publisher" -> "Apress"),
    Map("title" -> "Beginning Java", "publisher" -> "Apress")
)
```

If you run this Scala code in the REPL, you'll see the following output:

```
scala> val books = Array(
```

```
    |        Map("title" -> "Beginning Scala", "publisher" -> "Apress"),
    |        Map("title" -> "Beginning Java", "publisher" -> "Apress")
    | )
val books: Array[Map[String, String]] = Array(Map(title -> Beginning Scala,
publisher -> Apress), Map(title -> Beginning Java, publisher -> Apress))
```

Note that only the array and Maps were specified, not their types. As you can see in
the output in REPL, the Scala compiler inferred the types of the array and the Map. In this
way, you could let the type inferencer determine the type for you, which can help you
trim a lot of ceremonious code, thus keeping the code clean and lean and central to the
business logic.

Tip   Let the type inferencer determine the type; this helps you trim
ceremonious code.

This concept is not strange if you recently used Kotlin or Java 14 because they offer
something similar.

Think Expressions

As you learned in Chapter 4, expressions evaluate to a value, so there's no need for a
return statement. In Java, a return statement is commonplace, as shown here:

```
def phoneBanking(key: Int) : String = {
    var result : String = _
     key match {
        case 1 => result = "Banking service"
        case 2 => result = "Credit cards"
        case _ => result = "Speak to the customer executive"
    }
    return result
}
```

As you can see, the final result is stored in a result variable. The code, while flowing
through a pattern match, assigns strings to the result variable. To improve this code,

you need to follow an expression-oriented approach, which is explained in detail in Chapter 4. This can be done in the following way:

- As mentioned, the first and foremost way to adopt a functional style is to use val instead of var. You first change the result variable to a val.

- Instead of assigning through the case statements, use the last expression of the case statement for assigning the result.

Here is the code refactored to an expression-oriented pattern match:

```
def phoneBanking (key: Int) : String =
  val result = key match
    case 1 => "Banking service"
    case 2 => "Credit cards"
    case 3 => "Speak to the customer executive"
  return result
```

This code looks a lot more concise, but it can still be improved. You can remove the intermediate result variable altogether from the phoneBanking method. Here is the purely expression-oriented style:

```
def phoneBanking (key: Int) : String = key match
  case 1 => "Banking service"
  case 2 => "Credit cards"
  case 3 => "Speak to the customer executive"
```

It follows the expression-oriented approach. You can run the code in the REPL as shown:

```
scala> phoneBanking (3)
res8: String = Speak to the customer executive
```

Note   The key to using expressions is realizing that there's no need for a return statement.

Try to apply this concept not only in match expressions. You can apply this idea in try/catch expressions when something happens. Try to capture the exception to do something like log the error and after that provide a possible value (None/Some) for the method.

Focusing on Immutability

In Java, mutability is the default. Variables are mutable unless they're marked final. JavaBeans have getters and setters. Data structures in Java are instantiated, set, and passed along to other methods. Try changing the paradigm in your Scala code.

The first thing to do is to use immutable collections classes by default. If you choose to use a mutable collections class, make a comment in your code as to why you chose it. There are times when mutable collections make sense. For example, in a method where you are building a List, using ListBuffer is more efficient, but don't return the ListBuffer; return the List. This is like using a StringBuilder in Java but ultimately returning a String. So, use immutable collections by default, and use mutable data structures with a justification.

Use vals by default, and only use vars if there is a good reason that is justified by a comment. In your method, use val unless there's going to be a significant performance hit. Using val in methods often leads to thinking recursively. The following code shows a mutable implementation of a method that consumes all the lines from a BufferedReader:

```
def read1(in: java.io.BufferedReader): List[String] =
    var ret: List[String] = Nil
    var line = in.readLine
    while(line!=null)
        ret ::= line
        line = in.readLine
    ret.reverse
```

The code is readable but uses a couple of vars. Let's rewrite the code without vars and see how you can use tail recursion to give you a while loop:

```
def read2(in: java.io.BufferedReader): List[String] =
    val ret: List[String] = Nil
    doRead(in, ret)

def doRead(in: java.io.BufferedReader, acc: List[String]):List[String] =
```

```
in.readLine match
    case null => acc
    case s => doRead(in, s :: acc)
doRead(in, Nil).reverse
```

Look ma, no vars. You define the doRead method, which reads a line of input. If the line is null, you return the accumulated List. If the line is non-null, you call doRead with the accumulated List. Because doRead is in the scope of read2, it has access to all of read2's variables. doRead calls itself on the last line, which is a tail call. The Scala compiler optimizes the tail call into a while loop, and there will only be one stack frame created no matter how many lines are read. The last line of read2 calls doRead with Nil as the seed value for the accumulator.

Using vals in your code makes you think about alternative, immutable, functional code. This small example demonstrates that removing vars leads to refactoring. The refactoring leads to new coding patterns. The new coding patterns lead to a shift in your approach to coding. This shift in approach yields transformative code that has fewer defects and is easier to maintain.

Keeping Methods Short

If you keep methods short, then the logic in each method is more obvious when you or someone else looks at the code. See whether you can code methods in a single line. If not a single line, see whether you can code them in a single statement. Let's see how the previous code can be made into single statements.

```
def readLines(in:java.io.BufferedReader, acc:List[String]): List[String] =
    in.readLine match
        case null => acc
        case s => readLines(in,s :: acc)
```

```
def read3(in: java.io.BufferedReader): List[String] =
    readLines(in,Nil).reverse
```

When you code Scala, try not to have curly braces around the method body. If you can't write your code this way, you have to justify to yourself why your method should exceed a single statement. Keeping methods short allows you to encapsulate a single piece of logic in a method and have methods that build upon each other. It also allows you to easily understand the logic in the method.

Using Options Instead of Null Testing

The first benefit of using `Option` is the obvious avoidance of null pointer exceptions. You should never return null from a method: never, never, never. If you are calling Java libraries that may return null or throw an exception because of input problems, convert them to `Options`. You did this for parsing Strings to Ints. The pattern is basic: no nulls.

When you write code, ban null from your code. In the case of uninitialized instance variables, either assign a default value that is not null or, if there's a code path where the variable could be used prior to initialization, use `Option`, and the default value becomes None. If there's no logical value that can be returned from a method given legal input, the return type should be `Option`. The get method should never be called on an `Option`. Instead, `Options` should be unpacked using `map`/`flatMap`, the `for` comprehension, or pattern matching.

The second benefit is a little subtler. The use of `Option` and the transformative nature of mapping `Options` leads to a different style of code. The style is more transformative, more functional. The impact of repeatedly using immutable data structures will move your brain toward the functional side. You should be familiar with null pointer exceptions in Java. For example, consider the following Java method:

```
public Integer computeArea() { ... }
```

This `computeArea` method returns, as you might expect, the area of type `Int`, but it might return null, and you cannot tell just by looking at the method that it might return null. Because of this, the caller of the Java method is obliged to put null checks in their code and, if the caller is lucky and the method never actually returns null, the null checks merely clutter the caller's code. Scala solves this problem by getting rid of null altogether and provides a new type for optional values, that is, values that may or may not be present by means of the `Option` class. Here's you can write a `computeArea` method in Scala that may or may not return a value:

```
def computeArea: Option[Int] = { ... }
```

The return type of the `computeArea` method is `Option[Int]` and merely by looking at this return type, the caller of the `computeArea` method will know that it may not always return an `Int`. And to complete the picture, the `computeArea` method uses Some and None types to determine what to return, for example, in one implementation fragment example of the `computeArea` method.

```
computeArea match
  case Some(area) => ...
  case None => ...
```

Option, Some, and None used in this way are part of the unique features of Scala. It's how Scala is a state-of-the-art language. This also means that when a Scala function always returns a value, its return type is not an `Option` type but the type of the object that the method returns. If the Scala function never returns null, why is there a Null type in Scala? We take a brief pause here to let you envisage the answer. Good, that's correct. Scala supports Null types for compatibility with Java. None is the counterpart to Some, used when you're using Scala's `Option` class to help avoid null references.

As you read in previous chapters, the concept of `Option` exists in different languages but with another name. In Java, the same concept has the name of `Optional` and most developers use it to reduce `NullPointerExceptions`.

Refactor Mercilessly

In the beginning, you can write your Scala code as you would your Java code. It's a great place to start. Then, start applying the idioms you learned in the previous sections in this chapter. Start with the imperative code.

```
def validByAge(in: List[Person]): List[String] =
  var valid: List[Person] = Nil
  for (p <- in)
    if (p.valid) valid = p :: valid

  def localSortFunction(a: Person, b: Person) = a.age < b.age
  val people = valid.sort(localSortFunction _)
  var ret: List[String] = Nil

  for (p <- people)
    ret = ret ::: List(p.first)

  return ret
```

Turn your vars into vals, as illustrated here:

```
def validByAge(in: List[Person]): List[String] =
    val valid:ListBuffer[Person] = new ListBuffer // displaced mutability
    for(p<- in)
        if (p.valid) valid += p

    def localSortFunction(a: Person, b:Person) = a.age < b.age then 1 else 0
    val people = valid.toList.sort(localSortFunction)
    val ret:ListBuffer[String] = new ListBuffer
    for(p<- people)
        ret += p.first

    ret.toList
```

Turn your mutable data structures into immutable data structures.

```
def validByAge(in: List[Person]): List[String] =
    val valid = for (p<- in if p.valid) yield p
    def localSortFunction(a: Person,b:Person) = a.age < b.age
    val people = valid.sort(localSortFunction _)
    for(p<- people) yield p.first
```

Make your method into a single statement.

```
def validByAge(in: List[Person]): List[String] =
    in.filter(_.valid).sort(_.age < _.age).map(_.first)
```

While you can argue that this is too terse, you can refactor it another way.

```
def filterValid(in: List[Person]) = in.filter(p=> p.valid)
def sortPeopleByAge(in: List[Person]) = in.sort(_.age < _.age)
def validByAge(in: List[Person]): List[String] = (filterValid_ andThen
sortPeopleByAge_)(in).map(_.name)
```

Regardless of the refactoring choices you make, the business logic of your code is a lot more visible. The refactoring also moves you toward thinking about the transformations in your code rather than the looping constructs in your code.

Composing Functions and Classes

In the previous example, you composed `filterValid` and `sortPeopleByAge` into a single function. This function is the same as shown here:

```
(in: List[Person]) =>sortPeopleByAge(filterValid(in))
```

However, the composition of the two functions results in code that reads like what it does. You started by turning your methods into single statements. This makes testing easier and makes the code more readable. Next, you composed a new function by chaining together the two functions. Functional composition is a later stage Scala-ism, but it results naturally from making methods into single statements.

In Chapter 7, you explored how Scala's traits can be composed into powerful, flexible classes that are more type-safe than Java classes. As you evolve your Scala coding skills and begin to refactor classes rather than methods, start looking for common methods across your interfaces and traits. Move methods from concrete classes into traits. Soon, you'll likely find that many of your classes have little in them other than the logic that is specific to that class and the `vals` that are needed to evaluate that logic. Once you reach this level in your coding, you will likely find that your traits are polymorphic, that your traits represent logic that can be applied to a contained type, and then you can feel secure that your mind has completely warped into thinking Scala.

Once you're thinking Scala or thinking that you're thinking Scala, you might want to take the next advanced steps toward the goals of best practices.

Summary

Designing and building complex computer software is a serious business. Our livelihoods, and increasingly our whole society, depend on the stability and flexibility of our interconnected computer systems. Our cars and our banks and our grocery stores and our hospitals and our police departments all work better because they are interconnected by computer systems. Those systems run on the software we write.

If you want more information about this interesting topic, we suggest checking the sites of effective Scala[6] or the Scala Style Guide[7].

---

[6] http://twitter.github.io/effectivescala/
[7] https://docs.scala-lang.org/style/

We hope you have enjoyed the journey and are already thinking about new ways to reason about designing software and writing code. We want to end this journey by talking a bit about architecture.

Architecture is very important in overall system performance and team performance. Scala has a lot of the tools that allow for much better architectural decisions. It's kind of a *Zen and the Art of Motorcycle Maintenance* thing; you use the patterns that your language and its libraries make easiest. Scala makes it easier than Java or Ruby[8] for coders to implement architecturally solid designs.

---

[8] www.ruby-lang.org/es/

Index

A

add method, 206, 229, 230
Algebraic data types (ADT), 191
Anonymous function, *see* Function literal
Apache Ant, 248
Apache Ivy, 248, 258
apply method, 150, 161
Array, 30, 34–36
ArraryBuffer, 165
aScalaMethod method, 232

B

Backus–Naur Form (BNF), 245
@BeanProperty annotation, 227, 228
before/after method, 298, 299
Boolean type, 27
buffer methods, 165
Build definition, 257, 260

C

Call-by-name mechanism, 99, 100
Call-by-name parameter, 99, 101
Call-by-value, 99, 100
Case classes
    definition, 123
    mutable properties, 124
    nested pattern matching, 125
    Person class, 124
    Person instances, 124, 125
    read-only properties, 124
charityRun method, 184

Class
    Book.class, 57
    creation, 57
    definition, 54, 56
    instance, 57
    names, 56
    Scala 2, 57
    Scala 3, 57
Closure, 84, 85, 91, 92
Compiler optimization
    branch table, 120
    considerations, 122
    lookupswitch, 121, 122
    tableswitch, 121
computeArea method, 310, 311
Constructors
    auxiliary, 61, 62
    creation, 59
    default values, 62
    definition, 59
    field visibility, 60, 61
    javap-c Book.class, 59, 60
    private, 62
controllers package, 275
Control structures
    if/the/else expressions, 39
    for loops, 41, 42
    match expressions, 43, 44
    try/catch/finally blocks, 44
    while loops, 42
Covariant parameter types, 202
Curried functions, 93, 94

© David Pollak, Vishal Layka, and Andres Sacco 2022
D. Pollak et al., *Beginning Scala 3*, https://doi.org/10.1007/978-1-4842-7422-4

rint
e United States
aylor Publisher Services